WALKING
THE TALK

WALKING THE TALK

Reimagining Primary Health Care after COVID-19

Enis Barış, Rachel Silverman,
Huihui Wang, Feng Zhao,
and Muhammad Ali Pate

 **WORLD BANK GROUP**

Contents

Figures

Tables

Preface

The Universal Health Coverage (UHC) agenda has reached a crucial crossroads

The COVID-19 (Coronavirus) pandemic has laid bare the inherent weaknesses of health systems around the world. Confirmed global deaths are fast approaching 6 million and continue to climb. The pandemic brought the world economy to a standstill—costing trillions of dollars, eroding progress toward poverty elimination, and widening domestic and international inequalities. Vaccination campaigns now offer hope for a postpandemic future, but uneven rollouts have once again revealed staggering inequities across and between countries. Although it is still too early to offer a definitive postmortem on COVID-19, the early signs suggest failings at every level—from global governance all the way down to individual behavior. The pandemic has stolen the spotlight from the UHC agenda, even as it has reinforced the critical role of resilient national health systems as the very foundation of global stability and prosperity.

So where do we go from here?

In this report, we argue that a robust and reimagined primary health care (PHC) agenda, as part of a broader reinvigoration of UHC, must be part of the post-COVID-19 story—both to dig the world out of the COVID-19 ditch and to prevent similar catastrophes in the future. To be clear, we do not claim that the COVID-19 crisis was entirely or mostly the result of weak or nonfunctional PHC services. Yet PHC was often the weakest link in the national and community responses, despite its critical importance as a backstop to "flatten the curve" and prevent hospital saturation. Core PHC functions such as surveillance, testing, and contact tracing first fell through the cracks and then were ultimately assumed by newly created teams or by hospitals. Now we will again need PHC to close the COVID-19 chapter and make up for lost time—by administering vaccines against COVID-19; recouping losses to reproductive health, preventive care, and mental health; and building back better to meet the evolving needs of the global population.

Walking the Talk: Reimagining Primary Health Care after COVID-19 builds on the vast literature on PHC, revisiting the concept, its underpinnings, country experiences, and lessons learned. The report also is fully aligned with the 2018 Declaration of Astana on PHC as the main pillar of universal health coverage and the health-related Sustainable Development Goals, and it commits the World Bank to its global pursuit of health-for-all. Yet its emphasis is on the "how"—what it takes to build a fit-for-purpose primary health care service delivery platform—and it spells out how countries could reimagine it to "walk the talk," with the assistance of their global partners, including the World Bank Group.

We hope that the organizing framework presented in this report will add value to our dialogue with client countries for a better aligned and more effective path to universal health coverage by 2030. Indeed, the challenge before us is how to build and retain the PHC workforce with the right skills mix; to organize their care environment; and to ensure that they are well-resourced so that the services they provide are of the highest quality, comprehensive, coordinated, and integrated across all levels of care, yet affordable and sustainable. We extend an open invitation for collaboration to all of our partners in global health and reaffirm our commitment to the Global Action Plan PHC Accelerator to provide technical and financial assistance to make the recommendations of this report a reality.

Acknowledgments

This report was prepared under the Advisory Service and Analytics, "Reimagining Primary Health Care for UHC and HNP Strategy." This activity was coordinated by Huihui Wang (Senior Economist) and Lydia Ndebele (Health Specialist) and supervised by Muhammad Ali Pate (formerly Global Director, Health, Nutrition and Population Global Practice) and Feng Zhao (Practice Manager, Global Engagement, Health, Nutrition and Population Global Practice).

Enis Barış (Global Health Senior Advisor and Consultant) provided intellectual leadership in the conceptualization the report. He and Rachel Silverman (Consultant) coauthored all chapters. Other coauthors of the report include Huihui Wang (Senior Economist) for chapters 3, 4, and 5; Ece Özçelik (Consultant) for chapters 2 and 3; Manuela Villar Uribe (Health Specialist), Gianluca Cafagna (Health Specialist) for chapter 3; Federica Secci (Senior Health Specialist), Denizhan Duran (Young Professional), Sarah Alkenbrack (Senior Economist, Health), Roxanne Oroxom (Consultant), Muntaqa Umar-Sadiq (Consultant), and Roger Strasser (Consultant) for chapter 4; and Feng Zhao (Practice Manager) and Muhammad Pate (former Global Director, HNP) for chapter 5.

We acknowledge the helpful feedback received on the report drafts from the IINP leadership team and HNP colleagues throughout the process, as well as written comments provided for the decision meeting from John Paul Clark (Lead Health Specialist), Daniel Dulitzky (Regional Director), Susanna Hayrapetyan (Program Leader), Gayle Martin (Country Manager), Mark E. Cackler (Lead Agriculture Specialist), and Sherin Varkey (Senior Health Specialist). Chapters 3 and 4 have incorporated content from the World Bank's internal Frontlines First (FLF) series, developed in 2018 to commemorate the 40th anniversary of the Alma Ata Declaration. The team is also grateful to David Wilson (Program Director) and Mickey Chopra (Lead Health Specialist), Rachel Silverman (Consultant, lead author), Kojo Nimako (Consultant), and Danielle Fitzpatrick (Consultant) for their roles in compiling the FLF framework and briefs that have fed into this flagship report. We also acknowledge Jean-Olivier Schmidt (GIZ), Moritz Piatti (Senior Economist), Mengxiao Wang (World Bank consultant), and Alexandra Beith (World Bank consultant) for their contributions to chapter 4.

The team would like to express its appreciation for the very valuable guidance, external review, and feedback received from the Bill & Melinda Gates Foundation, which also generously supported the preparation of the flagship report; the World Health Organization; UNICEF; the Global Fund; and Gavi, The Vaccine Alliance.

The team also thanks Alexander Irvin for his incredibly skilled editorial assistance; Latifat Agharese Okara for her support in finalizing the report; and Ira Marina (Senior Executive Assistant), Marize de Fatima Santos (Program Assistant), and Kseniya Bieliaieva (Team Assistant) for their coordination and logistics support.

About the Authors

Enis Barış is Professor of Practice at the School of Population and Global Health, McGill University, Montreal, Canada, and President of GluonMed, a global health consultancy based in Washington, DC. He has been serving as a Senior Advisor to the World Bank, the New Development Bank (NDB), and The Global Fund, following retirement from the World Bank. During his two decades of service at the World Bank, he was an advisor to the Health, Nutrition and Population (HNP) Global Director and HNP Practice Manager in the East Asia and Pacific, Europe and Central Asia, and Middle East and North Africa Regions. He worked as Director of Country Health Systems at the European Regional Office of the World Health Organization, and he was Senior Advisor for Health at the International Development Research Centre of Canada. He also held the position of Adjunct Professor of Health Policy at the University of Montreal and the Duke Global Health Institute.

He is the author or coauthor of seven books, as well as more than 50 peer-reviewed research papers and book chapters, on comparative health systems, health and health care policy, and health and environment and disease control programs. Dr. Barış holds a medical degree from Turkey and an MSc and PhD from the Université de Montréal, Canada.

Muhammad Ali Pate is the Julio Frenk Professor of Public Health Leadership in the Harvard T. H. Chan School of Public Health. Until July 2021, he served as the Global Director, HNP, and as Director of Global Financing Facility for Women, Children, and Adolescents. Dr. Pate previously held several senior positions, including as the Chief Executive Officer of Big Win Philanthropy, based in the United Kingdom, and the Minister of State for Health in the Federal Government of Nigeria.

Dr. Pate is an MD who trained in both internal medicine and infectious diseases, with an MBA from Duke University. He also has a masters' degree in health system management from the London School of Hygiene & Tropical Medicine.

Rachel Silverman is a Policy Fellow at the Center for Global Development, where she leads policy-oriented research on global health financing and incentive structures. Her wide-ranging research currently focuses on the practical application of results-based financing, reimagining primary health care, global health transitions, efficient global health procurement, innovation models for global health, priority setting for universal health care, alignment and impact in international funding for family planning, and strategies to strengthen evidence and accountability. She has been affiliated with the Center for Global Development since 2011; earlier, she worked with the National Democratic Institute to support democracy and governance-strengthening programs in Kosovo.

She holds an MA in philosophy with distinction in public health from the University of Cambridge, which she attended as a Gates Cambridge Scholar. She also holds a BA with distinction in international relations and economics from Stanford University.

Huihui Wang is a Senior Economist at the World Bank. She has 20 years of experience working in low-, middle-, and high-income countries, with a focus on supporting them to achieve universal health coverage. She is currently involved in several global initiatives related to transforming and improving primary health care, knowledge programs on COVID-19 impact and response, and nutrition financing. She has also led the World Bank's lending operations and technical support in health system reforms in East Asia, Europe and Central Asia, and Sub-Saharan Africa regions. She joined the World Bank as a Young Professional in 2009.

She holds a medical degree from Beijing Medical University and an MA in economics and a PhD in health services and policy analysis from University of California at Berkeley.

Feng Zhao is Practice Manager, Strategy, Operations and Global Engagement, at the World Bank. He has more than 20 years of experience in public health, medicine, economics, and demography at the global, regional, and country levels. He has worked extensively on health policy dialogues, as well as technical work and operations, particularly in Europe and Central Asia and Sub-Saharan Africa. As the World Bank Practice Manager, he oversees the global health engagement program and is leading a strategy-refreshing exercise for the HNP program.

He serves as a faculty member for a number of universities, including as a faculty member for the Harvard Finance Minister Executive Leadership Program. He holds a PhD in population and health economics from the Johns Hopkins University, a masters of public health from University of California at Berkeley, and a medical degree from China.

Abbreviations

ACO	Accountable Care Organization
ADZU	Ateneo de Zamboanga University
ART	antiretroviral therapy
BHCPF	Basic Health Care Provision Fund
BHS	basic health services
BMPHS	Basic Minimum Package of Health Services
CBL	case-based learning
CCTs	conditional cash transfers
CEME	Community Engaged Medical Education
CHA	Cambridge Health Alliance
CHPS	Community-based Health Planning and Service
CHWs	community health workers
CMS	Center for Medicaid and Medicare Services
CNAMTS	Caisse Nationale d'Assurance Maladie des Travailleurs Salariés
CPC+	Comprehensive Primary Care Plus
CVD	cardiovascular disease
DAH	development assistance for health
DALY	disability-adjusted life years
DCP3	*Disease Control Priorities* (3rd edition)
DRG	diagnosis-related group
EAPHLNP	The East Africa Public Health Laboratory Networking Project
EBAIS	Equipos Básicos de Atención Integral de Salud
ECG	electrocardiogram
EHR	electronic health record
EPSS	Evaluación de la Prestación de Servicios de Salud
e-RS	e-referral system for specialist consultations
FFS	fee for service
FHS	Family Health Service (Brazil)
FHTs	family health teams

FPs	general practice/family medicine specialists
GAP	SDG3 Global Action Plan
GBD	Global Burden of Diseases, Injuries, and Risk Factors
GFF	Global Finance Facility for Women, Children and Adolescents
GIS	geographical information systems
GK	Gesundes Kinzigtal GmbH
GP	general practitioner
GSP	Global Skills Partnership
HALE	healthy life expectancy
HANSA	Health and Nutrition Services Access Project (World Bank)
HCP	Human Capital Project
hearScreen™	hearing screening smartphone-based application
HF	health financing
HIC	high-income country
HITAP	Health Intervention and Technology Assessment Program (Thailand)
HIV	human immunodeficiency virus
HLC	healthy living center
HMIS	health management information systems
HMO	health maintenance organization
HNP	Health, Nutrition, and Population
HPV	human papillomavirus
HRH Program	Human Resources for Health Program (Rwanda)
HSRS	Health Sector Reform Strategy
HTA	health technology assessment
IBRD	International Bank for Reconstruction and Development
ICL	integrated clinical learning
ICT	information and communications technology
IDA	International Development Association
IHME	Institute for Health Metrics and Evaluation
IT	information technology
JLN	Joint Learning Network for Universal Health Coverage

LGBT	lesbian, gay, bisexual, and transgender
LHINs	local health integration networks
LMICs	low- and middle-income countries
M&E	monitoring and evaluation
MA	medical administration
MBA	masters of business administration
MCH	maternal and child health
MDG	millennium development goal
MDR-TB	multidrug resistant tuberculosis
MEPI	Medical Education Training Partnership Initiative
mHealth	mobile health(care)
MoE	Ministry of Education
MoF	Ministry of Finance
MoH	Ministry of Health
MoI	Ministry of the Interior
MoL	Ministry of Labor
MoT	Ministry of Technology
MPA	multiphase programmatic approach
MPH	public health administration
MSM	men who have sex with men
NASF	Family Health Support Centers
NCDs	noncommunicable diseases
NEPI	Nursing Training Partnership Initiative
NHSC	National Health Service Corps (United States)
NICE	National Institute for Health and Clinical Excellence
NLC	Nurse Licensure Compact
NOSM	Northern Ontario School of Medicine
NPHWs	nonphysician healthcare workers
OECD	Organisation for Economic Co-operation and Development
P4P	pay-for-performance
PaRIS	Patient-Reported Indicator Surveys
PCMH	US-based Patient-Centered Medical Home

PFM	public financial management
PHC	primary health care
PHCPI	Primary Health Care Performance Initiative
PNG	Papua New Guinea
PPE	personal protective equipment
PPP	preferred primary care provider
PREM	patient-reported experience measures
PROM	patient-reported outcome measures
R&D	research and development
RMNCAH-N	Reproductive, Maternal, Newborn, Child and Adolescent Health and Nutrition
RMNCH	reproductive, maternal, newborn, and child health
RNs	registered nurses
SARS	severe acute respiratory syndrome
SDGs	Sustainable Development Goals
SHI	social health insurance
TB	tuberculosis
UHC	universal health coverage
UNICEF	United Nations Children's Fund
VAT	value added tax
WBOT	ward-based outreach teams
WDCs	ward development committees

OVERVIEW

Introduction

The world has waited long enough for high-performing primary health care (PHC). It is now time to deliver. Forty years ago, leaders embraced the promise of health for all people through PHC. That vision has inspired generations. For nearly half a century, however, countries have struggled to walk the talk on PHC. We have not built health systems anchored in strong PHC where they were needed most. Today, COVID-19 (Coronavirus) has brought the reckoning for that shared failure—but it has also brought the chance to do the job right at last.

The COVID-19 pandemic has shown policy makers and ordinary citizens why health systems matter and what happens when they fail. In doing so, it has created a once-in-a-generation chance for structural health system change. Bold reforms now can prepare health systems for future crises and bring goals like universal health coverage (UHC) within reach. PHC holds the key to these transformations. To fulfill that promise, the walk has to finally match the talk. This report charts an agenda toward reimagined, fit-for-purpose PHC. It asks three questions about health systems reform built around PHC: "why?," "what?," and "how?"

The "why?" of PHC reform: Confronting complex change

Since PHC has been around for decades, why write a report about it now? The answer is that the characteristics of high-performing PHC are precisely those that are most critical for managing the pressures coming to bear on health systems in the post-COVID world. The challenges include future infectious outbreaks and other emergent threats, as well as long-term structural trends that are reshaping the environments in which systems operate in noncrisis times. This report highlights three sets of megatrends that will increasingly affect health systems in the coming decades: demographic and epidemiological shifts, changes in technology, and citizens' evolving expectations for health care.

The trends most important for health systems include population growth in low- and middle-income countries (LMICs), population aging in advanced economies, and the worldwide explosion of noncommunicable diseases (NCDs). PHC has unique capabilities to help systems meet these challenges, but features of traditional PHC systems need to evolve to take full advantage of existing strengths and build new ones.

The "what?" of PHC reform: Four structural shifts

PHC is good, but it has to get better. What about it needs to change? To meet the demand for quality, people-centered, integrated health care in the 21st century, all countries—despite their many differences—will need to achieve four fundamental shifts in how PHC is designed, financed, and delivered. Some countries have already made bold strides on these agendas, providing evidence for others. The four shifts can be described as follows:

+ **From dysfunctional gatekeeping to quality, comprehensive care for all**: Its gatekeeping function makes PHC a cornerstone of efficiency in health systems. Often, however, patients—especially poor patients—perceive PHC gatekeeping as an exclusionary barrier shutting them out from the care they want. Some countries have transformed this dynamic by creating PHC teams attuned to local realities and skilled to deliver the quality services that communities require.

+ **From fragmentation to people-centered integration**: In high-income countries and LMICs alike, patients often experience health care as fragmented and impersonal. Strong local PHC teams can fix this. Accountable teams build care around patients' needs and preferences; treat all patients with respect; collaborate and communicate internally; and coordinate patients' movement through the health system, taking buck-stops-here responsibility for outcomes, no matter where their patients receive care.

+ **From inequities to fairness and accountability**: COVID-19 has under-scored inequities in health care access and outcomes between and within countries. Some countries are harnessing PHC's distinctive capacities to tackle inequities. They prioritize PHC-driven essential service packages and reward accountability for health outcomes in frontline PHC.

+ **From fragility to resilience**: In the wake of the pandemic, countries need to draw the lessons and undertake ambitious reforms. Achieving this will involve ensuring that PHC teams include public health surveillance and outreach capacity and that financial and human resource surge capacities are built into health sector planning and resource allocation at the local level.

The "how?" of PHC reform: Directions for action

After identifying high-level shifts that describe the outcomes that countries seek with PHC reform, this report presents evidence on the actions that countries can take—and are already taking—to bring these shifts about. Based on the available evidence, we emphasize three paths for action.

Priority reform 1: Multidisciplinary team-based care

Delivering PHC services through multidisciplinary teams is key to fulfilling the promise of PHC. In this model, a multidisciplinary team of health service providers—headquartered at a PHC hub facility but reaching out actively into the community—works collaboratively to serve a defined population that is assigned ("empaneled") to the team. The specific composition of the care team and the size of the catchment population vary between and within countries, reflecting local health needs and resources. The core PHC team generally consists of at least three types of providers—community health workers (CHWs), nurses, and general practice/family medicine specialists.

Although the evidence base on multidisciplinary collaborative care is nascent, emerging findings suggest substantial performance gains. Empanelment to dedicated care teams provides a strong foundation for care coordination and continuity, enabling long-term relationships between patients and providers. Patients with access to continuous, personalized care have been shown to receive better quality care, report higher satisfaction with health services, and incur lower health expenditures.

Proactive PHC teams can tackle barriers to care that disproportionately affect vulnerable constituencies. Engaging directly with communities, local teams can deliver health education and promotion; offer nutritional coaching and supplementation; identify subclinical illness; and help sustain adherence to treatment for diseases from diabetes to tuberculosis. This process may reduce health disparities.

Multidisciplinary team-based PHC platforms offer benefits for preparedness, response, and resilience in emergencies. These platforms can incorporate data collection, surveillance, and other public health functions. Syndromic surveillance coordinated with national public health authorities can help identify and contain outbreaks before they spread. Relationships of trust between the PHC team and community facilitate communication and behavior change during emergencies.

Priority reform 2: Building a multiprofessional health workforce

In many countries, the PHC workforce remains insufficient—in numbers, competencies, distribution, and/or mandate—to deliver quality team-based PHC. Bringing high-quality PHC to all people, particularly underserved populations, will require changes in how health workers are trained, deployed, managed, evaluated, and paid.

The transition to community team-based care requires a reorientation of medical education, particularly for physicians. Reforms can embed medical education within community clinical settings and orient medical graduates to generalist/primary care specialization. Educational content must evolve beyond clinical knowledge and skills, nurturing additional competencies that are crucial for community-focused care. For example, provider teams need strategic communication capacity to dialogue with communities about health needs and communicate the vision of PHC, along with interpersonal and political skills to build relationships with stakeholders that influence community health. These stakeholders may include government agencies, businesses, religious authorities, and community leaders.

Frontline strategies to get best results from the PHC workforce include task shifting, where selected care tasks are delegated to nonphysician health workers under physician supervision, optimizing the use of higher-skilled cadres. Evidence shows that CHWs and midlevel cadres can effectively deliver a range of health promotion and basic curative interventions, including management of common childhood illnesses; promotion of antenatal care and breastfeeding; and prevention and treatment for tuberculosis, malaria, and HIV. In countries including Nigeria and South Africa, CHWs have played a notable role in COVID-19 case detection and contact tracing.

Key areas for PHC workforce policy also include health worker performance evaluation and compensation. Primary care teams need quality measurement tools that promote accountable performance by rewarding team members for managing complexity, solving problems, and thinking creatively to address patients' specific circumstances. Priorities for outcome and performance management include people-centered reporting and metrics.

Priority reform 3: Financing public-health-enabled PHC

Financing is critical for the transition to high-performing PHC. Significant investments—not simply adjustments at the margins—are needed to put PHC at the center of health systems. Each country will identify its own locally relevant PHC policies, define a benefits package, and assess budget implications. Modeling from past studies suggests that most LMICs will need to substantially raise their government health expenditures to achieve strong PHC. Those investments can be expected to pay substantial dividends—by improving population health and human capital, advancing economic inclusion, and facilitating countries' competitiveness.

General government revenue is increasingly recognized as the best financing source for PHC. Using it facilitates equitable access to health services and improves financial protection for the population. When it comes to deciding how public resources for health should be spent, the best results come from prioritizing investment in the highest-impact health services within countries' budget constraints and ensuring that services reach the whole population. A prioritized health benefits package for primary care—customized to the local burden of disease, community values, and citizen preferences—helps justify allocating resources to PHC and can also facilitate accountability.

Traditional fee-for-service payments, line-item budgets, or capitation alone are increasingly seen as poorly aligned with team-based, integrated care models. Many countries have adopted financing innovations to foster team-based care; promote coordination and integration; and improve quality, outcomes, and efficiency. These emerging models, sometimes called "value-based" payments, shift clinical and financial accountability to providers by adjusting and conditioning reimbursement based on cost, quality, and patient-experience metrics.

Given the severe health-financing constraints in many lower-income countries, especially post-COVID, the donor community will have a crucial role in supporting PHC reform in these settings. Rethinking development assistance for health (DAH) can drive the investments and capacity building needed to deliver on the promise of people-centered PHC while also addressing problems of DAH fragmentation. A new era of development assistance will require shifting from investing in specific priority programs to investing in systems, including the capital investments and recurrent operational costs needed for stronger PHC. Many donors are signaling increased attention to investment in PHC systems and public financial management.

Policy recommendations

Each country will have its own road map for PHC reform that reflects national starting conditions, health and development priorities, and political economies. However, some policy priorities will apply across settings. This report formulates broad policy recommendations for governments and proposes actions for the global health community, including the World Bank.

Team-based care organization

1. **Assess health workforce strengths and gaps and plan the transition to team-based delivery**. Countries can jump-start their PHC team composition and empanelment strategies through a situation assessment and team-based care transition plan.

2. **Leverage information technology on the PHC frontlines**. Digital tools can foster transparency and accountability in PHC. Countries can score efficiency gains by upskilling data analysis capabilities within local care teams.

Multidisciplinary health workforce development

1. **Launch multidisciplinary medical education reforms**. Medical education strategies will build the skills for community-focused, team-based care.

2. **Reform provider compensation to promote rural practice and generalist care**. Countries can use evidence-based options to tackle compensation imbalances and redistribute the health workforce.

3. **Expand tiered accreditation systems tied to reimbursement policy**. Governments can engage with the private sector to leverage its workforce and infrastructure for PHC delivery, while improving care quality and affordability. Reimbursement and strategic purchasing policies can incentivize private sector participation in a tiered accreditation system.

Financing and resource mobilization

1. **Finance PHC through general government expenditure, without user fees**. Countries get the best results when they finance PHC through general government revenue. PHC services should be free at the point of care.

2. **Implement pro-health taxes**. Countries can often boost tax revenue by implementing or increasing pro-health taxes on harmful products, especially tobacco, alcohol, and sugar.

3. **Leverage payment reform to promote team-based care, coordination, and quality.** Countries can expand the use of strategic/value-based purchasing to facilitate team-based care models. Patients' voices should be heard when designing provider payment mechanisms.

4. **Create an accountability framework that links resources to results**. Resource mobilization tends to be more successful when accompanied by a strong accountability framework. Transparent measurement of PHC financing, which has been a weak link in many countries, is critical.

What the World Bank and its partners will do

The World Bank will use its lending, learning, and leadership to support countries in delivering the promise of reimagined PHC.

1. **Lending: accelerate access to funding for PHC reforms**. The World Bank will work with the Global Finance Facility (GFF) and other Global Action Plan (GAP) PHC Accelerator partners to facilitate countries' access to funds for PHC-oriented system reforms. Advancing PHC assertively in COVID-19 health system-strengthening operations and the GFF Essential Services Grants will be a "win-win" for countries and the World Bank's programs.

2. **Learning: mobilize practice-relevant PHC knowledge**. Together with analytic and financial partners, the World Bank will strengthen global knowledge hubs for PHC, including the Primary Health Care Performance Initiative (PHCPI), and ensure that they are equipped to achieve even more in the years ahead. World Bank technical assistance to countries will support the integration and operationalization of PHC knowledge in policies and programs.

3. **Leadership: develop country-specific policy options through dialogue**. To support national leadership in PHC reform and facilitate a multisectoral whole-of-government approach, the World Bank Health, Nutrition, and Population Global Practice, together with other global practices (such as Agriculture and Environment) and the Human Capital Project, will establish a dedicated platform for policy dialogue, advice, and technical assistance to ministries of health and ministries of finance. Dialogue will identify entry points and strengthen relationships for subsequent country-level technical collaboration and financial support, building on and further leveraging the GFF country leadership program.

Conclusions

With COVID-19, policy makers, health professionals, and ordinary citizens in most countries understand that business as usual in health care is no longer an option. Health systems need transformation on the scale of the crisis itself. COVID-19 has created a once-in-a-generation opportunity for sweeping systemic change backed by bold public investment and supported by broad social demand. The health care model that can drive this change is fit-for-purpose primary health care. This model is anchored in the values and lessons of the historical PHC movement—and it is reimagined for a world in which the pandemic has challenged much of what we thought we knew.

Nearly half a century after the Alma Ata Conference, PHC's proven benefits have still not reached hundreds of millions of people who urgently need them. When COVID struck, PHC's power to protect communities in health emergencies was not used. We need to keep talking about PHC. Above all, we need to walk the talk—fast. The distinctive strengths of PHC are vital to "build back better" in health after the pandemic. Countries that choose the path of ambitious PHC reform will reap powerful rewards: through lower health care costs; more resilient systems; stronger human capital; increased health literacy; higher economic productivity; and above all, longer, healthier, and more satisfying lives for people.

Chapter 1

Primary Health Care:

TIME TO DELIVER

Introduction

More than 40 years ago, policy makers from around the world launched the global primary health care (PHC) movement with the 1978 Declaration of Alma-Ata. The PHC vision has inspired successive generations, and PHC systems have powered remarkable health gains in many settings. Countries where the needs for PHC are greatest, however, have struggled to "walk the talk." Even before the COVID-19 (Coronavirus) crisis, most of the low- and middle-income countries (LMICs) lagged far behind the pace of change needed to achieve their health targets under the Sustainable Development Goals (SDGs), including universal health coverage (UHC) backed by strong primary care. Today, the COVID-19 crisis has stripped away the illusions and exposed the consequences of our collective negligence. By unmasking the latent failures of the status quo in health systems, the pandemic has created an opening for transformative change. The distinctive strengths of PHC are vital to "build back better" in health after COVID-19. For PHC to play this change-leading role, however, the walk finally has to match the talk.

An unfinished journey

Since the 1978 Declaration, some form of PHC has been implemented in virtually every country. Well-designed PHC services have demonstrated their capacity to deliver population health gains and improve health equity at manageable cost across a wide range of country contexts. The PHC evidence base has grown steadily stronger (Hone, Macinko, and Millett 2018).

Practice-focused global networks have formed, including the Primary Health Care Performance Initiative (PHCPI) and others, to support countries in reaching PHC goals. In 2018, World Health Organization (WHO) member states unanimously reaffirmed the foundational importance of PHC in a declaration marking the 40th anniversary of the Alma-Ata Conference, and they endorsed PHC as the cornerstone of UHC and sustainable health systems in the 21st century (WHO 2018).

Yet, along with its recognized successes, there is a widely shared sense that PHC has not yet fulfilled its potential (WHO 2019). Although PHC principles are sound, efforts to implement those principles have repeatedly fallen short of expectations, particularly in LMICs. Since the early days of the global movement, countries at all levels of income have struggled to "walk the talk" on PHC.

Well before the COVID-19 crisis, the consequences were visible in countries' health results. Under the SDGs, all countries have pledged to achieve UHC by 2030 to provide their people with quality essential health services and financial protection from excessive health care expenditures. As of 2016, however, over 3.6 billion people—roughly half of the world's population—still lacked access to basic health care (Billl & Melinda Gates Foundation 2021; WHO and World Bank 2017; WHO and World Bank 2019). Financial protection has also lagged, so that people who do obtain health services risk being driven into poverty as a result. Every year between 2000 and 2010, approximately 100 million people were pushed into extreme poverty, and over 800 million people suffered financial catastrophe as a result of paying for health care out of pocket. These figures have seen little improvement over time since then, and they have actually deteriorated since the onset of the COVID-19 pandemic (Bill & Melinda Gates Foundation 2021; WHO and World Bank 2019).

Countries have worked to narrow the gaps, but results are far too slow. At the rates of progress on service coverage and financial protection measured before COVID-19, the UHC goal was already practically beyond the reach of the majority of LMICs. Meanwhile, health systems in many higher-income countries have achieved broad service coverage but face shortfalls in the quality of care, chronic health disparities among social groups, and soaring health care costs.

Demographic, epidemiological, and socioeconomic trends show that even greater challenges lie ahead for health systems. Populations are rising fast in some of the poorest countries, and they are aging rapidly in higher-income settings. Many countries face a protracted epidemiologic transition, where stunting coexists with obesity, and surging noncommunicable disease burdens come atop persistent infectious threats. Rising citizen expectations for health care have followed urbanization and globalization, even as climate change, economic crises, institutional fragility, and conflict threaten to overwhelm fragile health gains in many countries.

The supply side of health care is also in flux, with new pressures and proliferating, often contradictory, proposals across all health system domains; these include financing, workforce dynamics, health technology, and organization of care. On the eve of COVID-19, while shortfalls in service coverage and financial protection persisted in many settings, health leaders faced insistent demands to raise care quality and strengthen equity, while simultaneously bringing costs under control and making systems more efficient. Experts argued that PHC was critical for tackling all of these challenges, yet many countries' PHC investments stagnated.

The shock of COVID-19

COVID-19 has exposed health system failures in countries around the world. In doing so, it has generated a powerful momentum for change. The pandemic exploited multiple weaknesses across health system platforms in rich and poor countries. Underresourced surveillance networks failed to promptly detect the spread of the virus in communities, so waves of severe cases seemed to surge out of nowhere, overwhelming hospitals in the process. Shortages of supplies and equipment quickly broke out, sparking bidding wars and leaving health workers without protective gear. System fragmentation hampered the efficient flows of patients, staff, and supplies.

Amid these cascading failures, the crisis was exacerbated by specific weaknesses in countries' PHC platforms—the predictable result of decades of benign neglect and chronic underinvestment in PHC. Few countries had connected PHC providers to technology-enabled event-based or syndromic surveillance systems. Many people in poor and rich countries alike lacked a regular PHC provider who could evaluate, counsel, and quickly refer them to testing or hospital care. Financial barriers in some countries kept many people from seeking early access to testing and care.

By stressing PHC networks that were already stretched thin, the pandemic diverted resources and interrupted the delivery of routine essential services, including vaccinations, maternal and child health interventions, and care for infectious diseases other than COVID-19. LMICs bore the brunt of these impacts. Nigeria, for example, saw a reduction of 50 percent in outpatient visits, antenatal care services, and immunization (World Bank 2020). Resilient PHC networks capable of responding to health emergencies could have facilitated control of the crisis and substantially reduced its human and economic costs.

Practical options for stronger PHC

Although flaws in health care organization may sometimes be apparent only to specialists, following COVID-19, few citizens of any affected country can be unaware of deep inadequacies in their health systems. This also means that countries emerging from the pandemic have an opportunity and a responsibility to undertake ambitious reforms. The time is right for reimagining PHC—not to redefine it abstractly but to clarify practical steps countries can take to make PHC fit-for-purpose in the 21st century, starting now.

The good news is that, even as COVID-19 laid bare the health system weaknesses—including underdeveloped PHC—it simultaneously inspired health leaders to think and act beyond established paradigms. Policy makers and citizens recognized anew the life-or-death importance of strong, well-resourced health systems, the heroism of the frontline health workforce, and the value of equitable access to health services in protecting the health of the whole population.

As the world emerges from the COVID-19 crisis, health systems will enter a period of critical risk and opportunity. Bold policy choices now can transform health systems for the decades to come, bringing goals like UHC within reach. In many countries, such decisions will enjoy unprecedented support from citizens. However, the deepening economic crisis is already putting pressure on health and social service budgets across the globe. Before austerity overwhelms ambition, there will be a brief window of opportunity to seize the momentum and launch the far-reaching reforms that are needed to fix underlying systemic problems rather than to simply treat superficial symptoms. Health leaders need to be prepared to act before that window closes.

This report looks to the past months of worldwide upheaval—added to 40 years of global PHC experience—to chart an agenda toward fit-for-purpose primary health care. It reflects a renewed understanding of global and local vulnerabilities in the post-COVID-19 world. It affirms the unique promise of PHC, while it analyzes deficiencies in PHC design, delivery, and financing that have reduced performance. And it seeks to harness the current global momentum with a practical reform agenda that takes existing constraints seriously and moves beyond business as usual.

This report pursues four objectives:

+ Contribute evidence to the growing consensus on PHC as the cornerstone of high-performing health systems, while also showing why PHC must evolve.

+ Identify structural shifts most PHC systems need to undertake to further improve outcomes and efficiency.

+ Propose proven reform steps and implementation strategies that countries can use to drive shifts in care organization, the health workforce, and health financing.

+ Show how countries can optimize domestic and external technical and financial resources to "walk the talk" on reimagined PHC.

Audiences

The report is addressed primarily to governments, in particular, policy makers and technical advisers in ministries of finance and ministries of health. Since PHC is most effective when supported by a whole-of-government approach to policy making, the report also aims to engage leaders in other government departments, clarifying how the recommended actions can advance some of those sectors' priority agendas. The report's recommendations prioritize options that are realistic for most LMICs. Adapted versions of these approaches are likely to yield solid results in many wealthier countries as well.

A second audience is the private sector entities, both for-profit and not-for-profit, which are on the front lines of providing essential health services in many countries. The aim is to persuade the sector entities that this approach to PHC has value for their work too and to engage in discussion on how they can align their efforts with that of public sector agencies that are responsible to implement the reforms.

The report also addresses a wide range of development partners—especially Global Action Plan (GAP) collaborators, who are committed to accelerate progress toward the achievement of health-related SDG goal and targets—but also the wider community of bilateral and multilateral agencies, foundations, and civil society organizations engaged in global health and development. The approach to PHC described here is informed by the technical work and leadership of many of these agencies, and this report is an invitation to deeper collaboration.

Finally, the report aims to advance collaboration on PHC within the World Bank Group itself. This includes promoting wider understanding of PHC as an effective platform to build and protect human capital within a multisectoral architecture, including One Health, as outlined in the World Bank's Health, Nutrition and Population Strategy Refresh (World Bank 2020; see also World Bank 2007). This report lays out the case for raising the profile of PHC in World Bank lending. The lending, learning, and leadership that the World Bank Group brings can substantially benefit countries advancing on the change paths described herein. The best results will come through broad collaborative alliances, with which the World Bank has long experience, including PHCPI, the Joint Learning Initiative for Universal Health Coverage (JLN), and others.

Looking back at the history of PHC is humbling. Visionary health leaders, innovative practitioners, and exceptional scholars have built the PHC literature and legacy over the past half century. Recently, leading institutions and new generations of researchers have offered compelling proposals on how PHC can evolve to meet today's health challenges. Against this background, the contributions of this report are necessarily modest. Nevertheless, building on frontline country experience and previous research, it organizes actionable evidence so that policy makers and implementers may use it practically to plan, fund, and implement PHC reforms.

Data sources and policy timeframe

This report draws on the peer-reviewed and gray literature, as well as data sources from the World Bank, Organisation for Economic Co-operation and Development (OECD), WHO, other specialized UN agencies, and the Institute for Health Metrics and Evaluation (IHME).

The report addresses a historical context in which policy makers and health-sector partners are grappling with the consequences of COVID-19. It offers specific recommendations for leveraging the distinctive capabilities of high-performing PHC in this context of urgent action. The report's technical and policy recommendations also look beyond crisis response and early-stage recovery to consider a longer timeframe appropriate for structural change in PHC systems. The report discusses actions and outcomes through 2030, the target year for the SDGs, including the countries' pledge to achieve UHC.

Limitations

It is important to acknowledge this report's limitations. One fundamental point concerns the availability of evidence and its applicability across different contexts. In general, relatively few studies compare different organizational and financing modalities of PHC systems in countries while controlling for other factors that may influence the outcomes of interest, such as political economy and features of the health workforce. The report's core arguments apply to countries at all levels of income; its main concern, however, is to suggest how LMICs can improve their health systems through fit-for-purpose PHC. Historically, a large share of PHC research has taken place in high-income countries (HICs). Accordingly, the report cites considerable evidence on PHC challenges and solutions from higher-income settings, while recognizing the transposition challenges involved in applying these findings elsewhere. Wherever possible, the report draws on the growing body of PHC evidence directly derived from LMIC settings. In recent years, PHC research in LMICs has gained remarkable momentum. Networks including the JLN, PHCPI, and others support high-quality research and have created repositories of evidence for investigators and practitioners. Supporting these networks to further develop the PHC learning agenda in lower-income settings is an important commitment for the World Bank.

Chapter 2 of the report discusses global megatrends that are increasingly affecting health systems today, posing challenges for performance and sustainability. The range of forces in this category is large, and only a few can be analyzed here. We have focused on trends—including shifts in the age distribution of human populations, mobility, urbanization, and rising noncommunicable disease burdens—that will affect all countries, although in different ways, and where the link to practical choices facing health policy makers is relatively clear. We have chosen not to focus in detail on other important topics—notably, climate change—that will also strongly impact health systems in the coming decades but where the implications for PHC policy and practice are currently less clear. Working cross-sectorally with countries and partners to better anticipate climate impacts on health and support climate-robust PHC is a key task for the future.

The conceptual architecture of this report involves identifying four high-level change goals for stronger PHC and charting three priority reform axes that countries can use to reach those goals. Both the change goals and directions for reform have been defined based on literature reviews; analysis of existing PHC performance assessment tools and change frameworks; documented country experiences; and expert consultation. Readers will recognize broad alignment between the conceptual architecture developed here and existing, widely cited frameworks for understanding and improving PHC. However, it is important to be explicit on two points.

+ First, while this report's agenda for fit-for-purpose PHC builds on and benefits from previous frameworks, research, and country experience, the fit-for-purpose PHC program is a new framing and therefore subject to caution. It is derived from ongoing original work, and the responsibility for its shortcomings rests entirely with the report team rather than with our sources.

+ Second, the construction of the fit-for-purpose PHC agenda is based on a primarily qualitative approach to prior frameworks and evidence. In foregrounding the promise of team-based PHC service delivery models, for example, we have not attempted to generate original quantitative estimates of the benefits that such models could produce in terms of population health indicators and health system cost savings in specific settings. Doing this is another important frontier for future learning.

What does PHC mean in this report?

Historically, defining PHC has been a difficult and often divisive problem. This report adopts the current definition of PHC formulated by WHO. In addition, the report formulates its own definition of fit-for-purpose primary health care (box 1.1). This definition reflects long-term aspirations in the spirit of the Declarations of Alma-Ata and Astana, but it also identifies practical priorities for PHC reform today.

Reimagining PHC

In addition to the WHO definition of primary health care, this report formulates a concept of "fit-for-purpose" to reimagine PHC. The term "fit-for-purpose" characterizes the PHC systems that countries establish progressively as they implement the reforms outlined in this report. Improving health outcomes and making health systems more efficient, equitable, and resilient can be understood as PHC's purpose. PHC platforms are "fit" to the extent that they achieve this purpose.

The definition of fit-for-purpose PHC is derived from the broader WHO definition and emphasizes a select set of attributes that appear particularly important for PHC in today's health system environments. We define fit-for-purpose PHC as follows:

A health- and social-service delivery platform uniquely designed to meet communities' health and health care needs across a comprehensive spectrum of services—including health services from promotive to palliative—in a continuous, integrated, and people-centered manner. Services provided by this platform are tailored to the socioeconomic and cultural ecology to which communities belong, as well as to the financial and human resources of the health system within which the platform operates resiliently and sustainably. The platform ensures equitable access to quality health care and other services throughout people's life course, advancing universal health coverage and contributing to sustainable development.

BOX 1.1
DEFINING PRIMARY HEALTH CARE

WHO Definition

The current World Health Organization (WHO) definition of primary health care (PHC) provides the foundation and clearest expression of the concept of PHC used in this report. The WHO definition has three interrelated components that, taken together, cover all aspects of PHC. Under this definition, primary health care accomplishes the following:

+ Meet[s] people's health needs through comprehensive promotive, protective, preventive, curative, rehabilitative, and palliative care throughout the life course, strategically prioritizing key health care services aimed at individuals and families through primary care and the population through public health functions as the central elements of integrated health services, and

+ Systematically address[es] the broader determinants of health (including social, economic, environmental, as well as people's characteristics and behaviors) through evidence-informed public policies and actions across all sectors, and

+ Empower[s] individuals, families, and communities to optimize their health, as advocates for policies that promote and protect health and well-being, as co-developers of health and social services, and as self-carers and care-givers to others (WHO 2018b).

What PHC Is Not

Related to WHO's positive PHC definition are certain negative stipulations, that is, the things that PHC is *not*. Primary health care has often been presented as synonymous with other health-service models that actually differ in crucial ways from PHC as defined by WHO. This conflation of dissimilar concepts—sometimes unintentional, sometimes deliberate—has often had negative consequences both for the credibility of PHC and for the health and lives of people receiving health services labeled as primary health care.

+ PHC does not mean basic or rudimentary health care.

+ PHC does not equal gatekeeping. The latter is often understood solely from the supply perspective, with a view to efficiency. The objective of providing appropriate care at the right level is eclipsed. As a result, patients and communities may tend to perceive gatekeeping (and PHC itself) as a hurdle to clear to access specialized care.

+ PHC is not equivalent to "primary care" or "comprehensive primary care," since these two terms in their most common usage do not cover the second and third components of the WHO definition cited. "Primary care" and "comprehensive primary care" as commonly understood do not fully encompass promotive, protective, rehabilitative, and palliative care throughout the life course. They largely focus on curative medical care, even if this is sometimes broadly defined (Peikes et al. 2018).

(Continued)

BOX 1.1 *(continued)*

+ Integrating primary care and public health to improve population health is not a supplementary enhancement of PHC. It is already part and parcel of PHC, properly understood (IOM 2012).

+ Integrating primary care and public health to improve population health is not a supplementary enhancement of PHC. It is already part and parcel of PHC, properly understood (IOM 2012).

+ Primary health care does not mean first-contact care, nor the first level of care in the health system. First-contact care could be emergency medical services. Historically, equating PHC with the first level of care has led to its being understood as low-quality health care, mainly for the poor. PHC should also not be seen as focusing only on first causes of community health problems, that is, the structural social and economic determinants. PHC recognizes the importance of health determinants and may support action to address them through multi-sectoral initiatives, but PHC's concern with underlying health determinants does not downplay the importance of quality personal health care services for those who need them (Frenk 2009).

+ "Selective PHC," a concept introduced shortly after the 1978 Alma-Ata Conference and widely applied subsequently, is *not* PHC. It distorts the concept of PHC by focusing on selected diseases rather than the whole person and the full spectrum of services from promotive to palliative (Kluge et al. 2018).

Defining what PHC is and is not has implications for the connection between PHC and universal health care (UHC). This report understands PHC as the main vehicle for the realization of UHC. Some authors note that the universal inclusivity highlighted in the term "UHC" was anticipated in the PHC vision expressed at Alma-Ata. From its inception, PHC was understood to involve equitable access to health services (Sanders et al. 2019). This was reflected in the PHC goal of Health for All and the commitment to put people at the center of health systems (Ghebreyesus et al. 2018).

The main use of this definition is to highlight specific structural features and processes that are integral to countries' success in the reform agendas described in the report, as well as to underscore the interdependence among some of these features. The term "platform" evokes a set of interlinked services and the delivery architecture required to provide them, including health-worker teams, the networks and resources that support them, and the infrastructure health workers use to deliver care to communities.

Structure of the report

The remainder of this report proceeds as follows. The report asks "Why?," "What?," and "How?" questions about PHC-driven health system reform. Chapter 2 shows why these reforms are urgent now. It analyzes trends in demographics, epidemiology, technology, and citizens' expectations for health care that pose daunting challenges for health systems today—challenges to which systems built around strong PHC will be best able to respond. Chapter 3 describes what PHC reforms aim to achieve. It identifies four systemic shifts that characterize fit-for-purpose PHC: boosting service quality while expanding coverage; achieving greater integration of people-centered care; enhancing fairness and accountability in PHC; and preparing PHC networks to tackle emergencies with resilience. Chapter 4 summarizes evidence on how countries can deliver these shifts. It describes three priority reform agendas: developing a multidisciplinary, team-based PHC platform; building a multiprofessional health workforce; and creating PHC financing solutions that can bring public health crisis response capabilities to the front lines, while strengthening routine PHC services. Finally, chapter 5 offers recommendations for countries and development partners to deliver PHC reforms and strengthen health system performance in the post-COVID world. It also explains how the World Bank is changing its work to support countries as they walk the talk on PHC.

References

Bill & Melinda Gates Foundation. 2021. "Goalkeepers Report." Bill & Melinda Gates Foundation, Seattle, Washington.

Frenk, Julio. 2009. "Reinventing Primary Health Care: The Need for Systems Integration." *The Lancet* 374 (9684): 170–73. https://doi.org/10.1016/S0140 -6736(09)60693-0.

Ghebreyesus, Tedros Adhanom, Henrietta Fore, Yelzhan Birtanov, and Zsuzsanna Jakab. 2018. "Primary Health Care for the 21st Century, Universal Health Coverage, and the Sustainable Development Goals." *The Lancet* 392 (10156): 1371–72 (October). https://doi.org/10.1016/S0140-6736(18)32556-X.

Hone, Thomas, James Macinko, and Christopher Millett. 2018. "Revisiting Alma-Ata: What Is the Role of Primary Health Care in Achieving the Sustainable Development Goals?" *The Lancet* 392 (10156): 1461–72 (October). https://doi .org/10.1016/S0140-6736(18)31829-4.

IOM (Institute of Medicine). 2012. *Primary Care and Public Health: Exploring Integration to Improve Population Health.* Washington, DC: The National Academies Press.

Kluge, Hans, Ed Kelley, Shannon Barkley, Pavlos N. Theodorakis, and Naoko Yamamoto, et al. 2018. "How Primary Health Care Can Make Universal Health Coverage a Reality, Ensure Healthy Lives, and Promote Wellbeing for All."

The Lancet 392 (10156): 1372–74 (October). https://doi.org/10.1016/S0140
-6736(18)32482-6.

Peikes, Deborah, Stacy Dale, Arkadipta Ghosh, Erin Fries Taylor, Kaylyn Swankoski,
et al. 2018. "The Comprehensive Primary Care Initiative: Effects on Spending,
Quality, Patients, and Physicians." *Health Affairs* 37 (6): 890–99. https://doi
.org/10.1377/hlthaff.2017.1678.

Sanders, David, Sulakshana Nandi, Ronald Labonté, Carina Vance, and Wim Van
Damme. 2019. "From Primary Health Care to Universal Health Coverage—One
Step Forward and Two Steps Back." *The Lancet* 394 (10199): P619–21 (August).
https://doi.org/10.1016/S0140-6736(19)31831-8.

WHO (World Health Organization) and World Bank. 2017. *Tracking Universal Health
Coverage: 2017 Global Monitoring Report.* Geneva and Washington, DC: WHO
and World Bank.

WHO (World Health Organization). 2018. "Declaration of Astana." WHO, Geneva.

WHO (World Health Organization). 2019. "The Global Action Plan for Healthy Lives
and Well-being for All." WHO, Geneva. http://www.who.int/sdg/global-action
-plan.

WHO (World Health Organization) and United Nations Children's Fund (UNICEF).
2018. "A Vision for Primary Health Care in the 21st Century: Towards Universal
Health Coverage and the Sustainable Development Goals." Geneva: WHO and
UNICEF.

WHO (World Health Organization) and World Bank. 2019. "Global Monitoring Report
on Financial Protection in Health 2019 (Advance copy)." Geneva: WHO and
World Bank.

World Bank. 2007. *Healthy Development : The World Bank Strategy for Health,
Nutrition, and Population Results.* Washington, DC: World Bank.

World Bank. 2020. "World Bank Country Team Assessment Reports 2020."
World Bank, Washington, DC.

Chapter 2

CHALLENGES FOR HEALTH SYSTEMS:

COVID-19 and Beyond

Introduction

The COVID-19 (Coronavirus) pandemic found health systems in most countries unprepared for a health threat that was widely predicted to be imminent: a newly emerging and deadly infectious disease capable of rapid global spread (Horton 2020). This preparedness lapse alone would justify far-reaching health system reforms. In the wake of a staggering public health system about which the world was warned well in advance and whose worst effects could have been prevented, previous ways of organizing, delivering, and paying for health services need to change.

But better preparedness for public health emergencies is only part of what health policy must now aim to achieve. The rationale—the "Why?"—of health system reform is more complex, because the challenges that health systems face extend far beyond the threat of future infectious outbreaks. To better understand the rationale for ambitious health system reform now, we need a broader sense of the key forces that will influence population health needs and health system response options in the coming years. To provide a portion of this background, this chapter asks two questions:

+ What are the forces that are likely to shape the evolution of countries' health ecosystems in the coming decade?

+ Are current health service delivery and financing models ready to manage those forces?

The chapter does not try to answer these broad questions comprehensively across all levels of care; rather, it focuses on selected aspects that are especially relevant to the discussion of health system reform led by primary health care (PHC).

Health system ecologies: Trends for the coming decade

Health systems reflect countries' unique histories and contexts. Today, however, health ecosystems worldwide are affected by a set of powerful trends that increasingly shape population health, the demands placed on health services, and the resources that policy makers have available to respond to health needs. This chapter focuses on three sets of trends: high-level demographic and epidemiological patterns, developments in technology, and citizens' evolving expectations for health services.

Before turning to those topics, it is important to acknowledge again the extent to which countries' choices about PHC reform will continue to be influenced by the fallout of COVID-19 and how leaders frame and manage the crisis politically. The pandemic has hit most countries with a double shock: a public health disaster rapidly overlaid by a brutal economic contraction that has spared few economies worldwide (Kurowski et al. 2021). More than a year into the pandemic, many hope that it will soon be brought under control, thanks in particular to the rapid development of vaccines. However, COVID-19's epidemiological trajectory is uncertain, and its economic impact threatens to be long lasting (World Bank 2020). Access to vaccines for most people in low- and middle-income countries (LMICs) remains a distant hope.

The pandemic's implications for health financing are complex. Following the substantial government outlays required for the emergency response, countries face crucial decisions on health spending in the years ahead. Pressures to rapidly rein in public sector health spending, in combination with other components of government expenditure, are already being felt. However, a compelling case can be made that countries that seize the crisis as an opportunity to invest in health—including but not limited to outbreak preparedness—will reap rewards, saving many lives and ultimately achieving a stronger economic recovery (figure 2.1).

Figure 2.1 Policy choices will be critical for health goals and economic recovery

Performance score of the UHC Effective Coverage Index

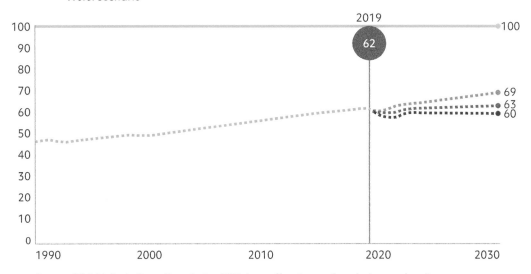

Source: Bill & Melinda Gates Foundation 2020, https://ww2.gatesfoundation.org/goalkeepers /downloads/2020-report/report_letter_en.pdf.

Note: UHC = universal health care.

Demographic and epidemiological trends

Today, few would question that health systems in most countries need to prepare better for emergencies and unforeseen events. In the decades ahead, however, many of the greatest pressures on health systems will continue to come from causes that are not unexpected. On the contrary, they are well known, persistent, and evolving in largely predictable ways. These include secular trends in the size, composition, and distribution of human populations, together with long-observed shifts in the burden of disease, the recurrent emergence and recrudescence of diseases of zoonotic origin, and the threats of "global public bads," such as antimicrobial resistance (World Bank 2017), environmental degradation (UNEP 2019), and climate change (Watts et al. 2019). These and related "public bads" will contribute appreciably to disease burdens, while they complicate health service delivery in the large majority of countries.

Population dynamics: Rapid growth in poorer regions, rapid graying among the rich

The global population will continue to increase in the coming decades, raising the pressure on health systems that are already overstretched. Since the Declaration of Alma-Ata, the global population has almost doubled, from about 4.2 billion in 1978 to 7.6 billion in 2018.[1] The world's population is projected to increase further, to 8.5 billion by 2030 and 9.7 billion by 2050, adding an estimated 83 million people each year (UN 2019a). Population growth rates differ sharply across regions, with the fastest rates in Sub-Saharan Africa and South Asia (GBD Collaborators 2018).

The bulk of the global population growth is projected to take place in LMICs, concentrating in the poorest countries across the globe. Populations of many Sub-Saharan African countries are expected to double by 2050. Eight of the nine countries that will account for more than half of global population growth in this period are LMICs (Democratic Republic of Congo, the Arab Republic of Egypt, Ethiopia, India, Indonesia, Nigeria, Pakistan, and Tanzania). Meanwhile, many high-income countries (HICs) are projected to experience modest growth or a decline in their populations (GBD Collaborators 2018; UN 2019a).

Populations in many high-income countries are growing older. Since the early 2000s, HICs have seen drops in the proportion of the working-age population, with the fall expected to continue: from 66.2 percent in 2015 to 58.3 percent in 2050. This trend coincides with an increase in the proportion of the population at and above the age of 65 (figures 2.2 and 2.3). The share of the elderly in the total population will expand from 16.7 percent to 26.9 percent over the same period (GBD Collaborators 2018). In contrast to HICs, most LMICs are expected to see an increase in the proportion of the working-age population in the years ahead. For instance, the working-age population share in low-income countries is estimated to have risen from 54.1 percent in 2005 to 62.7 percent in 2015, while the share of the population 65 years of age or older likely grew modestly from 3.2 percent to 5.4 percent. Recent work highlights that one-half the growth in working-age populations from 2020 to 2050 will occur in Sub-Saharan Africa (UN 2019b). However, while the proportion of older adults in LMIC populations will continue to grow modestly, the absolute numbers of people in this age category will expand substantially, placing important additional demands on health systems that must meet the complex care needs of large numbers of seniors. This trend is already marked in a few LMICs and most HICs.

The upshot of these population trends is concerning for health leaders everywhere. HICs face exploding health care costs linked to the care needs of

Figure 2.2 Percentage of working-age population (15–64 years of age), by income group and geographic location, 1950–2100

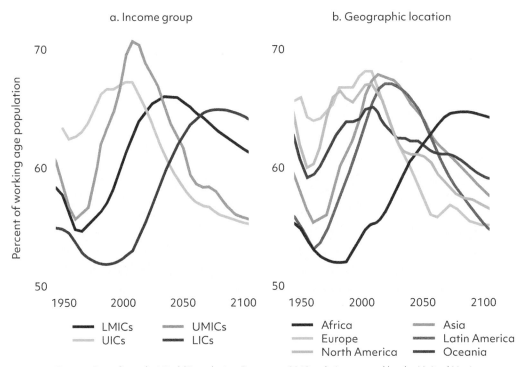

Source: Data from the World Population Prospects 2019 website curated by the United Nations Department of Economic and Social Affairs, Population Division (2019).

Note: HICs = high-income countries, LICs = low-income countries, LMICs = low- and middle income countries, and UMICs = upper-middle-income countries.

Figure 2.3 Percentage of population 65+ years of age, by income group and geographic location, 1950–2100

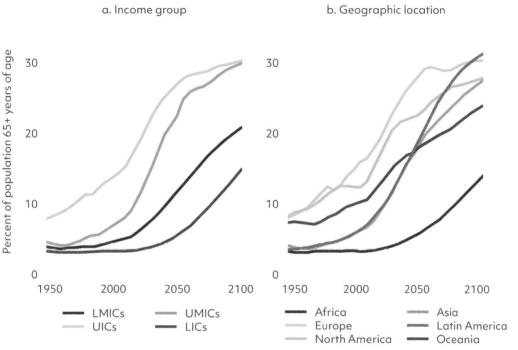

a. Income group

b. Geographic location

Source: Data from the World Population Prospects 2019 website curated by the United Nations Department of Economic and Social Affairs, Population Division (2019).

Note: HICs = high-income countries, LICs = low-income countries, LMICs = low- and middle-income countries, and UMICs = upper-middle-income countries.

aging populations, even as these countries' working-age populations shrink—exactly the demographic whose contributions would have been expected to finance the rising use of complex medical services among the aged. Under these conditions, health systems face powerful pressures to boost efficiency and rein in costs. The proven capacity of strong PHC to contain costs offers a crucial advantage. High-performing PHC has been regularly found to reduce unnecessary hospitalizations and costly emergency room visits, offering cheaper and better management of high-prevalence chronic conditions—for example, diabetes, asthma, hypertension, and congestive heart failure—in community settings at unit costs far below those that apply in higher-level health facilities (OECD 2020). The health promotion and disease prevention facets of PHC offer a powerful means to lower longer-term treatment costs and ensure the future solvency of systems.

Meanwhile, health systems in LMICs have an even more pressing need to make sure that limited health resources are used efficiently.

The promotion and prevention logic applies even more strongly in these contexts. So, increasingly, does the imperative to manage chronic conditions in community settings where costs are much lower. This argument gains strength as the absolute numbers of older citizens rise, together with the prevalence of multiple comorbidities and "lifestyle" diseases (such as obesity and diabetes) once seen largely in rich countries. In LMICs with rapidly growing younger populations, another key advantage of PHC is its capacity to efficiently deliver key maternal and child health services, along with promotive, preventive, and curative services that can boost the productivity of working-age populations; these services include nutritional supplementation, malaria prevention and treatment, treatment of minor injuries, and routine monitoring of vision and hearing. Such PHC services are critical to build and protect the human capital embodied in LMICs' young people and working adults—the cornerstone of the economic futures of the respective countries.

Longer, healthier lives—but not for all

Global average life expectancy at birth rose from 65.4 years in 1990 to 72.6 years in 2018. Low-income countries (LICs), however, lag more than a decade behind the global average, although the gap narrowed from 14.7 to 11.8 years during this period.[2] This persistent gap in life expectancy is driven by diverse factors, including high rates of maternal and child mortality, ongoing impact of the HIV pandemic, proliferating conflict and violence, and inadequate access to quality health care services.[3]

Healthy life expectancy (HALE) is a summary measure that combines changes in mortality and nonfatal health outcomes (Salomon et al. 2012). As such, HALE may provide a clearer snapshot of overall population health than life expectancy per se. Global average HALE at birth increased from 58.5 years in 2000 to 63.3 in 2016 (WHO 2019a). Although this is a welcome trend, the difference in 2016 between life expectancy and HALE at birth was some nine years, a stark reminder that many people will spend a substantial portion of their later lives afflicted by chronic illness that in many cases could have been prevented (figure 2.4). Wide disparities in HALE persist across countries at different income levels. In 2000, the average HALE in LICs was about 12.6 years below the global average. This gap narrowed to about nine years by 2016, but the contrast with HICs remains striking. The average HALE in HICs exceeds the global average by almost seven years. In this context, the proven capacity of high-performing PHC to narrow health equity gaps within and between countries takes on increased salience (Hone, Macinko, and Millett 2018). Multiple systematic reviews confirm the evidence base that associates strong PHC with lower health inequalities (Salomon et al. 2012).

Figure 2.4 Living longer, living sicker: Years lived in poor health, 1990 and 2019

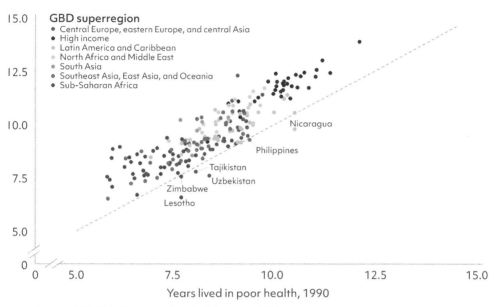

Source: GBD 2019 Demographics Collaborators 2020.

Note: The scatter plot shows years lived in poor health, calculated by subtracting HALE from life expectancy at birth, for 1990 and 2019. Datapoints are colored by GBD superregion. GBD = Global Burden of Diseases, Injuries, and Risk Factors Study; HALE = healthy life expectancy.

The changing burden of disease calls for reinforced PHC and action across sectors

The wide lag between HALE and overall life expectancy in all countries points to inadequate prevention and management of chronic diseases all along the country income spectrum. The global burden of noncommunicable diseases (NCDs) is rising steadily. The trend is particularly marked in LMICs, but all countries are affected (figure 2.5). This spells unprecedented challenges for health systems, many of which are already struggling to meet surging demand for NCD services while containing costs. The total number of deaths attributable to NCDs increased by 22.7 percent worldwide between 2007 and 2017. In 2017, NCDs accounted for 73.4 percent of all deaths, compared to 18.6 percent from communicable diseases and maternal, neonatal, and nutritional causes, and 8 percent due to injuries (IHME 2017). One recent study found that the absolute number of NCD deaths that could be averted with quality and timely provision of health care services increased by 49.3 percent, reaching 34.5 million in 2017 (Martinez et al. 2020). These averages mask substantial variation across countries and regions. About 40 percent of premature mortality due to avertable NCDs in 2017 was clustered in Southeast Asia, the Eastern Mediterranean, and

Figure 2.5 Noncommunicable diseases will test already-fragile health systems

Projected change from 2015 to 2040 in percentage of disease burden due to NCDs by score on the health system capacity index

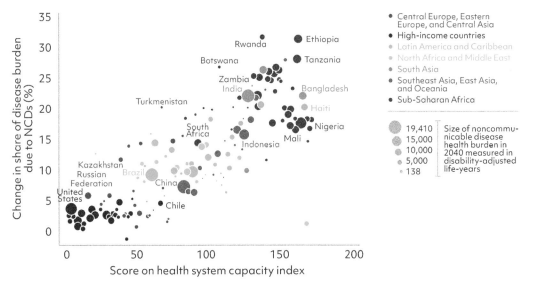

Source: Bollyky et al. 2017.

Note: NCD = noncommunicable disease.

Sub-Saharan Africa (Martinez et al. 2020). Feasible, cost-effective means exist to tackle this soaring burden of preventable suffering and death. The solution backed by the strongest evidence is reinforcing PHC networks to cover the whole population with the services required for prevention; early detection; and low-cost, high-quality community management of chronic NCDs, as some countries at all income levels have already found (Hone, Macinko, and Millett 2018).

Despite gains during the Millennium Development Goal (MDG) period, preventable diseases remain a major driver of mortality and morbidity in developing countries. Between 2000 and 2017, the proportion of global population with at least basic drinking water services increased from 82 percent to 90 percent. This trend was coupled with a rise in access to basic sanitation services from 56 percent to 74 percent of the population (UNICEF and WHO 2019). Despite these improvements, globally, 12.6 million deaths—corresponding to 23 percent of all deaths—are attributable to environmental risk factors modifiable by multisectoral policies, such as investment in water and sanitation services. Children under five years of age are particularly vulnerable; mortality due to environmental risk factors constituting 28 percent of global deaths for this age group.

For children, environmental factors contribute to the burden of infectious and parasitic diseases, neonatal and nutritional disorders, and injuries; for older adults, environmental risk factors primarily exacerbate the NCD burden (Neira and Prüss-Ustün 2016). The importance of hygiene practices and access to clean water and sanitation have again been highlighted by the COVID-19 pandemic. Simple public health measures, like hand hygiene, have become an integral part of efforts to curb the spread of COVID-19. However, in communities without reliable access to clean water, such measures cannot be consistently implemented.

The persistently high burden of preventable diseases highlights other opportunities for intersectoral action in areas critical for countries' human capital and economic development. For instance, over the past three decades, many countries made important strides in improving the food security for young children (Burns et al. 2010). The percentage of stunted children under five years of age stood at 21.3 percent in 2019, down from 39.3 percent in 1990. Yet important gaps in child nutrition persist. As of 2019, globally, an estimated 149 million children under five were stunted, 49.5 million suffered from wasting, and 40 million were overweight (UNICEF 2020). Rigorous evidence is mounting on the close links between health outcomes and a range of socioeconomic and environmental determinants, including housing security (Desmond and Kimbro 2015; Fink, Günther, and Hill 2014); access to water, sanitation, and hygiene (Piper et al. 2017); and vector control (Ng et al. 2017). Intersectoral action on health determinants has historically proven to be among the most difficult components of the classic PHC agenda for countries to implement and measure. However, a growing body of recent evidence suggests that the continuous, comprehensive care provided by well-trained, multidisciplinary PHC teams can be an effective way to tackle risk factors and other social determinants of health, which, in turn, improves equity of health outcomes (OECD 2020).

Urbanization brings new challenges for health service delivery

The global population has urbanized rapidly since the launch of the global PHC movement in the late 1970s. The proportion of the global population residing in urban areas is estimated to have increased from 39.3 percent in 1980 to 56.2 percent in 2020 (UN 2018). By 2050, some 70 percent of the global population will live in cities (figure 2.6) (Jungalwalla 1968). The degree of urbanization varies among countries across the development spectrum and across geographic regions. As of 2020, about 8 out of 10 people in HICs live in urban centers, compared with almost 6 out of 10 in middle-income countries. This contrasts with LICs, where only about 3 out of 10 people reside in cities. In North America, the world's most urbanized region, approximately

Figure 2.6 Urban populations continue to surge

Urban and rural population projected to 2050, World
Total urban and rural population, given as estimates to 2016, and UN projection to 2050. Projections are based on UN World Urbanization Prospects and its median fertility scenario.

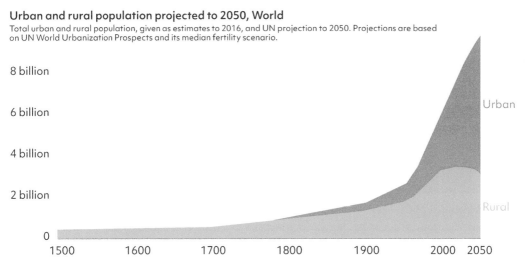

Sources: ourworldindata.org, based on UN 2018 and historical sources.

82.6 percent of the population lives in urban centers, compared to 81.2 percent in Latin America and the Caribbean and 74.9 percent in Europe. In contrast, many countries in Sub-Saharan Africa remain mostly rural, with only about 41.1 percent of the region's population residing in urban areas.[4]

Rapid urbanization poses major challenges for traditional models of health care delivery, especially in slums. In 2019, about 1 billion people, or almost 24 percent of urban populations, lived in slums.[5] People living in slum areas face multiple health threats related to socioeconomic and environmental factors, including housing insecurity; overcrowding; and absent or insufficient access to clean water, sanitation, and other essential services. Slum conditions pose new organizational and logistical challenges for PHC systems. Meanwhile, slum populations face disproportionate risks for some childhood diseases and greater prevalence of water-borne diseases, such as cholera and typhoid, among other health problems (UN-Habitat 2003).

Migration and forced displacement increase people's vulnerability and make them harder to reach with services

Migration has become a crucial element of global population trends. The number of international migrants has increased substantially in the past decade, from about 221 million in 2010 to 272 million people in 2019 (UN 2019c).

This trend suggests that the pace of international migration exceeded the growth in population globally during this period. The international migrant population is comprised predominantly of younger people; children and adolescents under 20 years of age and working-age individuals between ages 20 and 64 years represent 14 percent and 74 percent of all international migrants, respectively. Emerging evidence suggests that the major drivers of global migration trends are the rising demand for migrant workers, on the one hand, and violence, insecurity, and armed conflict, on the other hand (UN Department of Economic and Social Affairs 2019). In 2019, one-third of all international migrants were from 10 LMICs, including China, India, Mexico, the Russian Federation, and Syria. Only 20 countries, primarily HICs, hosted two-thirds of all international migrants.

In the past decade, the world has seen an unprecedented surge in the number of people who have been forcibly displaced from their homes. Rising conflict and violence across the globe displaced 79.5 million people during this period. Of those who are forcibly displaced, 26 million are estimated to be refugees. In 2018, 9 of the top 10 countries together hosting approximately 57.5 percent of all refugees were LMICs (UNHCR 2019). These included Colombia, Pakistan, and Turkey; Turkey hosts more than 14 percent of all refugees in the world. An estimated 45.7 million people are internally displaced within their own countries, including in Colombia, Democratic Republic of Congo, Syria, and Yemen. Forcibly displaced populations tend to be younger; children and adolescents under 18 years of age represent 40 percent of this population, and they often live in hard-to-reach areas that pose additional organizational and logistical challenges for health care services (UNHCR 2020). Forced population displacement due to climate change is expected to accelerate internal and international migration in the years ahead (McMichael, Barnett, and McMichael 2012).

New technologies can connect people—but only if the technologies are widely accessible

By many measures, the world is becoming increasingly connected. Yet the digital divide between underconnected and highly digitalized countries threatens to deepen existing inequities. In the world's least-developed countries, only 20 percent of people are online, compared to about 80 percent in developed countries. Exacerbating cross-country variation in digital connectivity, disparities exist within countries based on gender, income, geographic location, and level of education. On average, only about 63 percent of rural households in the least-developed countries have access to a mobile phone, compared to 89 percent of urban households. Similar connectivity gaps exist between genders. Globally, the share of women with online access is 12 percent lower than for men; this gap reaches 30 percent in the least-developed countries (United Nations Conference on Trade and Development 2019; WHO 2019a).

Disparities in digital connectivity has become all the more important during the COVID-19 pandemic, where the traditional face-to-face rendition of PHC services became problematic. Cognizant of the fact that access to a smart phone alone would not be of much help, many countries have been able to rapidly deploy digital solutions in the form of telekiosk, telemedicine, telehealth, or telecare to continue providing much needed PHC services to their citizens.

Rising expectations for health care—and lagging performance

In many countries, people now expect more from their health systems. Greater access to information has reinforced this pattern, along with some people's new experiences in seeking care in urban settings. Even if overburdened, the urban health care networks tend to be more physically accessible, better staffed, and better equipped, compared to rural settings. Rapid urbanization has also meant expanded job opportunities for many citizens, raising incomes and, in turn, tax revenues. As these trends continue, there will be greater expectations for high-quality public services, as well as greater demand for better governance, transparency, and control of corruption.

In some settings, the COVID-19 pandemic may have accelerated these shifts, prompting citizens to look to their governments for reliable information, public health guidance, and crisis leadership. Moving forward, citizens' expectations for high-quality health care will continue to rise. Yet confidence in health systems in many LMICs remains low. A recent study showed that only about 42.4 percent of people in 28 Sub-Saharan African countries were satisfied with the availability of high-quality health care in their areas of residence (Deaton and Tortora 2018). A survey spanning countries in Latin America found generally low confidence in PHC systems, although with substantial variation across countries. For instance, in Brazil, 32.1 percent of survey participants reported having confidence that they will receive effective treatment, including medications and diagnostic tests, compared to 54.9 percent in Colombia and 73.4 percent in Mexico (Guanais et al. 2019).

Trends in health care delivery and financing

As the global megatrends described impact health systems, core system components are necessarily changing. As the pressures on systems intensify, change will accelerate—for better or worse.

Prior to COVID-19, many countries had registered progress in the two key domains of universal health coverage: coverage with quality essential health services and financial protection from excessive health care costs. Even before the pandemic struck, however, gains had not been sufficient to keep most LMICs on track to achieve universal health care (UHC) and other Sustainable Development Goals (SDGs) health targets by 2030 (figure 2.7) (WHO 2019b).

On the service delivery front, traditional models of health care organization have helped reduce but not eliminate important gaps in the access, utilization, and quality of health care services in countries across the development continuum. Substantial gains have been achieved in ensuring access to essential health care services since 2000 (WHO 2019a), yet this progress slowed after 2010. It is estimated that in 2017, only 33 percent to 49 percent of the global population had access to essential health care services. Health service coverage is

Figure 2.7 Service coverage and financial protection worldwide: Slow progress even before COVID-19

Service coverage index (SDG 3.8.1, 2015)

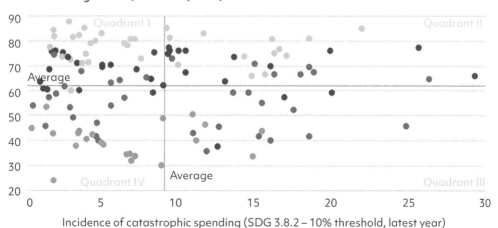

● Low ● Lower middle ● Upper middle ● High

Source: WHO 2019.

Note: SDG = Sustainable Development Goal.

especially low among vulnerable population groups, including poor women and women residing in rural areas. Current projections suggest that, if the pace of expanding service coverage does not pick up markedly, only between 39 percent and 63 percent of the global population will have access to essential health services by 2030, far below the UHC target. Moreover, these projections do not reflect the impact of COVID-19. Facing this stark shortfall, many countries urgently need to rethink the traditional organization of health care (WHO 2019b).

Before the pandemic, results in financial protection were also mixed (WHO 2019b). Out-of-pocket spending—the most inequitable and inefficient form of health financing—continues to dominate health financing in LMICs. Recent evidence shows that financial protection against debilitating health care costs worsened between 2000 and 2015. Globally, the number of people with out-of-pocket health expenditures exceeding 10 percent of their household income increased by 3.6 percent during this period, reaching 927 million in 2015. Similarly, the number of people who spent more than 25 percent of their household income on health was estimated at around 210 million (WHO 2019b). A closer look at the data reveals that progress toward providing better financial protection differed across the development continuum. Between 2000 and 2015, the sharpest increase in out-of-pocket expenditures occurred among upper-middle-income countries. In contrast, LICs started out in 2000 with the highest numbers of people spending 10 percent or 25 percent of their household budgets on health services but subsequently saw declines in this indicator. Importantly, these declines could stem from a variety of causes, including better coverage of basic health services, but also forgone health care because of people's inability or unwillingness to pay.

An important driver of rising out-of-pocket expenditures relates to the ways in which health care services are produced. Mounting evidence shows that, in many health systems, patients often do not receive the right type of health care service. Low-value care has been found across the care continuum, including overtesting, unnecessary surgical interventions (such as unnecessary caesarean sections), and imprudent use of antibiotics. Many health systems miss opportunities to reduce costs, for example, by using lower-cost inputs such as generic drugs that would provide the same benefits to patients as the more expensive options.

In many countries, hospital resources are being used for conditions that could be prevented by timely access to quality PHC services. Recent studies estimate that the inappropriate use of emergency department resources costs the United States approximately US$38 billion annually. Combined, this evidence demonstrates that it is paramount to move toward new ways of organizing care, so that patients get more health for their money rather than spend more money for health.

Implications for primary health care

Substantial challenges face health systems in the 21st century. COVID-19 has exacerbated many of those challenges and exposed underlying weaknesses in health systems in countries at all levels of income. In the years ahead, as known threats intensify, others will emerge in domains not yet foreseen.

PHC systems offer proven tools to tackle existing challenges, as well as the flexibility and creativity to confront new threats. The evidence base on PHC's contributions to population health has grown significantly since Alma-Ata. A substantial body of research from across the development spectrum shows the benefits of strong PHC systems for health outcomes (Macinko, Starfield, and Erinosho 2009), efficiency in service delivery (WHO 2019b), and quality of care (Friedberg, Hussey, and Schneider 2010). In many settings, comprehensive PHC approaches have been crucial to narrowing the health disparities (Macinko, Starfield, and Erinosho 2009). PHC offers the surest foundation for health system development to manage the trends that will shape health needs and opportunities in the decades ahead.

To fulfill this promise, however, PHC itself must evolve. In many cases, approaches that succeeded in the Alma-Ata period or even the MDG era cannot simply be transposed to today's health system contexts. The powerful trends described are shaping a novel global health landscape with new risks and new rules—but also new opportunities with advanced technology. The COVID-19 pandemic and the response thereto embody these transformations. The pandemic has provided an opportunity to rethink established health system paradigms, including the role of PHC.

Strengthening governance and accountability in PHC systems

Demographic and epidemiological changes, evolving health needs, and rising public expectations raise the stakes for better-functioning health systems. Repositioning PHC to meet the demands of the new health care ecology will require rethinking governance and accountability in PHC systems. Governance and accountability structures shape the processes by which patients, providers, and payers interact, mediating these stakeholders' divergent interests and power relationships.

Accountable PHC systems will need to be more responsive to meet people's expectations in their engagements with the health system, as embodied in professional ethics and human rights.

Achieving this will require PHC systems to enhance the structural aspects of care, including the quality of basic amenities, choice, prompt attention, and access to social support networks. It will also mean attention to interpersonal domains, including patient dignity and autonomy, better communication between providers and patients, and respect for patient confidentiality. PHC systems will need to invest in building relationships of trust with patients and communities to ensure that decisions are aligned with ethical standards and professional norms, as well as with societal and cultural values.

Building more accountable PHC systems will mean moving away from traditional ways of thinking about how to allocate scant resources. Although the evidence is still limited, global experience shows that, to improve PHC accountability, countries can employ a battery of strategic purchasing policies, including capitation, performance-based contracts, and global budgeting. Provider payment methods will need to reflect the care setting in which PHC services are provided, incorporating feedback from patients. It is paramount that payments to PHC providers signal a sense of fairness relative to the payments made to specialists.

Accountability hinges on the availability of accurate and relevant information to track performance over time and across providers. Transparency will need to be embedded as a core principle of accountable PHC systems. Greater transparency helps mitigate, if not eliminate, corruption and waste by facilitating closer monitoring of providers and payers and helping to realign provider incentives. Efforts to improve the transparency of PHC systems will entail instilling a culture of evidence-based, data-driven medical practice; tracking the most relevant data; and expanding venues for feedback from citizens. Facilitating input from system users may involve, for example, scaling up real-time feedback loops using culturally appropriate, patient-reported outcome measures and patient experience reports.

Reorganizing care delivery

Many people across the globe are living longer and healthier lives—and all aspire to do so. Rapid urbanization and increased digital connectivity will continue to fuel citizens' expectations for high-quality health care. As these trends converge, traditional health care organization models are coming under increasing strain. Health systems in LMICs, where global population growth is concentrated, already struggle with poor infrastructure and digital connectivity, stark human resource gaps, and weak supply chains, fueling shortfalls in service coverage, quality, efficiency, and equity. Many LMICs need new solutions to expand coverage of essential services while improving financial protection—the pillars of UHC. This new ecology of care magnifies the need to rethink traditional care models.

PHC systems have unique strengths to address the pressures caused by population growth, rising NCD burdens, population aging, and other trends that require more people to engage more often with the health system. However, some features of traditional PHC systems must be transformed to take full advantage of existing strengths and build new ones. This is particularly important for LMICs that bear a double burden of communicable and noncommunicable diseases. For instance, today, almost 8 in 10 patients receiving ART in LMICs reside in Sub-Saharan Africa. Thanks to recent efforts in HIV treatment (such as early ART initiation), many high-prevalence countries have achieved important gains in reducing HIV-related mortality. These gains, however, also generate new challenges for care delivery systems. The high prevalence of HIV/AIDS among working-age populations in Sub-Saharan African countries suggests that a greater proportion of the population will continue living with the disease, while concurrently confronting other chronic conditions. More generally, the double burden of disease coupled with the projected rise in working-age populations in LMICs will boost demand for sustained engagement with the health system, pushing up health spending.

These demographic and epidemiological trends underline the urgent need for additional investments in PHC systems. Population aging will require better integrated, long-term care that empowers health professionals to address both the expressed and unexpressed needs of populations (McConnell and Uwe 2019). Health expenditures are projected to escalate with a growing elderly population, because individuals tend to incur the highest medical costs closer to the end of their lives (Bloom et al. 2015). Compounding the effects of population growth and aging, health risks that are not addressed earlier in the life course will undermine health in older people and will increase the likelihood that a greater proportion of the aging population will be impacted by ill health, disability, and costly comorbidities.

New investments in curative care services alone are unlikely to curb these pressures on health systems. While some HICs are already scaling up long-term care programs, substantial work remains to be done to address the high degree of fragmentation, low-quality and low-value care, and waste. In many UMICs, efforts are needed to integrate primary care with other levels of care; address the chasm between service coverage and quality; and improve inefficiencies in service provision. Meanwhile, health systems in many LMICs

41

are unprepared to address the needs of their aging populations. Long-term care arrangements in these settings remain weak and poorly integrated with social services, placing elderly people and their families at high risk for catastrophic out-of-pocket health care expenditures.

The potential benefits of improving health care models extend beyond the health sector. In many of today's HICs, changes in the population age structure between the 1960s and 1990s enabled countries to reap a demographic dividend—faster economic growth due to drops in fertility and mortality, supported by economic and social policies to propel economic expansion. Today, many LMICs with young populations are poised to reap a similar demographic dividend—but its benefits will not be automatic. A strong body of evidence warns that changes in the population age structure, on their own, do not guarantee countries a demographic dividend. To secure it, LMICs need to deliver better education, health, and employment opportunities before their populations start aging. Building fit-for-purpose PHC systems is critical to ensure that people have access to high-quality care that meets their changing health needs over the life course. To achieve this, many LMICs urgently need to rethink their health care organization models. Their window of opportunity to do so is narrowing.

Harnessing the power of PHC in future public health emergencies

Among its many important lessons, the COVID-19 pandemic has highlighted the need for countries to reorganize existing health care delivery models so that they can better manage public health emergencies while meeting long-term health care needs. PHC provides the strongest platform to advance these changes, but few countries have yet made full use of this option. Global experience shows that PHC systems can curb the spread of outbreaks by disseminating reliable health information and prevention strategies, enabling rapid diagnosis of new cases, and contact tracing. During emergency response, effective PHC systems are also critical to ensure that people's routine health needs are met without disruption; these needs include vaccinations and other preventive services and the treatment of the full range of chronic conditions, including mental health conditions.

Positioning PHC systems as an effective first line of response to public health emergencies will require that PHC professionals have access to up-to-date information and tools. This includes reliable access to medical supplies (such as testing kits), equipment (such as personal protective equipment), and medicines. It will also mean harnessing new technologies on the PHC front lines.

Conclusion

Exceptional pressures will come to bear on health systems in all countries in the decade leading to 2030, the goal line year for major global health and development targets, including universal health coverage under SDG 3. Already, though, for health policy makers in countries facing the impacts of COVID-19, "exceptional pressure" is not a threat hovering in the future. It is right here, right now. Leaders also know that COVID-19 is not the only or even necessarily the most devastating health problem many of their countries face. The pandemic is part of a broader and more complex ecology of health risks and opportunities in the advancing 21st century. It is that ecology as a whole that policy makers have to manage.

One of the most powerful tools for this task is PHC. Yet PHC today remains a promise incompletely fulfilled. The early PHC movement mapped out a bold agenda of health action that included but went far beyond reorganizing the delivery of medical services. But in the decades following the 1978 Alma-Ata Conference, implementation of PHC stumbled, especially in some LICs. Key reasons for these shortfalls often included weak governance and account-ability mechanisms and inadequate financing. Poor results in some settings also reflected unresolved disputes about what is essential in PHC, how key implementation steps should be designed and sequenced, and what ultimately constitutes success in PHC.

Lessons have and are still being drawn from these experiences. It is also the case that, for nearly half a century, well-designed PHC models have demon-strated their capacity to deliver population health gains and improve health equity at manageable cost. Now, in a post-COVID-19 world shaped by complex and interacting megatrends, strong PHC networks offer the best platform for countries to solve old and new health challenges.

If PHC systems in most countries are not yet prepared to play this role, what will it take to get them ready? A series of recent publications has provided important evidence and analysis on this issue, while global networks such as Primary Health Care Performance Initiative (PHCPI) are reinforcing their efforts to help countries diagnose and tackle PHC gaps (OECD 2020).[6] In the next chapter, we build on that work to describe four high-level shifts to improve performance in PHC systems.

Notes

1. Data are from the World Bank's World Development Indicators database.
2. Data are from the World Bank's World Development Indicators database and Google Public Data Explorer.

3. Data are from the World Bank's World Development Indicators database and Google Public Data Explorer.

4. UN, *World Urbanization Prospects*.

5. https://unstats.un.org/sdgs/report/2019/goal-11/#:~:text=The%20 proportion%20of%20the%20urban,23.5%20per%20cent%20in%202018.

6. See the PHCPI website at "Strong Primary Health Care System Save Lives," accessed May 11, 2021, https://improvingphc.org/.

References

Bill & Melinda Gates Foundation. 2020. 2020 Goalkeepers Report, https://ww2 .gatesfoundation.org/goalkeepers/downloads/2020-report/report_letter_en.pdf.

Bloom, David E., Somnath Chatterji, Paul Kowal, Peter Lloyd-Sherlock, Martin McKee, Bernd Rechel, Larry Rosenberg, and James P. Smith. 2015. "Macroeconomic Implications of Population Ageing and Selected Policy Responses." *The Lancet* 385 (9968): 649–57. (February), https://doi.org/10.1016/S0140-6736(14)61464-1.

Bollyky, Thomas J., Tara Templin, Matthew Cohen, and Joseph L. Dieleman. 2017. "Lower-Income Countries That Face the Most Rapid Shift in Noncommunicable Disease Burden Are Also the Least Prepared." *Health Affairs* (Project Hope) 36 (11): 1866–75, https://doi.org/10.1377/hlthaff.2017.0708.

Burns, C., B. Kristjansson, G. Harris, R. Armstrong, S. Cummins, A. Black, and M. Lawrence. 2010. "Community Level Interventions to Improve Food Security in Developed Countries." *Cochrane Database of Systematic Reviews* 12 (December), https://doi.org/10.1002/14651858.CD008913.

Deaton, Angus S., and Robert Tortora. 2018. "People In Sub-Saharan Africa Rate Their Health and Health Care among the Lowest in the World." *Health Affairs* 34 (3): 519–27, https://pubmed.ncbi.nlm.nih.gov/25715657.

Desmond, Matthew, and Rachel Tolbert Kimbro. 2015. "Eviction's Fallout: Housing, Hardship, and Health." *Social Forces* 94 (1): 295–324, https://doi.org/10.1093/sf /sov044.

Fink, Günther, Isabel Günther, and Kenneth Hill. 2014. "Slum Residence and Child Health in Developing Countries." *Demography* 519 (4): 1175–97, https://doi .org/10.1007/s13524-014-0302-0.

Friedberg, Mark W., Peter S. Hussey, and Eric C. Schneider. 2010. "Primary Care: A Critical Review of the Evidence on Quality and Costs of Health Care." *Health Affairs* (May), https://doi.org/10.1377/hlthaff.2010.0025.

GBD 2017 Population and Fertility Collaborators. 2018. "Population and Fertility by Age and Sex for 195 Countries and Territories, 1950–2017: A Systematic Analysis for the Global Burden of Disease Study 2017." *The Lancet* 392 (10159): 1995–2051, https://doi.org/10.1016/S0140-6736(18)32278-5.

GBD (Global Burden of Disease) 2019 Demographics Collaborators. 2020. "Global Age-Sex-Specific Fertility, Mortality, Healthy Life Expectancy (HALE), and Population Estimates in 204 Countries and Territories, 1950–2019: A Comprehensive Demographic Analysis for the Global Burden of Disease Study 2019." *The Lancet* 396 (10258): 1160–203, https://doi.org/10.1016/S0140 -6736(20)30977-6.

Guanais, Frederico, Ferdinando Regalia, Ricardo Pérez-Cuevas, and Milagros Anaya. 2019. *From the Patient's Perspective: Experiences with Primary Health Care in Latin America and the Caribbean.* Washington, DC: Inter-American Development Bank.

Hone, Thomas, James Macinko, and Christopher Millett. 2018. "Revisiting Alma-Ata: What Is the Role of Primary Health Care in Achieving the Sustainable Development Goals?" *The Lancet* 392 (10156): 1461–72.

Horton, Richard. 2020. *The COVID-19 Catastrophe: What's Gone Wrong and How to Stop It Happening Again.* Cambridge: Polity Press.

IHME (Institute for Health Metrics and Evaluation). 2017. "Findings from the Global Burden of Disease Study 2017." IHME, Seattle, WA.

Jungalwalla, N. 1968. "Urbanization and Health." *Israel Journal of Medical Sciences* 4 (3): 532–43, https://doi.org/10.4038/jccpsl.v14i1.2941.

Kurowski, Christoph, David B. Evans, Ajay Tandon, Patrick Hoang-Vu Eozenou, Martin Schmidt, Alec Irwin, Jewelwayne Salcedo Cain, Eko Setyo Pambudi, and Irina Postolovska. 2021. *"From Double Shock to Double Recovery: Implications and Options for Health Financing in the Time of COVID-19."* Health, Nutrition and Population Discussion Paper. World Bank, Washington, DC. https://openknowledge.worldbank.org/handle/10986/35298. License: CC BY 3.0 IGO.

Macinko, James, Barbara Starfield, and Temitope Erinosho. 2009. "The Impact of Primary Healthcare on Population Health in Low- and Middle-Income Countries." *Journal of Ambulatory Care Management* 32 (2): 150–71, https://doi.org/10.1097/JAC.0b013e3181994221.

Martinez, Ramon, Peter Lloyd-Sherlock, Patricia Soliz, Shah Ebrahim, Enrique Vega, Pedro Ordunez, and Martin McKee. 2020. "Trends in Premature Avertable Mortality from Non-Communicable Diseases for 195 Countries and Territories, 1990–2017: A Population-Based Study." *The Lancet Global Health* 8 (4): e511–23, https://doi.org/10.1016/S2214-109X(20)30035-8.

McConnell, Margaret A., and Sunde Uwe. 2019. "Ageing into Risk Aversion? Implications of Population Ageing for the Willingness to Take Risks. In *Live Long and Prosper? The Economics of Ageing Populations,* edited by David Bloom. London: Centre for Economic Policy Research.

McMichael, Celia, Jon Barnett, and Anthony J. McMichael. 2012. "An Ill Wind? Climate Change, Migration, and Health." *Environmental Health Perspectives* 120 (5): 646–54, https://doi.org/10.1289/ehp.1104375.

Neira, M., and A. Prüss-Ustün. 2016. "Preventing Disease through Healthy Environments: A Global Assessment of the Environmental Burden of Disease." *Toxicology Letters* 259: S1, https://doi.org/10.1016/j.toxlet.2016.07.028.

Ng, Marie, K. Ellicott Colson, Nancy Fullman, Laura Dwyer-Lindgren, Tom Achoki, Matthew T. Schneider, Peter Mulenga, Peter Hangoma, Felix Masiye, and Emmanuela Gakidou. 2017. "Assessing the Contribution of Malaria Vector Control and Other Maternal and Child Health Interventions in Reducing All-Cause under-Five Mortality in Zambia, 1990-2010." *American Journal of Tropical Medicine and Hygiene* 97 (3): 58–64, https://doi.org/10.4269/ajtmh.15-0315.

OECD (Organisation for Economic Co-operation and Development). 2020. *Realising the Potential of Primary Health Care.* OECD Health Policy Studies, OECD Publishing, Paris, https://doi.org/10.1787/a92adee4-en.

Piper, Joe D., J. Chandna, E. Allen, K. Linkman, O. Cumming, A. J. Prendergast, and M. J. Gladstone. 2017. "Water, Sanitation and Hygiene (WASH) Interventions: Effects on Child Development in Low- and Middle-Income Countries." *Cochrane Database of Systematic Reviews* 3 (March), https://doi.org/10.1002/14651858.CD012613.

Salomon, Joshua A., Haidong Wang, Michael K. Freeman, Theo Vos, Abraham D. Flaxman, Alan D. Lopez, and Christopher J. L Murray. 2012. "Healthy Life Expectancy for 187 Countries, 1990–2010: A Systematic Analysis for the Global Burden Disease Study 2010." *The Lancet* 380 (9859): 2144–62, https://doi.org/10.1016/S0140-6736(12)61690-0.

UN (United Nations). 2018. *World Urbanization Prospects: The 2018 Revision* (ST/ESA/SER.A/420). New York, NY: United Nations.

UN (United Nations). 2019a. "World Population Prospects 2019: Highlights." Department of Economic and Social Affairs, United Nations, New York, NY.

UN (United Nations). 2019b. "World Population Prospects." Department of Economic and Social Affairs, United Nations, New York, NY, http://www.ncbi.nlm.nih.gov /pubmed/12283219.

UN (United Nations). 2019c. "International Migrant Stock 2019 in Oman." United Nations Population Division 1–2., https://www.un.org/en/development/desa /population/migration/data/estimates2/countryprofiles.asp.

UNEP (United Nations Environment Programme). 2019. "Healthy People and More Information." *Global Environment Outlook—GEO-6: Healthy Planet, Healthy People*. Cambridge: University Printing House, https://doi .org/10.1017/9781108627146.

UN-Habitat (United Nations Human Settlements Program). 2003. *The Challenge of Slums: Global Report on Human Settlements 2003*. Nairobi: UN-Habitat.

UNHCR (United Nations High Commissioner for Refugees). 2019. "Global Trends: Forced Displacement in 2018." UNHCR, Geneva.

UNHCR (United Nations High Commissioner for Refugees). 2020. "Global Trends in Forced Displacement in 2020." UNHCR, Geneva.

UNICEF (United Nations Children's Fund). 2020. "Global Nutrition Report." UNICEF, New York, NY, https://globalnutritionreport.org/reports/2020-global-nutrition-report.

UNICEF (United Nations Children's Fund) and WHO (World Health Organization). 2019. "Progress on Drinking Water, Sanitation and Hygiene 2000–2017: Special Focus on Inequalities." Report. UNICEF, New York, NY.

United Nations Conference on Trade and Development. 2019. *Digital Economy Report 2019: Value Creation and Capture: Implications for Developing Countries*. New York: United Nations Publications.

United Nations Department of Economic and Social Affairs. 2019. "International Migrant Stock 2019 Ten Key Messages," September. United Nations, New York, NY.

Watts, Nick, Markus Amann, Nigel Arnell, Sonja Ayeb-Larkssoon, Kristine Belesova, Maxwell Boykoff, Peter Byass, Wenjia Cai, Diarmid Campbell-Lendrum, Stuart Capstick, et al. 2019. "The 2019 Report of *The Lancet* Countdown on Health and Climate Change: Ensuring That the Health of a Child Born Today Is Not Defined by a Changing Climate." *The Lancet* 394 (10211): 1836–78, https://doi .org/10.1016/S0140-6736(19)32596-6.

WHO (World Health Organization). 2019a. *World Health Statistics 2019: Monitoring Health for the Sustainable Development Goals*. Geneva: WHO. https://apps.who .int/iris/handle/10665/324835. License: CC BY-NC-SA 3.0 IGO.

WHO (World Health Organization). 2019b. "Global Monitoring Report on Financial Protection in Health 2019." WHO, Geneva.

WHO (World Health Organization). 2019c. "Primary Health Care on the Road to Universal Health Coverage: 2019 Monitoring Report. WHO, Geneva.

World Bank. 2017. "Drug-Resistant Infections: A Threat to Our Economic Future, Volume 2: Final Report." HNP/Agriculture Global Antimicrobial Resistance Initiative, World Bank, Washington, DC.

World Bank. 2020. *Poverty and Shared Prosperity 2020: Reversals of Fortune*. Washington, DC: World Bank.

Chapter 3

Reimagined PHC:

WHAT WILL IT LOOK LIKE?

Introduction

Chapter 2 explores complex forces reshaping today's health ecosystems. A consensus is growing among health policy makers, scholars, and practitioners that the best health systems solutions to these new challenges will be anchored in primary health care (box 3.1). Chapter 2 also argues that, to drive ambitious reforms in health systems, primary health care (PHC) in many countries must undergo important changes.

Calls to transform PHC have emerged frequently over the decades. It has been relatively easy to describe plausible ways to make PHC work better, but to successfully implement these plans has been more challenging.

BOX 3.1

PHC AND HEALTH SYSTEM REFORM IN THE 21st CENTURY: A GROWING CONVERGENCE AND STRONG ALLIANCES

Recent landmark studies have presented visions and practical guidance for primary health care (PHC) reform. Some of these emerge from innovative global networks that are supporting countries to take PHC performance to the next level, including the Primary Health Care Performance Initiative (PHCPI)[a] and the Joint Learning Network (JLN) for Universal Health Coverage. This report builds on these important contributions and introduces additional data and analysis that can help countries implement PHC reforms successfully.

In preparation for the 40th Anniversary of the Declaration of Alma-Ata, the World Health Organization (WHO) and United Nations Children's Fund (UNICEF) developed *A Vision for Primary Care in the 21st Century,* stressing the three components of PHC to meet evolving health needs: (1) integrated health services with an emphasis on primary care and essential public health functions; (2) empowered people and communities; and (3) strengthened multisectoral policy and actions (WHO and UNICEF 2018). An accompanying operational framework includes 14 levers for action, building on the 2008 World Health Report, *Primary Health Care: Now More Than Ever* and the related *Framework on Integrated, People-Centered Health Services* geared to engaging and empowering people and communities; reorienting care models; and coordinating services within and across sectors, supported by governance reforms (WHO 2008; WHO 2016).

At an operational level, PHCPI's *Strategies for Improving Primary Health Care* offer step-by-step, evidence-based guides to upgrade and reform specific PHC components or inputs. The Organisation for Economic Co-operation and Development's (OECD) *Realising the Potential of Primary Healthcare* has recently emphasized team-based care models, smart economic incentives, and patient empowerment as "necessary changes" in PHC systems (OECD 2020).

a. "Strong Primary Health Care Saves Lives in Times of Crisis and Calm," https://improvingphc .org/.

This chapter spells out in clear terms the high-level shifts that evidence suggests many PHC systems need to undertake today. Chapter 4 then marshals data on how countries can make these changes happen. It recognizes the serious difficulties that await these efforts, especially in low- and middle-income countries (LMICs), and shows how some countries have been able to address them successfully.

Four high-level shifts for stronger PHC

To meet the evolving demand for quality, people-centered, integrated health care in the 21st century, all countries—despite their many differences—will need to achieve four fundamental shifts in how PHC is designed, financed, and delivered.

This chapter describes those shifts. They involve progressively reconfiguring key aspects of care delivery, patient-provider relationships, workforce composition and preparation, and financing. One way to think about these shifts is as the outcomes of change processes in PHC systems—the results that health leaders aim for when they introduce PHC reforms. The importance of most of these outcomes is intuitively clear and has often been affirmed in the history of PHC. Some countries have made remarkable progress toward reaching these outcomes over the years; many more, however, have struggled, made limited gains, and at times gone backward. Following COVID-19 (Coronavirus), these specific high-level shifts are once again critical for PHC systems to be able to respond, recover, and "build back better." Box 3.2 presents short definitions of the shifts.

BOX 3.2

FOUR SHIFTS TO IMPROVE PERFORMANCE IN PHC

The four high-level shifts described in this chapter can be summarized as follows:

+ **From dysfunctional gatekeeping to quality, comprehensive care for all**: High-performing primary health care (PHC) networks carefully assess patients' needs, ensuring that people receive the care they require at the most appropriate level of the health system. This gatekeeping role makes PHC a cornerstone of efficiency in health systems. Often, however, patients experience PHC gatekeeping in a very different way. Since at least the 1990s, surveys in many countries find that patients tend to perceive PHC as low-quality health care for poor people and local PHC personnel as unskilled and disrespectful. This form of dysfunctional gatekeeping

(Continued)

BOX 3.2 *(continued)*

becomes an adversarial relationship that complicates patients' access to "real" health care in advanced clinics and hospitals. The solution is an ambitious shift that strengthens the range and quality of services that people can obtain at their local PHC facilities. Some countries have scored impressive gains by creating multiskilled local PHC teams and rewarding them for delivering high-quality services that meet the bulk of health needs in communities. These PHC teams practice "positive gatekeeping," more appropriately termed "personalized care coordination."

+ **From fragmentation to people-centered integration**: In high-income countries (HICs) and low- and middle-income countries (LMICs) alike, patients often experience the search for health care as a solitary, bewildering journey. Many patients must patch together their care from multiple institutions and providers who are physically dispersed and systemically uncoordinated, practice inconsistent pricing regimes, may give different answers to the same diagnostic and therapeutic questions, and provide services of variable quality. Health service fragmentation and the absence of stable, trusting patient-provider relationships are cited in many surveys as key reasons for people's dissatisfaction with health care. This situation demands a shift to cohesive local PHC teams that build care around patients' needs and preferences; treat all patients with respect; collaborate and communicate internally; and coordinate patients' movement through the health system and back to their communities.

+ **From inequities to fairness and accountability**: COVID-19 has underscored the stark inequities in health care access and outcomes that exist globally, within countries, and often from one urban neighborhood to the next. Shared anger at such inequities was one of the main reasons that the original PHC movement was launched and gained global support. Today, PHC's potential to tackle equity gaps remains unfulfilled in many settings. However, strong examples exist of countries that have harnessed PHC's distinctive capacities to address inequities in health and health care. These countries have made policy and implementation choices that support the equitable, efficient delivery of a PHC-driven essential service package and that foster and reward accountability for health outcomes in frontline PHC.

+ **From fragility to resilience**: COVID-19 revealed the vulnerability of underresourced PHC systems to public health threats and showed the consequences for people and economies of health systems insufficiently prepared for infectious outbreaks. In the wake of the pandemic, countries need to draw the lessons and undertake ambitious reforms. At the PHC level, this will involve, for example, ensuring that PHC teams include public health surveillance and outreach capacity, and that financial and human resource surge capacities are built into health sector planning and resource allocation at the local level.

Shift 1: From dysfunctional gatekeeping to quality comprehensive care for all

The concept of gatekeeping as a core function for primary health care first gained prominence in some high-income countries (HICs) in the 1980s and 1990s. The concept has spurred recurrent controversy in policy debates. Proponents argue that gatekeeping at the primary level streamlines health care so that the right services will be provided at the right level of the system. A clear aim of gatekeeping in PHC is to reduce unnecessary referrals to more expensive higher-level specialists. This helps to limit the burdens on hospital outpatient and inpatient services and to contain costs, especially in health care settings where geographic and financial access to care is less of a concern, and patients have greater freedom to choose their providers.

The gatekeeping function, broadly understood, is a feature of any rationally organized health system, except where it exists as a result of shortage of trained practitioners (Reibling and Wendt 2012). Coordinating care by using this function well improves service quality, as well as efficiency, and it is likely to produce better patient outcomes. The term "gatekeeping" as commonly used, however, refers above all to managed care in a pluralistic health care environment, with a multiplicity of providers and insurers, where cost-containment is a dominant concern, as in the United States (Forrest 2003; Velasco Garrido, Zentner, and Busse 2011) (box 3.3).

Although changing words does not yet change reality, some have found it use-ful to refer consistently to care coordination rather than gatekeeping. There are at least two good reasons for this. First, in modern health system ecology, people seeking health care tend to be more demanding, better informed, and more empowered to participate in shared decision-making with their providers than in the past. As populations age, and noncommunicable dis-eases (NCDs) and multiple comorbidities become more prevalent—requiring advanced medical skill sets and a multiplicity of complex interventions—care coordination and care integration best capture the sense of what care seekers need and demand. Second, the benefits packages now envisioned for universal health care (UHC) in many countries render the care coordination function increasingly vital. As described in the *Disease Control Priorities Third Edition* (*DCP3*), these packages typically involve several service delivery platforms for the provision of a large set of essential health interventions, whereby four of the five cited platforms (Watkins et al. 2017) and 198 of the 218 interventions are meant to be delivered at the PHC level (Watkins et al. 2018). The vocabu-lary of care coordination keeps us reminded of how pivotal and challenging this function is in today's health care landscapes.

BOX 3.3

WHAT HAS TO CHANGE: DYSFUNCTIONAL GATEKEEPING AND QUALITY GAPS

Despite some gains in access to basic services, enormous gaps in the quality and comprehensiveness of primary care persist in many countries. Increasingly, individuals' most pressing health challenges relate to noncommunicable diseases, mental health, nutritional disorders, and injuries, many of which lie outside the traditional remit of primary health care (PHC). In low- and middle-income countries (LMICs), over 75 percent of individuals with diabetes (Manne-Goehler et al. 2019) and 90 percent of individuals with hypertension (Mills et al. 2016) receive zero or inadequate care to control their conditions (Thornicroft et al. 2017). Sixty percent of health care-preventable deaths in these countries can be attributed to poor-quality care—substantially more than the total attributable to nonutilization of the health system (Kruk et al. 2018).

Unqualified providers have proliferated in unregulated LMIC markets, and the adherence of PHC providers to clinical guidelines can be low. With limited ability to solve patients' problems and perceived poor quality deterring care-seeking, PHC services can be inefficient and unproductive. Some PHC providers often see extremely low caseloads despite high burdens of disease—only 1.4 outpatient visits per day in Nigeria, 5.2 per day in Madagascar, and 6 per day in Uganda[a]—while absentee rates frequently exceed 25 percent.[b]

Low- and middle-income countries: In rural India, 76 percent of all primary care providers and 65 percent of self-identified "doctors" have no formal medical training (Centre for Policy Research 2011). In eight Sub-Saharan African countries, providers complete less than one-half of the relevant history and physical examination questions, given a patient's symptomatic presentation,[c] and frequently misdiagnose common conditions.[d] Among women giving birth in facilities in rural Tanzania, more than 40 percent bypassed their local health clinic to seek care in hospitals, despite substantially higher costs. They were more likely to do so if they were relatively wealthy, the local facility was in poor physical condition, or if the perceived (and actual) quality of care was low (Kruk et al. 2014).

Upper-middle-income countries: Although major depressive disorder should be treatable in a primary care setting, less than one in ten people with major depression receive minimally adequate treatment in Bulgaria, Lebanon, or Mexico (Thornicroft et al. 2017).

High-income countries: In Riyadh, Saudi Arabia, 75 percent of survey respondents in a sample of PHC centers reported that they do "not make primary health care their first choice." They most frequently cite the limited scope of services and mistrust to explain their preferences (Olasunbo et al. 2016).

a. Data from PHCPI, "Caseload per Provider (Daily)," accessed May 10, 2021, https://improvingphc .org/indicator/caseload-provider-daily#?loc=64,77,86,93,120,130,129&viz=0&ci=false.

b. Data from PHCPI, "Provider Absence Rate," accessed May 10, 2021, https://improvingphc.org /indicator/provider-absence-rate#?loc=&viz=0&ci=false.

c. Data from PHCPI, "Adherence to Clinical Guidelines | PHCPI," accessed May 10, 2021, https:// improvingphc.org/indicator/adherence-clinical-guidelines#?loc=&viz=0&ci=false.

d. Data from PHCPI, "Diagnostic Accuracy | PHCPI," accessed May 10, 2021, https://improvingphc .org/indicator/diagnostic-accuracy#?loc=&viz=0&ci=false.

What is meant by high-quality comprehensive care?

Health care quality can be succinctly defined as "the degree to which health care services for individuals and populations increase the likelihood of desired health outcomes and are consistent with current professional knowledge" (Larson 1991). As such, care quality encompasses two key domains: (1) ensuring effectiveness, that is, providing appropriate care based on scientific knowledge and safety, and (2) avoiding harm through inappropriate or inadequate care. Beyond these core features, some authors have broadened the concept of care quality to include criteria such as timeliness, efficiency, equity, and patient centeredness, among many others (Agency for Healthcare Research and Quality, n.d.). Some have recommended including quality of inputs as well as patient outcomes as proxy indicators, in addition to measuring quality at the service/output level (Donabedian 1988; Joyce, Moore, and Christie 2018).

A classic definition of comprehensiveness evokes "the provision of integrated, accessible health care services by clinicians who are accountable for addressing a large majority of personal health care needs," within the broader context of primary care (IOM 1996). PHC is the appropriate level to marry the two concepts of quality and comprehensiveness of care. Doing this moves the discussion away from focusing on gatekeeping to envisioning a platform to provide a comprehensive set of essential services (Watkins et al. 2017).

What are the drivers of quality, comprehensive care?

Fundamental to building high-quality, comprehensive primary health care is a systems approach (Bargawi and Rea 2015). WHO experts note that quality improvement efforts often tend to focus on the micro level of local facilities and staff performance. Although crucial, this approach needs to be supported by systemic action, since the quality of local primary health care is deeply affected by the prevailing culture and environment of the health system. System-level interventions to improve quality of care include the following: national workforce strategies; registration and licensing mechanisms; service delivery and care platform redesigns; external evaluation or accreditation; public reporting and benchmarking mechanisms; and national regulatory bodies for medicines, medical devices, and other health products. Health information systems to measure and drive quality of care, as well as financing methods to support provision of high-quality care, are also essential (Bargawi and Rea 2015).

Recent WHO technical guidance on quality in PHC notes that the organization of PHC providers in cohesive multidisciplinary teams is increasingly recognized as a driver of quality, comprehensive care. Effective primary care is now being delivered in many settings by multidisciplinary teams that provide a comprehensive package of services using more holistic models of care. Improving the quality of services requires equal attention to both clinical skills and nonclinical functions, such as effective community engagement, leadership, communication, and innovation (Bargawi and Rea 2015).

Leadership and governance underpin all efforts to improve quality across the health system. Strong commitment to and leadership for quality is required at all levels to ensure that all stakeholders work together to create the enabling environment needed to provide high-quality PHC (Bargawi and Rea 2015). Key characteristics of systems with strong leadership and governance include evidence-based policy making, efficient and effective service provision arrangements, regulatory frameworks and management systems, responsiveness to public health needs and the preferences of citizens, transparency, institutional checks and balances, and clear and enforceable accountability (Brinkerhoff and Bossert 2008). Leadership can be cultivated and exercised at all levels of the health system, from ministries of health to local governments and PHC facilities (Daire and Gilson 2014).

Shift 2: From fragmentation to people-centered integration

By its nature, health care delivery involves an asymmetry of information between those who provide services and those who receive them. Nevertheless, the "delivery" of effective care should not be seen as a one-way transfer from provider to patient;[1] instead, the delivery requires providers to work as partners and collaborators in empowering the people they serve. This approach, in turn, often requires a mindset shift—from solving an acute health problem on the patient's behalf to building long-term, trusting partnerships to strengthen health and wellbeing across the life course.

Three global trends in health care knowledge and delivery are sharpening this imperative.

+ First, as noted, patients and populations are increasingly informed about their own health and therapeutic options. Many enjoy rapid access to data and general information, an extensive understanding of their own medical conditions, and the ability to triangulate external information and knowledge with the information shared by their care providers.

+ Second, transparency of provider performance and patient outcomes is fast becoming the norm, allowing people to make informed choices among providers.[2]

+ Finally, increasingly urbanized, educated, and informed populations across the world expect technical excellence to cure their illness, as well as respect for their dignity, wholeness as a person, preferences, and constraints.

These secular trends are particularly relevant for PHC—typically the first point of contact with health care outside of emergency settings. PHC practitioners are not only expected to be healers but also managers, coordinating the health care needs of the care seekers,[3] their families, and the entire communities in which they reside.

What is meant by people-centeredness in PHC?

The United States Institute of Medicine (which became the National Academy of Medicine in 2015) classically defined patient-centered care as "providing care that is respectful of, and responsive to, individual patient preferences, needs and values, and ensuring that patient values guide all clinical decisions" (IOM 2001). As such, it comprises eight components: (1) respect for the patient's values, preferences, and expressed needs; (2) coordination and integration of care; (3) information and education; (4) physical comfort; (5) emotional support and alleviation of fear and anxiety; (6) involvement of family and friends; (7) continuity and transition; and (8) access to care, mainly in relation to amenities (O'Neill 2015).

The basic tenet of people-centeredness is that the organizational model of health care, with PHC at the center, revolves around the health, health care, and broader psychosocial needs of the person, both as a care seeker and as a member of the community. Health and nutrition promotion and prevention are given as much importance as episodic, curative care, with the goal of enhancing lifelong health and quality of life (box 3.4). Achieving this also requires full integration with secondary and tertiary care; people-centeredness must go hand-in-hand with integrated care. The role of PHC is paramount as first point of care and coordinator across all health care levels. People-centeredness is an evolving concept. An expanded definition includes additional dimensions of structural and interpersonal responsiveness to ensure that health services are provided without discrimination on the basis of income, ethnicity, language, gender, or other factors (Murray and Evans 1990).

BOX 3.4

WHAT HAS TO CHANGE: DISCONTINUOUS DELIVERY

More than one-half of the global disease burden can be attributed to ongoing behavioral or metabolic risk factors occurring in the household or community (GBD Risk Factor Collaborators 2018), yet most primary health care (PHC) platforms remain oriented to episodic disease treatment rather than prevention and promotion. Without empowering individuals, families, and communities to take charge of their own health and its determinants—and without serving as a connection point, tracking and managing a patient's journey across the entire health system—PHC can only address the tip of the iceberg of acute disease presentations through interventions that lack the power to drive major population health improvements.

Discontinuities in care are associated with departures from clinical best practice, preventable hospitalizations, and far higher total health care expenditure (Frandsen et al. 2015). Lack of engagement with patients also undermines chronic and infectious disease treatment. The World Health Organization (WHO) estimates that adherence to long-term therapies is just 50 percent in high-income countries, and far lower across low- and -middle-income countries (WHO 2015); chronic disease patients say mistrust, confusion, and alienation from the treatment planning process are barriers to treatment adherence (Pagès-Puigdemont et al. 2016). Limited information-sharing between providers, including following discharge from higher-level care, further exacerbates the risks of fragmentation, leading to duplication, errors, and patient safety risks (Schoen et al. 2009).

Low- and middle-income countries: In Sierra Leone, less than one percent of febrile patients completed referrals to health facilities after testing negative for malaria on a rapid diagnostic test (Thomson et al. 2011).

Upper-middle-income countries: In Peru, only 21 percent of survey respondents report that the last doctor they saw "knows me as a person," while 34 percent say they "know what to expect from this doctor," and 31 percent report that they "feel totally relaxed with this doctor" (Ipsos 2018).

High-income countries: A 2016 survey across 11 countries found that 19 to 35 percent of all patients had experienced at least one problem with care coordination over the past two years—for example, medical records not being shared with a specialist, duplication of testing, or receiving conflicting information from multiple health care professionals (Commonwealth Fund n.d.). In Japan, 60 percent of patients reported that their regular doctor had not spent enough time with them during consultations (OECD 2019). In the United States, 50 percent of primary care physicians do not know if their patients have completed referrals (Mehrotra, Forrest, and Lin 2011).

What are the drivers of people-centeredness in PHC?

The mission and values of the health system as a whole, and the PHC network in particular, can be formulated and applied in a way that drives the system toward people-centeredness. This happens when guiding values are egalitarian and inclusive and are fully aligned with the aims of optimizing population health outcomes and equitable access to care.

Care delivery is fundamental to people-centeredness and best serves it when care is collaborative, integrated, and coordinated by the PHC team. Along with patients' medical care needs, practitioners are responsible to give high priority to care-seekers' physical comfort, emotional well-being, dignity, and care preferences.

The PHC team's willingness to listen and respond to care seekers and families is at the heart of people-centered practice. Care-seeker and family viewpoints need to be not simply heard but genuinely respected and incorporated in decisions. The physical organization of care settings can also support or undermine people-centeredness. People-centeredness is present when basic amenities of the care setting are designed in a way that respects care seekers' dignity, autonomy, and confidentiality, while enabling the prompt provision of health and social support services.

A wide range of factors can enable the translation of people-centeredness from abstract principle into provider behavior and care-seekers' experience. Such enablers include governance policies and tools, such as the formulation of a PHC mission statement and its rigorous application and establishing performance-based incentives for care providers. Effective incentives can be financial or nonfinancial. The training of PHC teams is another crucial means to instill people-centeredness as a guiding value and teach team members how they can put it systematically into practice. Regulatory measures can lend support to people-centered care, for example, by ensuring patient confidentiality and establishing enforceable norms for patient safety.

Tools that encourage health practitioners to listen to care-seekers' voice and act on their concerns play a key enabling role. These tools may include an accountability framework that gauges people-centeredness and empowerment, for example, through the Patient-Reported Indicator Surveys (PaRIS), incorporating patient-reported experience measures (PREM) and patient-reported outcome measures (PROM). Community and care-seeker information, education, and communication are also crucial. By definition, people-centered communication is not a one-way download of information and instructions from health providers and experts to patients. It is an interactive process that engages people as knowledgeable and responsible agents in their own health. Communication flows both ways, between attentive health professionals, on the one hand, and empowered care seekers and communities, on the other hand. Technology and information platforms can enable and accelerate these interactive relationships.

Shift 3: From inequities to fairness and accountability

Some inequalities in health are unavoidable, since they stem from genetic differences or other factors beyond control. Health inequities, in contrast, are defined by WHO as "avoidable, unfair, or remediable differences among groups of people, whether those groups are defined socially, economically, demographically, or geographically or by other means of stratification" (WHO 2021). The goal of health equity implies that "everyone should have a fair opportunity to attain their full health potential and that no one should be disadvantaged from achieving this potential" (WHO 2021). Most observed health and health care inequities—between individuals and between populations—could be reduced or even eliminated by addressing the structural determinants of health along with disparities in health care resource allocation (box 3.5).

What is meant by fairness and accountability in PHC?

Fairness in health and health care refers to the absence of structural and systemic inequities that could be addressed through health promotion, disease prevention, and medical care. Fairness also encompasses the just distribution of the burden of health care costs according to people's ability to pay—precluding any out-of-pocket payments, no matter how minimal, at the point of service. Finally, fairness entails a respectful and appropriate response to the nonmedical needs, rights, and expectations of those seeking and obtaining health care, delivered through a dignified interaction with providers (World Bank 2013). Fairness is thus closely linked to people-centeredness.

Accountability, in its simplest form, is the obligation to ensure that health and health care services are timely, effective, safe, appropriate, cost-conscious, and people-centered. As such, it requires a level playing field in the nexus of interactions among communities and care seekers, health care providers, and payers, often mediated through governance, that is, institutions, laws, and regulations.

PHC can address inequities in health and health care in multiple ways. One means—limited but important—is through primary care as the preferred first point of patients' contact with clinical services to address illness, sickness, or disease (World Bank 2013). PHC networks can also deploy, contribute to, or promote a comprehensive set of community-based interventions to

> **BOX 3.5**
>
> ## WHAT HAS TO CHANGE: HEALTH FINANCING GAPS WIDEN HEALTH CARE INEQUITIES
>
> Few governments fund comprehensive, universal primary health care (PHC) services at adequate levels to equitably meet population health needs; most governments in low- and middle-income countries (LMICs) cover well under half of the PHC costs through general government revenue. Beyond absolute resource constraints, the allocation of scarce resources is often skewed toward hospitals and relatively advantaged urban populations. In this context, patients must often pay out of pocket for critical health needs, pushing about 100 million people into poverty each year (WHO 2019b). Although many associate catastrophic health expenditure with unexpected hospitalization, most out-of-pocket expenses across LMICs and the World Health Organization's (WHO) European region go to outpatient care and medicines, both of which fall within the remit of PHC (WHO 2019b). Even when PHC services are financially accessible, patients commonly report disrespectful, impersonal, or even abusive care (Larson et al. 2019; McMahon et al. 2014; Wang et al. 2015). Such substandard care experience particularly affects marginalized populations, including migrants, racial minorities, sexual minorities, and youth. Financial barriers can also deter poor or marginalized families from seeking care early, leading to preventable hospitalizations and death.
>
> **Low- and middle-income countries**: Among households in rural Malawi where a family member required chronic disease medication, two-thirds incurred at least some out-of-pocket expenditure; the poorest quartile of households spent up to one-half of its monthly income on chronic disease care (Larson et al. 2019).
>
> **Upper-middle-income countries**: In Russia, 27 percent of patients report that they were not treated with "respect for [their] values, preferences, and expressed needs" during their last consultation; and 34 percent report that care was not "personalized to reflect [their] needs and choices" (Ipsos 2018).
>
> **High-income countries**: In the United States, over one-third of surveyed adults and almost two-thirds of uninsured adults skipped needed medical care in the past year due to cost barriers (Commonwealth Fund 2019). Families under the poverty line are more than three times as likely as the wealthiest families to delay or forgo care for their children due to cost or lack of insurance coverage (Wisk and Witt 2012).

reduce socioeconomic and cultural disparities that act as distal or proximal determinants of health. However, there are few well-documented instances globally in which PHC services have fully incorporated this function. In many settings, PHC still stands for a limited set of health care services, too often provided only to those who can afford to pay and/or who live in close proximity.

What are the drivers of fairness and accountability in PHC?

At the PHC level, fairness is achieved by eliminating or at least mitigating avoidable inequities in health and health care through accurate targeting of public health and primary care services to those most in need, while protecting the empaneled population from catastrophic health expenditure or health-related impoverishment. Fairness also means responding to people's expectations for humane, respectful, and dignified care, without any discrimination based on age, gender, income, area of residence, sexual orientation, disability, or other factors. This would imply not only that PHC is available, but that it is also geographically, socio-culturally, economically, and organizationally accessible to all.[4]

Accountability in PHC could be operationalized as the mandate and capacity to hold relevant health care institutions, facilities, and health professionals to account for their performance in providing people-centered, appropriate, comprehensive, continuous, safe, timely, and cost-conscious care to their empaneled population. As such, it would require an accountability results framework and a set of metrics mutually agreed by providers, payers, and the empaneled population alike.

In this sense, fair and accountable PHC rests on a social contract with the community it serves (the empaneled population). It also requires a transparent mechanism to collect, compile, analyze, and interpret data for continuous improvement and summative evaluation. The most useful data will include patient-reported experience and outcome measures (PREM and PROM) and input from the community at large. Measures would need to be customized considering community baseline characteristics (epidemiologic, demographic, socio-cultural, and economic), the level of ambition (goals, anticipated health outcomes), the time frame, and the rules and regulations pertaining to broader health system governance. Most important is a realistic estimation of resource needs—and the effective provision of resources based on those estimates. The estimation and the provision include both human resources (numbers, skills mix, and the applicable incentives to recruit and retain) and financial resources for full functionality regardless of short-term surges in demand. Planning and resource estimation need to be demand oriented, that is, derived through an assessment of a community's needs and expectations, rather than supply driven.

Shift 4: From fragility to resilience

Pandemics like COVID-19—as well as other shocks, including conflict or natural disaster—can devastate health systems and reverse years of hard-won health, development, and economic progress. "Health security" refers to the activities required to minimize the danger and impact of health shocks. Neither health security nor UHC can be achieved without building resilient health systems (UHC 2030 and SHFA 2020); WHO has reminded countries that the best foundation for resilient systems is PHC (WHO 2020a).

What is meant by resilience in PHC?

There is as yet no universally agreed definition of health system resilience. This report follows the influential definition proposed by Kruk et al. (2015) and widely adopted by the community of organizations working to advance UHC:

> *Health system resilience can be defined as the capacity of health actors, institutions, and populations to prepare for and effectively respond to crises; maintain core functions when a crisis hits; and, informed by lessons learned during the crisis, reorganize if conditions require it. Health systems are resilient if they protect human life and produce good health outcomes for all during a crisis and in its aftermath.*

Kruk et al.'s model characterizes resilient systems in terms of five fundamental attributes. Resilient health systems are (1) aware, (2) diverse, (3) self-regulating, (4) integrated, and (5) adaptable (Kruk et al. 2015).

Resilience is closely related to another concept widely discussed in the current health systems literature: preparedness (IWG 2017). Linguistically and practically, "preparedness" emphasizes pre-crisis actions to anticipate health emergencies, while "resilience" as defined by Kruk encompasses preparation, response, and post-crisis recovery. In this sense, preparedness can be considered as a stage of the continuous cyclical process to improve health system resilience (Rajan et al. 2021).

The overall definition of health system resilience and its conception as a cyclical process also apply to PHC. A PHC system is resilient if

+ It is well prepared for health emergencies.

+ It effectively responds to health emergences and maintains access to high-quality routine PHC services, as well as to public-health services during an emergency.

+ It recovers promptly once the health emergency is over by making the necessary adjustments, revising emergency action plans accordingly, and resuming its core functions.

A distinctive feature of a resilient PHC system is that, for each stage of the continuous cyclical process described, it maintains and reinforces three interconnected core functions: service delivery, surveillance, and communications (box 3.6).

Service delivery refers to the capacity of PHC to deliver both routine and emergency-related health services. Emergency-related PHC services have included, in the case of the COVID-19 pandemic, basic treatment and follow-up care for patients with mild symptoms, provision or facilitation of laboratory tests, triage, referral to hospitals, and mental health services. Routine PHC services typically include reproductive, maternal, newborn, and child health (RMNCH) services; infectious disease services (for example addressing HIV, tuberculosis, and sexually transmitted infections); and noncommunicable disease services. In many countries, COVID-19 forced overstretched health systems to suspend many PHC-level routine services in order to manage the waves of acutely ill coronavirus patients. The result, especially but not only in LMICs, has been large numbers of excess deaths caused not by the virus itself but by its effects on overall health service provision (box 3.7).

Surveillance mainly relates to the collection and reporting of high-quality and timely data on the disease burden and on the services delivered to the population. Especially for emergencies related to an infectious outbreak, passive surveillance—data collection and reporting activities—is usually accompanied by active surveillance—testing, contact tracing, and isolation management activities.

Communications refers to PHC's capacity to conduct an ongoing dialogue with the community to promote trust, healthy behaviors, and actions for

---

BOX 3.6

WHAT HAS TO CHANGE: FRAGILITY TO SHOCKS

During natural disasters, outbreaks, or conflict, vulnerabilities in infection control, supply chains, and surveillance can drive up the immediate death toll. In some settings, the second-order health impact of primary health care (PHC) interruptions can also approach or even exceed the direct mortality and morbidity caused by the outbreak.

Low- and middle-income countries: In Sierra Leone, in addition to the almost 4,000 deaths directly attributed to the 2014–15 Ebola epidemic (CDC, n.d.), another 3,600–4,900 stillbirths, neonatal deaths, and maternal deaths can be attributed to decreased utilization of essential maternal and neonatal health care (Sochas, Channon, and Nam 2017), along with additional morbidity and mortality from interruptions to HIV, tuberculosis, and malaria programs (Phillips et al. 2016).

In Nigeria, the COVID-19 pandemic has led to a 50 percent reduction in outpatient visits, antenatal care services, and immunization. In Bangladesh and Guinea-Bissau, vaccination and maternal health services delivered through outreach have been interrupted due to lack of personal protective equipment, and telemedicine has not been scaled up. In Papua New Guinea, immunization rates have declined; in addition, because mobile X-ray machines were reserved for COVID-19 patients, tuberculosis screening has also faced significant reductions.[a]

Upper-middle-income countries: Modeling from South Africa shows that even relatively modest and short-lived (three month) COVID-19-related disruptions to HIV treatment enrollment, viral load monitoring, and prevention could lead to over 30,000 excess new infections over the next five years (Jewell, Smith, and Hallett 2020).

High-income countries: In the United States, surveillance data show that routine measles immunization plummeted by more than one-half during the first month of the COVID-19 pandemic, leaving communities vulnerable to measles outbreaks (Santoli et al. 2020).

a. World Bank Country Team Assessment Reports, 2020.

BOX 3.7

THE COST OF *NOT* BUILDING FIT-FOR-PURPOSE PHC: COLLATERAL MORTALITY IN COVID-19

Along with COVID-19's direct health impacts, many low- and middle-income countries (LMICs) have seen a rise in mortality from other causes, associated with the curtailment of health services for non-pandemic-related conditions. Robust, resilient primary health care (PHC) systems would have been able to support the COVID-19 response, while maintaining the provision of essential preventive, promotive, and curative care of other kinds. Weak PHC systems in most LMICs have exposed populations to substantial additional risks across a broad range of health conditions:

(Continued)

BOX 3.7 *(continued)*

+ **Vaccine-preventable diseases**: Due to COVID-19, 14 major vaccination campaigns for polio, measles, cholera, human papillomavirus (HPV) yellow fever, and meningitis had already been postponed as of June 2020, resulting in 13.5 million people missing vaccinations in 13 of the poorest countries. Across 37 countries, the disruptions of measles campaigns could lead to 117 million children missing their vaccines, reversing gains in herd immunity.

+ **Nutrition**: COVID-19 is interrupting nutritional interventions, even as the pandemic is expected to double the number of people facing acute food insecurity, from 135 million at end-2019 to 265 million by end-2020. The United Nations Children's Fund (UNICEF) has reported severe disruptions in treatment coverage for acute malnutrition and vitamin A supplementation.

+ **Maternal health**: A 45 percent coverage reduction for six months would result in 1.16 million additional child deaths and 56,400 additional maternal deaths. This would represent a 9.8 percent to 44.7 percent increase in under-five child deaths per month, and an 8.3 percent to 38.6 percent increase in maternal deaths per month.

+ **Malaria**: The suspension of distribution campaigns for insecticide-treated nets and the disruption of malaria treatment could lead to as many as 225 million additional malaria cases across Sub-Saharan Africa in 2020 alone. This disruption could allow malaria in Sub-Saharan Africa to return to levels seen 20 years ago.

+ **Tuberculosis**: Multidrug resistant tuberculosis (MDR-TB) incidence is likely to worsen due to delays in diagnosis and contact tracing, along with reduced treatment adherence due to access and affordability barriers. Cases could increase by up to 11 percent globally between 2020 and 2025 under a three-month-lockdown, with delays in the resumption of services.

+ **HIV**: A six-month disruption of antiretroviral treatment (ART) globally is expected to lead to an approximately two-fold increase in HIV-related deaths over a one-year period.

+ **Noncommunicable diseases (NCDs)**: Although NCDs can be risk factors for COVID-19, reductions in physical activity, patient management, access to fresh food, and isolation due to the pandemic can lead to increased incidence of obesity, cardiovascular disease, and other chronic NCDs (Roberton et al. 2020; Stop TB Partnership 2020; World Food Programme 2020).[a]

Sources: Jewell, Smith, and Hallett (2020); Roberton et al. (2020); Stop TB Partnership (2020); WHO (2020b); https://www.wfp.org/news/covid-19-will-double-number-people-facing-food-crises-unless-swift-action-taken; https://www.unicef.org/media/82851/file/Global-COVID19-SitRep-11-September-2020.pdf.

a. For Refugees, "UNICEF GLOBAL COVID-19 Situation Report UNICEF COVID-19 UNICEF COVID-19 Response in GHRP Countries UNICEF GLOBAL COVID-19 Situation Report UNICEF Appeal 2020," no. 11 (2020).

prevention and emergency control, for example, handwashing and physical distancing. It also refers to the ability to communicate with other actors in the health system, such as public health institutions and hospitals, to maximize coordination along the care pathway, as well as with other sectors involved in the provision of emergency-related services, such as transportation and social protection.

What are the drivers of resilience in PHC?

Resilience in PHC depends on the ability to restructure core service delivery functions during an emergency and then reconfigure when the crisis is over. During an emergency, resilient PHC systems can adapt and maintain both routine and emergency-related health services. To maintain essential service delivery, PHC systems can provide outreach services through home visits or telemedicine, increase or redistribute health worker roles through task shifting, remove user fees, and/or extend opening hours (Hollander and Carr 2020). In the recovery stage, PHC systems should be prepared to handle a surge in demand due to care needs that were deferred during the emergency or ongoing needs among those who became ill. This surge may result in an above-normal workload for PHC providers. This also means that resilient PHC systems need the flexibility to rapidly adjust the size, distribution, and skill mix of their workforce based on changing needs.

Comprehensive routine data are a cornerstone of resilience, as they enable evidence-based managerial, organizational, and operational decisions. Resilient PHC systems play a key role in disease surveillance by collecting and reporting high-quality, timely data on local disease trends and service provision. The best tools for this purpose are digital data systems that (1) take patients rather than illnesses or services as their unit of reporting/analysis, (2) are integrated into a single platform, and (3) feed quality data continuously to health authorities. Well-integrated information systems allow PHC providers and facilities to closely monitor populations, identifying changes in disease patterns and service demand in real time.

COVID-19 has underscored the importance of stock management in health emergencies. Effective stock management requires adequate stockpiling plans and processes; strong supply chains and distribution channels; and robust, adaptable stock information systems for tests, vaccines, medicines, consumables, spare parts, and other inputs. Stocks should reflect the forecasted needs for different types of emergencies; be strategically distributed according to risks; and be available regardless of climatic, geographic, and other existing or emerging constraints, even during crises.

Communication and engagement with the community have proven to be an effective strategy to change behaviors and thereby reduce the impact of emergencies. When a crisis strikes, PHC systems with strong communications capacities are able to provide clear and up-to-date information on all aspects of the threat, helping people protect themselves and, in the case of an infectious epidemic, prevent disease spread. PHC systems are able to tailor messaging to the communities they serve, based on characteristics such as language, culture, age, gender, and education.

Certain enabling environmental conditions can facilitate the development of a resilient PHC system. The most fundamental of these include a fit-for-purpose governance model for agile responses. Such a governance model promotes coordination and local autonomy to rapidly respond to changing population needs. Also essential is the presence of a well-developed, costed, and tested emergency action plan. Well-developed plans specify clear emergency roles and responsibilities for all health system actors, including PHC facilities and outreach services in both the public and private sectors (WHO 2020b). To be ready to implement the plan, PHC leaders and managers can benefit from complementary training in leadership for crisis management, communication, and safety.

The ability to access extra-budgetary funds as required can be catalytic for strong PHC performance under emergency conditions. The extra-budgetary funds could flow from a range of sources, including changes to program budget allocations or external funds from donors or those made available by ministries of finance. This ability to adjust funding levels and flows is particularly important in the recovery stage to manage resurgent demand for noncrisis health services.

Building and maintaining trust-based community engagement also supports resilience in the long term. Community-centered PHC models, in which community health workers (CHWs) often play a key role, can facilitate a resilient PHC system. In an emergency, community-centered PHC models tend to provide more effective and clearer messages on emergency status, along with prevention and treatment recommendations that people can easily understand and follow. Community engagement strategies should be tailored to the local context and enhance messages that promote trust, such as those that highlight facility and health-worker adherence to safety standards and people-centered approaches to care.

Foundations for change: Enabling multisectoral action in PHC

The four fundamental shifts described map an ambitious change agenda for many PHC systems. The shifts will demand investment and effort from health leaders and stakeholders that are sustained over time. Fortunately, as noted at the start of the chapter, policy makers and PHC practitioners in many countries are already engaged in change processes like the ones discussed, and some countries have achieved impressive advances. Their experiences can enable others to seize opportunities, avoid pitfalls, and accelerate progress. We will shortly turn to analyzing evidence from those country experiences.

In closing this chapter, we briefly consider a subject that has potential importance for the four high-level shifts in PHC. It also has a prominent place in the history of PHC. The topic is multisectoral action for health, recently often conceptualized as a whole-of-government approach to health action. A strong case can be made that all four shifts described here could be accelerated by forms of collaborative action that reach across sectors of government and society. Country experience suggests that some strategies of this type are feasible under current conditions.

Since the Alma-Ata conference, multisectoral action for health has been an enduring concern of the PHC movement, as well as one of its greatest challenges. Like PHC itself, multisectoral or intersectoral action has suffered from a problem of conceptual tensions and competing definitions.[6] Without entering into the details of those debates, it is clear that multisectoral action related to health can take numerous forms and be carried out at many different levels, from the highest tiers of central government to the front lines of community-based health service delivery. However, in part because of the vast range of possible approaches, successfully delivering multisectoral action and measuring its impacts have proven challenging. An influential 2018 study of successes and failures in PHC, written for the 30th anniversary of Alma-Ata, concluded that, among the core components of PHC described at Alma-Ata, two had consistently proven most difficult to implement: intersectoral action for health and community participation (Lawn et al. 2008).

To systematically analyze the large literature on multisectoral action for health, including One Health, is beyond the scope of this report. Here, we present a short reflection on two aspects of multisectoral stewardship that are pertinent to the high-level PHC shifts. The first concerns linking primary care and public health services at the community level. The second looks at what the concept of multisectoral stewardship entails, as a dimension of leadership in PHC.

Linking primary care and public health

Debates on the place of multisectoral action in PHC began even before the Alma-Ata conference. The distinction between primary care and primary health care emerged in the late 1960s, when the term "primary health care" was first used by the Christian Medical Commission (Starfield, Shi, and Macinko 2005), prior to being adopted by WHO and others. At the time, "primary health care" was meant to replace the existing term "basic health services" (BHS), while enlarging its meaning (Cueto 2004). The importance assigned to multisectoral action became a key factor distinguishing PHC from other models of health service provision.

The Alma-Ata authors affirmed multisectoral engagement as a central pillar of PHC. Many reasons supported a broader, multisectoral conceptualization. Growing evidence at the time suggested that vertical disease control programs, like the costly and disappointing malaria eradication campaigns of the period, would not succeed in substantially reducing the burden of illness in LMICs. Tackling one disease at a time, such programs could not address the breadth and complexity of health needs in these settings. Medical advances alone, in any form, would fall short in these contexts without concomitant improvement in nutrition and living conditions (Levine 1976).

Support for multisectoral action was by no means universal. Alma-Ata was rapidly followed by attempts to circumscribe PHC to a limited package of basic services under the rubric "selective PHC" (Cueto 2004). This was presented as a means to make PHC concrete and align it to the health care needs and, above all, the delivery capacities of poor countries. Meanwhile, some HICs, especially in North America, embraced their own narrower model of "primary care," decoupling it from population-based services and limiting it to individualized essential care connected to a gatekeeping function. Despite these tensions, the broader concept of PHC—incorporating multisectoral action—has endured, linked to recurrent efforts to integrate primary care with public health (Rawaf 2018).

Integrating primary care and public health on the PHC front lines is a foundational step to make multisectoral engagement concrete and support healthier living in communities. For that integration to occur, however, PHC needs to be viewed not only as patients' first point of contact with health services, but as a "set of values and principles for guiding the development of health systems," anchored in social justice, solidarity, the right to health, people-centered health care, and community participation (Gauld et al. 2012). The emphasis on community participation implies a bottom-up approach to multisectoral action that is aligned with Alma-Ata principles. The driving force for work across sectors in this approach is community health needs as expressed by communities themselves, not only a desire among policy makers to break down ministerial silos and make government work more efficiently.

The importance of linking clinical services and public health action at the grassroots has practical implications for how local PHC teams are composed and how frontline PHC practitioners are trained. Bringing primary care and public health together means integrating epidemiologists and disease control specialists, nutritionists, pharmacists, social workers, and community health workers into expanded primary health care teams. Bringing collaborators with these skill sets to the PHC front lines can avoid placing the main burden for managing multisectoral partnerships on overworked clinicians. Multidisciplinary PHC teams can be composed, trained, empowered, and compensated to advocate with other sectors for healthy public policy and interventions.

Providing the PHC team with capacities and incentives to connect with the empaneled community in a proactive manner further enables multisectoral work at the community level. Achieving this will allow teams to more accurately track the prevalence and distribution of the main illnesses in the community. It also will enable the team to gain understanding of local health determinants, for example, lifestyle and behavior patterns, that can be targeted with customized multidisciplinary action. Proper undergraduate, graduate, and in-service training to raise awareness and build competencies for the latter is key, as are the communication skills and the financial and nonfinancial incentives for high performance (European Observatory on Health Systems and Policies and Rechel 2020). Finally, following the principle that "You manage what you measure," an expanded accountability framework for health outcomes can facilitate multisectoral initiatives by incorporating outcomes that depend on changes in health determinants, not simply on the results of clinical interventions. A framework that highlights outcomes that are sensitive to behavioral change may be especially useful.

Multisectoral stewardship in PHC

Although the bottom-up, community-driven dynamic is important, the success and sustainability of local multisectoral initiatives ultimately depend on support from central governments. Human, financial, and other resources directed from higher levels of the state to support local efforts can make the difference between promising pilot projects that fade, on the one hand, and models that maintain their momentum, that steadily improve their procedures and results, and that can be taken to scale, on the other hand. Conditions for success include values and principles supportive of multisectoral action in

PHC, governance structures that reflect them, and leaders who are willing to invest the necessary resources. Ideally, this includes central institutions able to adopt a whole-of-government approach.

The most ambitious efforts to advance health goals across sectors involve new partnerships and ways of working at the ministerial level. Achieving this, in turn, requires top health leaders to exercise stewardship in driving these high-level efforts politically. This stewardship corresponds to a key dimension of health system stewardship as defined by WHO: "Beyond the formal health system, stewardship means ensuring that other areas of government policy and legislation promote—or at least do not undermine—peoples' health" (WHO 2010).

In the case of multisectoral action linked to PHC, stewardship is a challenging political art that involves setting ambitious but winnable goals at the central governance level, while ensuring that high-level decisions are informed by the needs and aspirations of local communities. To practice this art, health leaders need to persuade partners in other government departments that those partners' own agendas will be served by the results that multisectoral action can bring. In other words, they need to offer plausible perspectives for "win-win" outcomes. In this sense, stewardship for multisectoral action in PHC involves a distinct understanding of leadership in health: one based not on top-down, command-and-control authority, but on partnership building, shared decision-making, and the capacity to set policy directions that can align the interests of varied stakeholders, including low-income and vulnerable communities.

Multisectoral stewardship becomes increasingly vital in the new health ecosystems where globalization, urbanization, population mobility, and aging are prominent. In this context, disease burdens are increasingly driven by factors that include poverty, poor quality of diets, inadequate access to education, and disenfranchisement due to stratifiers, such as ethnicity, gender, and rural location. These determinants powerfully shape the growing burden of NCDs in particular. Such shifts in health and health care needs cannot be tackled solely at the point of service delivery; they require action on distal and proximal determinants of healthy living [box 3.8].

As demographic and epidemiological trends drive rising care demands and surging health care costs in many countries, leaders seek a new balance between health promotion, disease prevention, and curative services. Shifting the weight to prevention and promotion would already enable short-term cost savings, and it is the only way to ensure health systems' financial

BOX 3.8

WHAT HAS TO CHANGE: SECTORAL SILOS INHIBIT COLLABORATION

The structural, social, and behavioral determinants of health span sectoral boundaries; likewise, improved physical and mental health offers cross-sectoral benefits. Housing, traffic, environment, and education policy, among many others, have an important role to play in tackling the leading causes of mortality and morbidity. Yet government ministries and the health system are poorly constructed for effective cooperation. Siloed financing flows, organizational hierarchies, and lines of accountability disincentivize joint action. Nonhealth ministries are tasked with achieving sector-specific goals and granted sector-specific funds; they may discount the health value of an intervention if it does not relate to the ministry's core business. The converse also holds true; an overmedicalized health sector may not consider the entire range of nonhealth benefits offered by health system interventions. Both phenomena can lead to substantial underinvestment and allocative distortions (McGuire et al. 2019). In emergencies, organizational siloes also slow and complicate the effort to mount an effective response, leading to unnecessary health losses.

Low- and middle-income countries: The Sub-Saharan African region is home to only 3 percent of the world's motor vehicles but accounts for 20 percent of global road traffic deaths (272,000 each year), due to poor infrastructure, inadequate vehicle safety standards, and a lack of legislation and enforcement to control speeding, drunk driving, and seatbelt/helmet use (WHO Regional Office for Africa 2018).

Upper-middle-income countries: In China, where 52 percent of men are daily smokers, recent measures have increased cigarette taxes to 56 percent of the total price—yet taxes are still far below WHO-recommended levels to deter tobacco use. No complete smoke-free laws have yet been applied to public spaces, including health care facilities, schools, restaurants, or indoor workplaces (WHO 2019c).

High-income countries: In WHO's European region, more than one-quarter of childhood asthma deaths and disability-adjusted life years (DALYs) in children are attributable to poor housing quality, including mold and dampness (Braubach, Jacobs, and Ormandy 2011).

sustainability in the longer term. PHC is the platform to make these changes work. PHC's importance for multisectoral and whole-of-government action will grow as multisectorality evolves from predominantly technological interventions in areas like water and sanitation, food security and the food supply chain, and transportation to engage problems driven by complex behavioral determinants, where technology alone will not provide solutions. The costliest of these problems in economic and public health terms include smoking, poor diet, obesity, harmful alcohol use, and interpersonal violence. Accordingly, some of the most successful recent examples of "win-win" multisectoral policy making involve measures such as raising excise taxes on health-damaging products, notably, tobacco (Bloomberg Philanthropies Task Force on Fiscal Policy for Health 2019).

Conclusion

This chapter has discussed the broad directions for policy action to adapt PHC systems to countries' new health care ecologies. Fundamental directions include the following:

+ Moving from a gatekeeping model of PHC to a focus on quality, comprehensive care for all

+ Reconnecting fragmented delivery mechanisms around people-centered care

+ Building fairness and accountability into the system's deep structures to reduce inequities

+ Making PHC more resilient to future emergencies while boosting its contribution to system-wide crisis response.

The chapter has also noted growing interest in some whole-of-government policy models to advance pro-health action across sectors, locally, nationally, and globally.

These shifts resonate strongly with other recent proposals for PHC reform; in many cases, they reflect principles and policy objectives articulated by PHC leaders and implementers throughout PHC's history. The critical question, now as then, is how these high-level policy directions can be translated into action in countries, especially where health resources are constrained. This chapter has contributed to that question by identifying the drivers for each broad shift in PHC. Drivers represent entry points for policy action. However, the diversity of levers raises the problem of how countries can best sequence and coordinate their use. The next chapter takes up the "how" issues that countries will face in setting out to improve PHC. It contains no simple recipes, but it describes a suite of coordinated actions that countries can use to move forward.

Notes

1. "People at the Centre: OECD Policy Forum on the Future of Health," n.d. https://www.oecd.org/health/ministerial/policy-forum/.

2. This is becoming the case in most middle- and upper-middle-income countries, in addition to high-income countries.

3. "Health (care) seeker is used instead of 'patient,' since all those who seek care are not patients, for example, a healthy individual seeking information before travel, a healthy pregnant woman seeking antenatal care, or a child to be immunized.

A distinction also needs to be made between an illness, as perceived by an individual, a sickness as perceived by the care provider and others, and a disease, referring to a medical condition rather than the individual. Finally, we also draw a distinction between health needs, i.e., behavioral input for healthy living, and healthcare needs which are related to a discomfort expressed by an individual requiring medical attention."

4. "In practical terms, this means that a PHC unit would have all necessary means (facility, equipment, digital platform, consumables, drugs) to provide the comprehensive set of services in an integrated, continuous, and resilient manner (community outreach, surveillance, case detection, primary care, multisectoral advocacy for health promotion and disease prevention); have a full team of professionals trained and competent in people-centered health, medical, and psycho-social care (doctors, nurses, midwives, social workers, dieticians, laboratory and other auxiliary staff); and that services are provided and managed in adherence with all structural and interpersonal domains of responsiveness, without imposing financial hardship. Responsiveness is understood to include quality of basic amenities, choice, access to social support networks, and prompt attention as structural domains, while dignity, autonomy, communication, and confidentiality are seen as interpersonal domains of responsiveness."

References

Agency for Healthcare Research and Quality. n.d. "Understanding Quality Measurement." https://www.ahrq.gov/patient-safety/quality-resources/tools/chtoolbx/understand/index.html.

Alzaied, Tariq Ali M. and A. Alshammari. 2016. "An Evaluation of Primary Healthcare Centers (PHC) Services: The Views of Users Abstract." *Indian Journal of Gerontology* 29: 1–9. https://www.semanticscholar.org/paper/An-Evaluation-of-Primary-Healthcare-Centers-%28PHC%29-Alzaied-Alshammari/f3605ef6fd57428ac6c54281d8685b37fccc9602.

Bargawi, Amina A., and David M. Rea. 2015. "Quality in Primary Health Care." *Health Policy and Planning*, 37–40.

Bloomberg Philanthropies Task Force on Fiscal Policy for Health. 2019. "Health Taxes to Save Lives: Employing Effective Excise Taxes on Tobacco, Alcohol, and Sugary Beverages: The Task Force on Fiscal Policy for Health." *Bloomberg Philanthropies*: 1–28. https://tobacconomics.org/files/research/512/Health-Taxes-to-Save-Lives-Report.pdf.

Braubach, Matthias, David E. Jacobs, and David Ormandy. 2011. "Environmental Burden of Disease Associated with Inadequate Housing: Summary Report." World Health Organisation Europe, Copenhagen.

Brinkerhoff, Derick W., and Thomas J Bossert. 2008. "Health Governance: Concepts, Experience, and Programming Options." Brief, United States Agency for International Development, February.

CDC (Centers for Disease Control and Prevention). n.d. "2014–2016 Ebola Outbreak in West Africa." CDC, accessed May 11, 2021, https://www.cdc.gov/vhf/ebola/history/2014–2016-outbreak/index.html.

Centre for Policy Research. 2011. "Mapping Medical Providers in Rural India: Four Key Trends." Policy Brief, Centre for Policy Research, 3–6.

Collins, Sara R., Herman K. Bhupal, and Michelle M. Doty. 2019. "Health Insurance Coverage Eight Years After the ACA."

Commonwealth Fund. n.d. "International Health Policy Survey," accessed May 10, 2021, https://www.commonwealthfund.org/publications/issue-briefs/2019/feb/health-insurance-coverage-eight-years-after-aca.

Cueto, Marcos. 2004. "The Origins of Primary Health Care and Selective Primary Health Care." *American Journal of Public Health* 94, 1864–74, https://doi.org/10.2105/AJPH.94.11.1864.

Daire, Judith, and Lucy Gilson. 2014. "Does Identity Shape Leadership and Management Practice? Experiences of PHC Facility Managers in Cape Town, South Africa." *Health Policy and Planning* 29 (Suppl 2): ii82–97, https://doi.org/10.1093/heapol/czu075.

Donabedian, A. 1988. "The Quality of Care. How Can It Be Assessed?" *The Journal of the American Medical Association* 260 (12): 1743–48, https://doi.org/10.1001/jama.260.12.1743.

European Observatory on Health Systems and Policies and Bernard Rechel. 2020. "How to Enhance the Integration of Primary Care and Public Health? Approaches, Facilitating Factors, and Policy Options." World Health Organization. https://apps.who.int/iris/handle/10665/330491.

Forrest, Christopher B. 2003. "Primary Care in the United States: Primary Care Gatekeeping and Referrals: Effective Filter or Failed Experiment?" *British Medical Journal* 326 (7391): 692–95, https://doi.org/10.1136/bmj.326.7391.692.

Frandsen, Brigham R., Karen E. Joynt, James B. Rebitzer, and Ashish K. Jha. 2015. "Care Fragmentation, Quality, and Costs among Chronically Ill Patients." *American Journal of Managed Care* 21(5): 355–62.

Gauld, Robin, Robert Blank, and Claus Wendt. 2012. "The World Health Report 2008: Primary Healthcare: How Wide Is the Gap between Its Agenda and Implementation in 12 High-Income Health Systems?" *Healthcare Policy* 7 (3): 38–58, https://doi.org/10.12927/hcpol.2013.22778.

GBD Risk Factor Collaborators. 2018. "Global, Regional, and National Comparative Risk Assessment of 84 Behavioural, Environmental and Occupational, and Metabolic Risks or Clusters of Risks for 195 Countries and Territories, 1990–2017: A Systematic Analysis for the Global Burden of Disease Study 2017." *The Lancet* 392 (10159): 1923–94, https://doi.org/10.1016/S0140-6736(18)32225-6.

Hollander, Judd E., and Brendan G. Carr. 2020. "Virtually Perfect? Telemedicine for Covid-19," https://www.nejm.org/doi/full/10.1056/nejmp2003539.

IOM (Institute of Medicine Committee on the Future of Primary Care). 1996. *Primary Care: America's Health in a New Era*, edited by M. S. Donaldson, K. D. Yordy, K. N. Lohr, and N. A. Vanselow. Washington, DC: National Academies Press, https://doi.org/10.17226/5152.

IOM (Institute of Medicine Committee on Quality of Health Care in America). 2001. *Crossing the Quality Chasm: A New Health System for the 21st Century*. Washington, DC: National Academies Press, https://doi.org/10.17226/10027.

Ipsos. 2018. "Global Views on Cyberbullying," http://pressoffice.mg.co.za/ipsos/PressRelease.php?StoryID=284412#author.

IWG (International Working Group on Financing Preparedness). 2017. "From Panic and Neglect to Investing in Health Security: Financing Pandemic Preparedness at a National Level." Working paper (English). World Bank, Washington, DC.

Jewell, Britta, Jennifer Smith, and Timothy Hallett. 2020. "The Potential Impact of Interruptions to HIV Services: A Modelling Case Study for South Africa," 1–9. https://www.medrxiv.org/content/10.1101/2020.04.22.20075861v1.

Joyce, Pauline, Zena Eh Moore, and Janice Christie. 2018. "Organisation of Health Services for Preventing and Treating Pressure Ulcers," *Cochrane Database of*

Systematic Reviews 12: 691–729, https://doi.org/10.1002/14651858.CD012132 .pub2.

Kruk, Margaret E., Sabrina Hermosilla, Elysia Larson, and Godfrey M. Mbaruku. 2014. "Bypassing Primary Care Clinics for Childbirth: A Cross-Sectional Study in the Pwani Region, United Republic of Tanzania." *Bulletin of the World Health Organization*, Geneva.

Kruk, Margaret E., M. Michael Myers, S. Tornorlah Varpilah, and Bernice T. Dahn. 2015. "What Is a Resilient Health System? Lessons from Ebola." *The Lancet* 385 (9980): 1910–12, https://doi.org/10.1016/S0140-6736(15)60755-3.

Kruk, Margaret E., Anna D. Gage, Catherine Arsenault, Keely Jordan, Hannah H. Leslie, Sanam Roder-DeWan, Olusoji Adeyi, et al. "High-Quality Health Systems in the Sustainable Development Goals Era: Time for a Revolution," *The Lancet Global Health Commission* 11: E1196–1252, https://doi.org/10.1016/S2214 -109X(18)30386-3.

Larson, Elaine. 1991. "Medicare: A Strategy for Quality Assurance." *Journal of Nursing Care Quality* 5 (4): 83, https://doi.org/10.1097/00001786-199107000 -00013.

Larson, Elysia, Godfrey Mbaruku, Stephanie A. Kujawski, Irene Mashasi, and Margaret E. Kruk. 2019. "Disrespectful Treatment in Primary Care in Rural Tanzania: Beyond Any Single Health Issue." *Health Policy and Planning* 34 (7): 508–13, https://doi.org/10.1093/heapol/czz071.

Lawn, Joy E., Jon Rohde, Susan Rifkin, Miriam Were, Vinod K. Paul, and Mickey Chopra. 2008. "Alma-Ata 30 Years On: Revolutionary, Relevant, and Time to Revitalise." *The Lancet* 372 (9642): P917–27, https://doi.org/10.1016/S0140 -6736(08)61402-6.

Levine, David. 1976. *Thomas McKeown, The Modern Rise of Population*. New York /San Francisco: Academic Press.

Manne-Goehler, Jennifer, Pascal Geldsetzer, Kokou Agoudavi, Glennis Andall-Brereton, Krishna K. Aryal, Brice Wilfried Bicaba, Pascal Bovet, et al. 2019. "Health System Performance for People with Diabetes in 28 Low- and Middle-Income Countries: A Cross-Sectional Study of Nationally Representative Surveys." *PLoS Medicine* 16 (3): 1–21, https://doi.org/10.1371/journal.pmed.1002751.

McGuire, Finn, Lavanya Vijayasingham, Anna Vassall, Roy Small, Douglas Webb, Teresa Guthrie, and Michelle Remme. 2019. "Financing Intersectoral Action for Health: A Systematic Review of Co-Financing Models." *Globalization and Health* 15 (1: 1–18, https://doi.org/10.1186/s12992-019-0513-7.

McMahon, Shannon A., Asha S. George, Joy J. Chebet, Idda H. Mosha, Rose N. M. Mpembeni, and Peter J. Winch. 2014. "Experiences of and Responses to Disrespectful Maternity Care and Abuse during Childbirth: A Qualitative Study with Women and Men in Morogoro Region, Tanzania." *BMC Pregnancy and Childbirth* 14 (268): 1–13, https://doi.org/10.1186/1471-2393-14-268.

Mehrotra, Ateev, Christopher B. Forrest, and Caroline Y. Lin. 2011. "Dropping the Baton: Specialty Referrals in the United States." *Milbank Quarterly* 89 (1): 39–68, https://doi.org/10.1111/j.1468-0009.2011.00619.x.

Mills, Katherine T., Joshua D. Bundy, Tanika N. Kelly, Jennifer E. Reed, Patricia M. Kearney, Kristi Reynolds, et al. 2016. "Global Disparities of Hypertension Prevalence and Control: A Systematic Analysis of Population-Based Studies from 90 Countries." *Circulation* 134 (6): 441–50, https://doi.org/10.1161 /CIRCULATIONAHA.115.018912.

Murray, Christopher J. L., and David B. Evans, editors. 1990. *Health Systems Performance Assessment: Debates, Methods and Empiricism*. Geneva: World Health Organization.

OECD (Organisation for Economic Co-operation and Development). 2019. *Health at a Glance 2019, Organización Para La Cooperación y El Desarrollo Económicos* 2019, https://www.oecd-ilibrary.org/social-issues-migration-health/health-at -a-glance_19991312.

OECD (Organisation for Economic Co-operation and Development). 2020. "Realising the Potential of Primary Health Care." OECD Health Policy Studies, OECD Publishing, Paris, May 30), https://doi.org/10.1787/a92adee4-en.

O'Neill, Niall. 2015. "The Eight Principles of Patient-Centered Care: Oneview Healthcare." Blog, accessed May 10, 2021, https://www.oneviewhealthcare.com /blog/the-eight-principles-of-patient-centered-care/.

Pagès-Puigdemont, Neus, Maria Antònia Mangues, Montserrat Masip, Giovanna Gabriele, Laura Fernández-Maldonado, Sergi Blancafort, and Laura Tuneu. 2016. "Patients' Perspective of Medication Adherence in Chronic Conditions: A Qualitative Study." *Advances in Therapy* 33 (10): 1740–54, https://doi .org/10.1007/s12325-016-0394-6.

Phillips, Steven Joseph, Kim J. Brolin Ribacke, Dell D. Saulnier, Anneli Eriksson, and Johan von Schreeb. 2016. "Effects of the West Africa Ebola Virus Disease on Health-Care Utilization: A Systematic Review," https://doi.org/10.3389 /fpubh.2016.00222.

Rajan, Selina, Kamlesh Khunti, Nisreen Alwan, Claire Steves, Trish Greenhalgh, Nathalie MacDermott, Alisha Morsella, et al. 2021. "In the Wake of the Pandemic Preparing for Long COVID." Policy Brief 39, European Observatory on Health Systems and Policies, http://www.euro.who.int/en/about-us/partners/.

Rawaf, Salman. 2018. "A Proactive General Practice: Integrating Public Health into Primary Care." *London Journal of Primary Care* 10 (2): 17–18, https://doi.org /10.1080/17571472.2018.1445946.

Reibling, Nadine, and Claus Wendt. 2012. "Gatekeeping and Provider Choice in OECD Healthcare Systems." *Current Sociology* 60 (4): 489–505.

Roberton, Timothy, Emily D. Carter, Victoria B. Chou, Angela R. Stegmuller, Bianca D. Jackson, Yvonne Tam, Talata Sawadogo-Lewis, and Neff Walker. 2020. "Early Estimates of the Indirect Effects of the COVID-19 Pandemic on Maternal and Child Mortality in Low-Income and Middle-Income Countries: A Modelling Study," *The Lancet Global Health* 8 (7): e901–08, https://doi.org/10.1016/S2214 -109X(20)30229-1.

Santoli, Jeanne M., Megan C. Lindley, Malini B. De Silva, Elyse O. Kharbanda, Matthew F. Daley, Lisa Galloway, Julianne Gee, et al. 2020. "Effects of the COVID-19 Pandemic on Routine Pediatric Vaccine Ordering and Administration— United States, 2020." *Morbidity and Mortality Weekly Report* 69 (19): 591–93, https://doi.org/10.15585/mmwr.mm6919e2.

Schoen, Cathy, Robin Osborn, Sabrina K. H. How, Michelle M. Doty, and Jordan Peugh. 2009. "In Chronic Condition: Experiences of Patients with Complex Health Care Needs, in Eight Countries, 2008," *Health Affairs* 27 (Suppl. 1), https://doi.org/10.1377/hlthaff.28.1.w1.

Sochas, Laura, Andrew Amos Channon, and Sara Nam. 2017. "Counting Indirect Crisis-Related Deaths in the Context of a Low-Resilience Health System: The Case of Maternal and Neonatal Health during the Ebola Epidemic in Sierra Leone." *Health Policy and Planning* 32 (Suppl 3): 32–39, https://doi.org/10.1093 /heapol/czx108.

Starfield, B., L. Shi, and J. Macinko. 2005. "Contribution of Primary Care to Health Systems and Health." *The Milbank Quarterly* 83 (3): 457–502, https://www.ncbi.nlm.nih.gov/pmc/articles/PMC2690145/.

Stop TB Partnership. 2020. "Step Up for TB 2020," accessed June 6, 2021, http://stoptb.org/suft/.

Thomson, Anna, Mohammed Khogali, Martin de Smet, Tony Reid, Ahmed Mukhtar, Stefan Peterson, and Johan von Schreeb. 2011. "Low Referral Completion of Rapid Diagnostic Test-Negative Patients in Community-Based Treatment of Malaria in Sierra Leone." *Malaria Journal* 10 (94): 1–7, https://doi.org/10.1186/1475-2875-10-94.

Thornicroft, Graham, Somnath Chatterji, Sara Evans-Lacko, Michael Gruber, Nancy Sampson, Sergio Aguilar-Gaxiola, Ali Al-Hamzawi, et al. 2017. "Undertreatment of People with Major Depressive Disorder in 21 Countries," *British Journal of Psychiatry* 210 (2): 119–24, https://doi.org/10.1192/bjp.bp.116.188078.

UHC 2030 and Sustainable Health Financing Accelerator (SHFA). 2020. "How COVID-19 Is Reshaping Priorities for Both Domestic Resources and Development Assistance in the Health Sector: UHC2030." Blog, accessed May 11, 2021, https://www.uhc2030.org/blog-news-events/uhc2030-blog/how-covid-19-is-reshaping-priorities-for-both-domestic-resources-and-development-assistance-in-the-health-sector-555362/.

Velasco Garrido, Marcial, Annette Zentner, and Reinhard Busse. 2011. "The Effects of Gatekeeping: A Systematic Review of the Literature." *Scandinavian Journal of Primary Health Care* 29 (1): 28–38, https://doi.org/10.3109/02813432.2010.537015.

Wang, Qun, Alex Z. Fu, Stephan Brennan, Olivier Kalmus, Hastings Thomas Banda, and Manuela De Allegri. 2015. "Out-of-Pocket Expenditure on Chronic Non-Communicable Diseases in Sub-Saharan Africa: The Case of Rural Malawi." *PLoS ONE* 10 (1): 1–15, https://doi.org/10.1371/journal.pone.0116897.

Watkins, David A., Dean T. Jamison, Anne Mills, Rifat Atun, Kristin Danform, Amanda Glassman, et al. 2017. "Universal Health Coverage and Essential Packages of Care." In *Disease Control Priorities, Third Edition (Volume 9): Improving Health and Reducing Poverty*, 43–65, edited by Dean T. Jamison, Hellen Gelband, Susan Horton, et al. Washington, DC: World Bank, https://doi.org/10.1596/978-1-4648-0527-1_ch3.

Watkins, David A., Gavin Yamey, Marco Schaferhoff, Olusoji Adeyi, George Alleyne, Ala Alwan, Seth Berkley, et al. 2018. "Alma-Ata at 40 Years: Reflections from the *Lancet* Commission on Investing in Health." *The Lancet* 392 (10156):1434–60, https://doi.org/10.1016/S0140-6736(18)32389-4.

WHO (World Health Organization). 2008. *The World Health Report 2008: Primary Health Care Now More Than Ever*. Geneva: WHO.

WHO (World Health Organization). 2010. *The World Health Report: Health Systems Financing: The Path to Universal Coverage*. Geneva: WHO, https://apps.who.int/iris/handle/10665/44371.

WHO (World Health Organization). 2015. *Adherence to Long-term Therapies: Evidence for Action*. Geneva: WHO.

WHO (World Health Organization). 2016. "Framework on Integrated, People-Centred Health Services: Report by the Secretariat." World Health Assembly, No. A69/39: 1–12.

WHO (World Health Organization, Regional Office for Africa). 2018. "Status of Road Safety in the African Region." No. 1: 1–4.

WHO (World Health Organization). 2019a. "Primary Health Care on the Road to Universal Health Coverage: 2019 Monitoring Report," https://www.who.int/healthinfo/universal_health_coverage/report/uhc_report_2019.pdf.

WHO (World Health Organization). 2019b. "WHO Report on the Global Tobacco Epidemic, 2019: Country Profile," 17–19, https://www.who.int/publications/i/item/9789241516204.

WHO (World Health Organization). 2020a. "Primary Health Care and Health Emergencies." Technical Series on Primary Health Care, Brief. WHO, Geneva, https://www.who.int/docs/default-source/primary-health-care-conference/emergencies.pdf?sfvrsn=687d4d8d_2.

WHO (World Health Organization). 2020b. "Strenghtening the Health System Response to COVID-19: Maintaining the Delivery of Essential Health Care Services While Mobilizing the Health Workforce for the COVID-19 Response." Copenhagen: WHO Regional Office for Europe, April.

WHO (World Health Organization). 2021. "Social Determinants of Health," accessed May 10, 2021, https://www.who.int/health-topics/social-determinants-of-health#tab=tab_1.

WHO (World Health Organization) and United Nations Children's Fund (UNICEF). 2018. "A Vision for Primary Health Care in the 21st Century: Towards Universal Health Coverage and the Sustainable Development Goals." WHO, Geneva, https://apps.who.int/iris/handle/10665/328065.

Wisk, Lauren E., and Whitney P. Witt. 2012. "Predictors of Delayed or Forgone Needed Health Care for Families with Children." *Pediatrics* 130 (6): 1027–37, https://doi.org/10.1542/peds.2012-0668.

World Bank. 2013. "Fairness and Accountability: Engaging in Health Systems in the Middle East and North Africa: The World Bank Health Nutrition and Population Sector Strategy for MENA (2013–2018)," World Bank, Washington, DC, https://openknowledge.worldbank.org/handle/10986/16109.

World Food Programme. 2020. "COVID-19 Will Double Number of People Facing Food Crises Unless Swift Action Is Taken," accessed June 6, 2021, https://www.wfp.org/news/covid-19-will-double-number-people-facing-food-crises-unless-swift-action-taken.

Chapter 4

MAKING IT HAPPEN

Introduction

Chapter 3 described four high-level shifts to strengthen primary health care (PHC) services. This chapter presents evidence from many countries to show how these shifts can happen—and are already happening—in practice. Although large gaps in the evidence base persist, knowledge is available to guide priority reform actions to bring these shifts about in the post-COVID-19 (Coronavirus) context.

This chapter focuses on three priority reform agendas. The first concerns the organization of PHC services at the community level and in relation to the wider health system. The heart of this agenda is creating a multidisciplinary team architecture for PHC delivery that is tailored to countries' priorities and available resources. The second reform axis concerns the changes in medical training and health workforce policies needed to support multidisciplinary PHC practice. The third priority reform area is PHC financing.

The chapter is organized according to the framework in table 4.1. It relates the four high-level shifts and outcomes discussed in chapter 3 to the three priority reform agendas. Using this framework, this chapter explains how each of the reforms contributes to advancing each of the four shifts to improve results in PHC.[1] The chapter unpacks the framework step by step, describing the policy and implementation challenges that countries face in each area and summarizing the evidence on practical solutions.

Priority Reform 1: Fit-for-purpose multidisciplinary team-based organization

From dysfunctional gatekeeping to quality, comprehensive care for all

Dedicated multidisciplinary teams for community and primary care are the backbone of modern PHC. Informed by international evidence (box 4.1), team-based care models are quickly emerging as the preferred PHC service delivery platform, forming the backbone of a PHC system that offers integrated, responsive, continuous, and community-oriented care. Team-based models offer additional human resources; a more robust mix of skills; and a stronger mandate to provide a universal, comprehensive package of PHC services to an assigned ("empaneled") population.

Table 4.1 Reimagining a PHC fit-for-purpose: Outcomes and priority reforms

"HOW?": PRIORITY REFORMS		
"WHAT?": OUTCOMES		**Multidisciplinary Team-Based Organization**
	1. From dysfunctional gatekeeping to quality comprehensive care for all	Multidisciplinary teams align clinical services to meet the full range of local health needs. Clinical services address acute illnesses and injuries and manage chronic conditions, including mental health needs. Teams expand community health education, health and nutrition promotion, and disease prevention.
	2. From fragmentation to people-centered integration	Multidisciplinary teams build long-term trust with empaneled communities, collaborate and communicate internally, and coordinate patients' movement through the health system and back tc the community.
	3. From inequities to fairness and accountability	Empanelment creates accountability for health outcomes. Financing and other mechanisms reinforce accountability. Team composition reflects local health and health care needs and socio-economic determinants. Both patient and health outcomes are embedded in the accountability framework.
	4. From fragility to resilience	PHC teams include public health surveillance an outreach capacity. Team structure helps buffer provider absences. Service-delivery organizatio and leadership ensure team capacity to manage the unexpected.

(Continu

Table 4.1 Reimagining a PHC fit-for-purpose: Outcomes and priority reforms
(continued)

"HOW?": PRIORITY REFORMS	
Multiprofessional health workforce development	Resource mobilization for public health-enabled primary care
Multiprofessional health education builds generalist knowledge, skills, and competencies. Curriculum and practicum reforms facilitate creating multidisciplinary PHC teams.	Allocation of financial and human resources is based on evidence of local disease burden, socio-economic conditions, and demographic characteristics. Financing rewards community engagement and supports a tailored essential service package, including primary care and public health.
Multiprofessional education emphasizes "soft" skills to promote shared medical decision-making; empower patients for self-care; contribute to patient satisfaction; and support teamwork and care coordination.	Data and IT platforms enable telehealth functions and support EHRs for the empaneled community. EHRs smoothly exchange data with the rest of the health care system, and users can access records confidentially.
Reformed multiprofessional education creates a culture of transparency and social accountability through leadership and team-based performance. PHC teams serve communities without discrimination based on gender, ethnicity, income, sexual orientation, or other factors.	Priority setting through a fair, participatory, and transparent process ensures that the essential service package is equitably and efficiently delivered to all. The service package takes account of socio-economic determinants of health and is not subject to ad hoc or geographic rationing.
Health workforce training prepares multidisciplinary PHC teams to prevent, detect, and respond to health emergencies. PHC teams are an effective first level of health system preparedness and response.	Financial and human resource surge capacity is built into health sector planning and resource allocation at the local level.

Source: Original table prepared for this publication.

Note: EHR = electronic health records; IT = information technology; PHC = primary health care.

BOX 4.1
WHY TEAM-BASED CARE?

Multidisciplinary care teams for empaneled populations have been endorsed as the preferred primary health care (PHC) service delivery platform by the Organisation for Economic Co-operation and Development (OECD), the World Health Organization (WHO), and the United Nations Children's Fund (UNICEF) (OECD 2020a; WHO 2016; WHO 2018a). Intuitively, team-based models offer several advantages over individual providers or less integrated networks.

+ First, the multidisciplinary nature of the team allows for an efficient and appropriate division of labor, with different provider types deploying their complementary skills and competencies to meet the full (and increasingly complex) health and wellness needs of individuals and families.

+ Second, the team offers a supportive and accountable structure for management and supervision. Team members offer each other coaching, encouragement, mentorship, and discipline, while the team as a whole can be held responsible for the health outcomes and satisfaction of the empaneled population.

+ Third, through empanelment to a dedicated care team, individuals and families can build long-term, trusting relationships with their health providers, with continuity of care further enhanced through complete and accessible health records.

+ Finally, team-based organization may offer some structural efficiencies, for example, lower overhead, built-in critical mass for quality assurance and improvement, and lower administrative costs.

Although the evidence base on multidisciplinary collaborative care is surprisingly sparse (Lutfiyya et al. 2019), emerging evidence appears to confirm these intuitions. A literature review on interprofessional collaborative practice identified 20 relevant studies, cumulatively pointing to improvements in chronic disease care, better medication adherence, reduced hospitalizations, and cost savings (Lutfiyya et al. 2019). Systematic reviews have found that the US-based Patient-Centered Medical Home (PCMH)—a multidisciplinary team-based model emphasizing patient-centered, coordinated, and comprehensive care—improves patient experience, care processes, and clinical outcomes for chronic disease (Jackson et al. 2013; John et al. 2020). The deployment of primary care teams within several centers in Canada, based on the PCMH, has been linked in several small studies to less frequent visits to emergency departments and reductions in avoidable hospitalization (Carter et al. 2016). In Brazil, the expansion of the Family Health Strategy team-based care model has been strongly associated with reductions in child mortality and (somewhat more tentatively) linked to reductions in hospitalization for conditions amenable to primary care-based prevention (Bastos et al. 2017). Several countries in Europe and Central Asia adopted multidisciplinary team-based care models under a family-centered PHC approach in the 1990s (World Bank 2005).

Under this model, a dedicated multidisciplinary team of health service providers—headquartered at a PHC hub facility but reaching out actively into the community—works collaboratively to serve a clearly defined catchment population. These local teams feed into larger clusters that form a more expansive network of services while maintaining a team orientation. Specialized services may be located at different nodes in the network rather than in one large center. Regional or urban hospitals and specialists assist and support the local PHC health team by supplementing the scope of clinical services and offering continuing education and professional development.

Patients are empaneled to dedicated PHC professionals who facilitate access to comprehensive PHC services and coordinate care with the other levels of the health system. Empanelment promotes more proactive management of the needs of patients and communities by assigning responsibility to providers, regardless of whether the patient seeks care.

The PHC team: Roles, composition, and catchment area

At the local level, the core PHC team consists of at least three categories of members working collaboratively—community health workers (CHWs), registered nurses (RNs), and general practice/family medicine specialists (FPs). Beyond these three core provider types, expanded team-based care models may include other specialized providers, such as midwives, dentists, optometrists, pharmacists, nutritionists, social workers, auxiliary health professionals such as laboratory and radiology technicians, and mental health counselors, as well as administrative support staff.

The PHC team works together in a community clinic setting that provides the full range of ongoing community-level care. This includes public health programs (such as for immunizations, screening, health promotion, and preventive care), as well as all first-contact health care for acute and chronic health problems. Mental health care and first response to emergencies are provided for the entire empaneled population. The PHC team has primary responsibility for referrals to higher levels of care, including information sharing and follow-up after a specialist consultation. Optimal team-based care models require clear role delineation and well-defined scope of practice—both to ensure efficient use of scarce physician time and to ensure low- and mid-level cadres deliver care appropriate to their level of training, under supervision.

Within this general approach, the specific composition of the care team and the size of the catchment population will vary between and within countries and will necessarily reflect local health needs and resource availability. Rigorous evidence to guide the optimal construction of the primary care team is limited; however, case studies have highlighted the importance of the clear delineation of responsibilities. Different health systems have taken different approaches to construction of care teams and assignment of tasks (table 4.2). In Costa Rica, primary health teams (called the Equipos Básicos de Atención Integral de Salud, or EBAIS) consist of a doctor, nurse, CHW, and pharmacist—each with a clearly defined role and set of responsibilities (Pesec et al. 2017). For example, CHWs perform home visits to deliver health promotion and household screening; nurses undertake basic clinical tasks

Table 4.2 Team-based care models around the world

	DESCRIPTION	CATCHMENT POPULATION	TEAM COMPOSITION
Brazil	The Family Health Program, launched in 1994, created family health teams (FHTs) responsible for the health of residents in a defined territory, including health promotion, education, and control of neglected tropical diseases. By 2015, the program covered 63% of the Brazilian population (almost 123 million individuals). Substantial evidence shows the program has improved health outcomes and system efficiency (Aquino, De Oliveira, and Barreto 2009; MacInko et al. 2010; Rasella et al. 2014; Rocha and Soares 2010).	The maximum is 1,000 households (4,000 residents).	At a minimum, the team consists of a physician, nurse, nurse technician, and four to six full-time community health agents. Additional incentives are available for adding other team members, including oral health workers, physiotherapists, and managers.
Costa Rica	Costa Rica's Basic Teams for Primary Health Care (EBAIS) began operating in 1994. As of December 2018, the country is organized in 7 regions; 106 health areas; and 1,048 PHC teams. Each PHC team offers health promotion, prevention, treatment, and rehabilitation.	It varies according to the availability of personnel, sector population, budget, and other variables. As of end-2018, an average of 4,474 inhabitants (range: 2,343-7,480) were assigned per PHC team.	The team includes at least one medical doctor (GP), one nursing assistant, and one technical assistant in primary care.

(Continued)

Table 4.2 Team-based care models around the world *(continued)*

	DESCRIPTION	CATCHMENT POPULATION	TEAM COMPOSITION
Turkey (Sumer, Shear, and Yener 2019)	Healthy living centers (HLCs), introduced in 2017, provide multidisciplinary services across health promotion, prevention, and disease management. Healthy living centers complement the family medicine system; family medicine physicians can refer their patients onward to receive their services.	About 200 HLCs across Turkey each serve a population of about 75,000.	The team includes an HLC manager, physician, dentist, nurse, midwife, medical secretary, social worker, dietician, child development specialist, psychologist, and care coordinator.
Ontario (Canada) (MOHLTC, n.d.)	Relatively generous capitation-based payment packages encourage family doctors to join FHT group practices. Some, including the provincial government, now argue that capitation rates were set too high and have resulted in unsustainable overpayment of family medicine physicians (Boyle 2019).	Patients voluntarily enroll with FHTs and agree to use their designated provider for all local, nonemergency care. 184 teams currently serve 3 million Ontario residents (about 15,000 patients per practice team).	It varies; typically, it includes at least doctors, nurse practitioners, and nurses. It may also include social workers, dietitians, and other health workers.
South Africa	Ward-Based Outreach Teams, established in 2020, are linked to PHC facilities and are intended to extend care into the community.	250–400 households per CHW (Naledi, Barron, and Schneider 2011).	It has a team leader (typically a professional nurse) plus five or more CHWs.
Ghana	Preferred Primary Care Provider (PPP) Networks link several Community-based Health Planning and Service (CHPS) compounds to single hub, for example, a health center or district hospital. Preliminary results suggest the program has improved referral feedback and service delivery coverage (Atim, Awoonor, and Hammah 2019).	It consists of 10 pilot networks (42 health facilities). The size of catchment population for each PPP network varies substantially (from ~5,000 to ~25,000).	It varies substantially.

Source: Original table compiled for this publication.

Note: CHW = community health worker; HLCs = healthy living centers; PHC = primary health care.

and counseling; and physicians lead management of acute and chronic conditions. In Thailand, primary health "matrix teams" consist of four care providers working at different levels within the health system: a family doctor (district hospital level), nurse (subdistrict level), community health worker (village level), and family member or caregiver (Alliance for Health Policy and Systems Research and Bill & Melinda Gates Foundation 2015). Recognizing the complexity of community support for chronic disease management, other models have sought to broaden the primary health care team to include allied health practitioners or to support greater integration with social services. From 2008, for example, the Brazil Family Health Service (FHS) introduced Family Health Support Centers (NASF), where interdisciplinary teams (including psychologists, for example) deliver extended care to support the family health team (Macinko, Harris, and Rocha 2017).

The COVID-19 experience highlights additional roles and competencies that may be desirable within the primary care team—either as permanent members of the care team or as temporary surge capacity during emergencies. Basic laboratory capacity to support diagnosis and surveillance may be brought in-house or otherwise assigned to a cluster of PHC teams. PHC teams could also introduce public health officers tasked with designing and leading public health campaigns; performing syndromic surveillance and reporting within the catchment areas; and directing contact tracing efforts during infectious disease outbreaks. A public health officer should interface closely with the broader PHC team, his or her counterparts in neighboring catchment areas, and central public health authorities.

Empanelment and transition to multidisciplinary care teams in mixed health systems

The transition from solo practice to empaneled multidisciplinary care teams can be complicated—particularly in mixed health systems, where care is fragmented across a variety of public sector, for-profit, and not-for-profit private providers. Empanelment, in particular, is often understood as a top-down, public-sector process (for example, applied on a geographic basis); however, alternative empanelment strategies can incorporate private sector providers.

Geographic empanelment is easily understood in the public sector context, wherein each public sector team serves a population within a defined geographic catchment area. In mixed health systems, it requires a public-private partnership design, in which patients are identified and assigned to private multidisciplinary care teams (such as provider networks) using existing geographic catchment areas or municipal boundaries, typically as part of a publicly financed strategic purchasing or contracting arrangement for underserved jurisdictions (Bearden et al. 2019; Montagu and Goodman 2016). For example, local health integration networks (LHINs) are community-based nonprofit organizations that receive funding from the Ministry of Health in Ontario, Canada, to plan, fund, and coordinate public health care services delivered by hospitals, long-term care homes, community care access centers, community support service agencies, mental health and addiction agencies, and community health centers. The LHINs conduct extensive needs mapping of subpopulations in a particular geographic or catchment area (for example, the elderly; the homeless; refugees; immigrants; and the lesbian, gay, bisexual, transgender [LGBT] community) through focus group sessions that allow the LHINs to identify challenges leading to shortfalls in the health outcomes of these subgroups relative to the rest of the population. Once LHINs identify gaps, they tender requests for proposals from private local health care providers, offering them government funding to provide the missing health care service in underserved geographies. LHINs outline clear expectations for these contracted health care providers to use various team-based care models, which are reinforced by performance measurement and evaluation systems that are transparent to the public (Aiyenigba et al. 2016; Montagu and Goodman 2016).

Insurance-based empanelment involves arrangements where patients are assigned or opt into accredited public or private provider networks or care teams, based on their enrollment in specific insurance schemes that may be public (for example, social or national health insurance schemes) or private (for example, through health management organizations) (PHCPI 2019). The insurer may have a gatekeeping scheme in place that can be used to support the development and implementation of clinical pathways and dual referral systems (Bearden et al. 2019). They may also encourage and incentivize promotive and preventive care through payment models, including partial or full capitation or fee-for-service models. This can be coupled with incentives to better use data and patient records for more proactive population management across specific patient populations (Aiyenigba et al. 2016).

In the United States, for example, patients benefiting from Medicare (a publicly financed insurance program for the elderly) can opt to join an accountable care organization (ACO), which would subsequently be responsible for the patient's whole-of-person care and health outcomes—including through financial incentives.[2] In Thailand, individuals covered by national health insurance are free to choose the primary care provider with whom they wish to register. Providers are then paid on a capitated basis; patients have four opportunities each year to change their provider network, facilitating an element of patient choice, provider accountability, and portability for seasonal migrants. In practice, however, choice in most rural areas is limited by geographic monopoly, as only a single provider is available within the geographic area (Tangcharoensathien et al. 2015). In Nigeria, the Hygeia health management organizations offer patients access to services through a corporate network of 1,608 hospitals and clinics. The network of private hospitals and clinics is bound by a capitation model, which incentivizes them to provide primary, preventive care through multidisciplinary care teams to a large segment of the Nigerian population (Aiyenigba et al. 2016).

Finally, where population-wide empanelment is not possible in the immediate term, interim policy measures can help make incremental progress toward a team based care model, for example, by incentivizing provider collaboration or forming and integrating networks of individual providers.

Private sector intermediary networks can organize private, independent health care providers and facilities into quality-assured networks of multidisciplinary teams. The networks connect small-scale private providers to interact with governments, patients, and vendors while performing key health system functions that are challenging for individual private providers to accomplish on their own, for example, proactive population management, quality improvement, management capacity, and integration into payment systems and universal health coverage (Aiyenigba et al. 2016).

Examples abound across highly diverse contexts. In a German pilot project, for example, a third-party health management company works in conjunction with the statutory private insurance companies and providers to offer population-based, integrated care across a specific catchment area; the program is financed by cost savings realized by the insurance providers. The program has improved patient experience and population health outcomes while reducing hospitalizations and health care costs (Busse and Stahl 2014; Pimperl et al. 2017). In Ghana, where individual Community-Based Health Planning and Services health centers still struggle to provide full PHC services due to lack of infrastructure, medicine, supplies, and human resource capacity, a pilot project (the Preferred Primary Provider Network) links four to five small CHPS zones (spokes) to a larger, more capacitated health center (hub)—thereby forming a decentralized group practice (Atim et al. 2019). In France, the Communautés Professionnelles Territoriales de Santé program connects geographically proximate health providers into a collaborative network with the overall objective of progressively eliminating solo primary health care practices that are often associated with isolation (OECD 2020a).

In some settings, where dedicated care teams are not yet the norm, narrowly constructed care teams have been set up to support patients with specific health needs. In Kazakhstan, for example, pregnant women are supported by a multidisciplinary team that includes social workers and psychologists in addition to health professionals; financial incentives help reinforce strong team performance, as evidenced by maternal and newborn health outcomes (Sukhanberdiyev and Tikhonova 2017).

Multidisciplinary care teams are the preferred standard of care for the human immunodeficiency virus (HIV). In the United States, the inclusion of pharmacists, care coordinators, social workers, nurses, and non-HIV primary care providers within the team has been associated with higher adherence to antiretroviral therapy (Horberg et al. 2012), while extensive international evidence associates inclusion of a pharmacist specifically with better adherence and clinical outcomes (Saberi et al. 2012). In the long run, these teams would ideally be "de-verticalized" from a single disease area/health need and integrated with generalist primary care for all health needs across the life course.

From fragmentation to people-centered integration

Empanelment to dedicated care teams: A strong foundation for care continuity

The literature distinguishes between three types of care continuity (Haggerty et al. 2003):

+ *Informational continuity* refers to the providers' accumulated understanding of patient history, values, and preferences. Such information can be vested in provider memory, written or electronic medical records, or some combination of the two—but it must be easily accessible and applicable at the point of care.

+ *Management continuity* refers to the coherent and coordinated planning and execution of patient care for complex or chronic disease.

+ *Relational continuity* refers to established interpersonal relationships between specific providers or care teams and the patients they serve (Haggerty et al. 2003).

Empanelment to dedicated care teams provides a strong foundation for all three types of care coordination and continuity. The effects span patients' health needs and life courses, both within PHC service delivery and across the health system. Empanelment enables continuity by creating a single PHC hub for each patient's care and disease management; offering an opportunity to build trusted long-term relationships with PHC providers; and building both written and informal repositories of information about patients. This matters because patients with access to continuous care have been shown to receive better quality care (Romano, Segal, and Pollack 2015), report higher satisfaction with health services (Reddy et al. 2015), and incur lower health expenditures (Hussey et al. 2018). In the United States, increases in the continuity of care have been linked to reductions in the utilization of specialist care (Nyweide et al. 2013), reductions in hospitalizations and emergency department use (Pourat et al. 2015), as well as reductions in medical errors (Gandhi et al. 2006). In Brazil, in areas with stronger PHC systems, a greater proportion of the population reported having a usual source of care, particularly in the poorest regions in the north and northeast (Dourado, Medina, and Aquino 2013).

Care continuity is clearly enhanced by the retention of care providers, and it is compromised by staff (or practice) attrition. High-staff turnover has been shown to reduce the probability of receiving preventive care services, weaken the coordination across different levels of care (Juliani, MacPhee, and Spiri 2017), and lower patient satisfaction scores (Reddy et al. 2015). PHC disruptions due to the retirement of primary care practitioners also lead to declines in the use of PHC services and increases in the number of medical tests and hospitalizations (Zhang, Salm, and van Soest 2018). In Denmark, the closure of primary care practices has been linked to increased utilization of emergency care (Simonsen et al. 2019), suggesting challenges in the transition of patients to new PHC providers.

When team-based networks function optimally, nonemergency access to higher levels of care is based on referrals from local PHC teams. PHC teams are accountable for prompt and appropriate referrals based on a patient's health needs and their informed clinical judgment. In turn, regional referral centers accept the responsibility and accountability for health outcomes within their catchment areas; they willingly receive requests for assistance and transfers when judged necessary by local care and take responsibility for communicating the results of a referral back to the PHC team. This approach fosters respectful and trusting relationships between PHC team members and specialist service providers. This is a true collaborative health system model that endorses the preeminence of cost-effective local comprehensive PHC services and preserves high-cost specialist services for those who need this level of care. It also recognizes the expertise of local PHC teams and their communities as being of equal value to the specialist expertise in regional referral centers.

Better two-way referrals: From primary care to specialists, and back into the community

The most effective PHC systems operate not as dysfunctional gatekeepers—a chokepoint before patients can access "real" care from secondary and tertiary providers—but as traffic dispatchers, triaging patients across different levels of care in an agile manner and in accordance with their health needs. The care coordination function helps direct patients to the appropriate care providers within the PHC team, and, as necessary, to external specialists. Equally important, it tracks the results of specialist consultations or hospitalizations and ensures appropriate follow-up care upon return to the community.

In some cases, specialist providers may physically co-locate with a PHC team on a part- or full-time basis. In theory, physical co-location of general practitioners with specialist providers extends the benefits of the PHC care team to a broader range of care—helping streamline referral processes, integrate medical records, and create better continuity of care across multiple types of health providers. In Canada, for example, a primary care physician can refer patients to a mental health counselor and/or psychiatrist, who are preferably physically co-located; the different providers then work collaboratively to provide whole-of-person care for low-acuity mental health needs (OECD 2020a). Cross-country survey data in Organisation for Economic Co-operation and Development (OECD) countries finds highly variable rates of co-location between general practitioners and other health professionals; rates of co-location can be as low as 5 or 6 percent (Czech Republic, Denmark, Germany, and Slovak Republic) and as high as 90–99 percent (Iceland and Lithuania) (Bonciani et al. 2018). Evidence on the results of co-location is limited and mixed. Analysis of survey data suggests that the co-location of general practitioners with specialists, midwives, physiotherapists, dentists, or pharmacists is significantly associated with improved coordination with secondary care; however, in countries with weak primary care systems, co-location is significantly associated with worse patient perceptions of care continuity, accessibility, and comprehensiveness (Bonciani et al. 2018).

Some low- and middle-income countries (LMICs) currently lack the capacity to rapidly create dedicated PHC teams able to work with and track individuals across the life course. In these settings, end-to-end, same-day services across diagnosis and treatment may offer a stopgap to increase referral completions and limit attrition. Studies show potential applications of same-day services to eye care and to the diagnosis and treatment of sexually transmitted infections; however, the approach has not been systematically evaluated and may be difficult to finance and integrate within routine services. In India, outreach camps provided by the philanthropically funded Aravind Eye Care System offer comprehensive eye exams and same-day provision of nonsurgical treatment (for example, glasses or a medicine prescription); patients in need of cataract surgery or other specialty services are counseled and transported to a nearby hospital for immediate admission (Aravind Eye Care System 2015). In Cameroon, a pilot study for cervical cancer screening returned test results for the human papillomavirus (HPV) within one hour of sample submission, offering same-day coagulation treatment to eligible patients; loss to follow-up was only 1 percent (Kunckler et al. 2017). A similar approach in Tanzania yielded promising results for the diagnosis and treatment of syphilis; testing for syphilis jumped more than 12-fold, treatment rates for diagnosed cases increased from 46 to 95 percent, and women reported savings as a result of averted transportation costs (Nnko et al. 2016).

When specialist services are not co-located or provided as integrated single-day services, technological solutions can play a useful role in strengthening referral processes. Although evidence is limited, a few available studies suggest that direct appointment booking services, typically over an online portal, have been associated with substantial reductions in the waiting time for nonurgent specialist services, though not with cost reductions (Frandsen et al. 2015). Such platforms are increasingly being adopted at scale within countries in the OECD. In the United Kingdom, all National Health Service providers were required to adopt an e-referral system for specialist consultations (e-RS) by October 2018; the platform enables patients to book a specialist appointment from their general practitioner's office at the time of referral or to do so from their personal computer after returning home (NHS 2018). An initial pilot study suggests that the new system can reduce waiting times for a specialist appointment by an average of eight days (Kripalani et al. 2007).

Electronic consultations (e-consults), defined as "asynchronous, consultative, provider-to-provider communications within a shared electronic health record (EHR) or web-based platform," can allow general practitioners to directly access specialist expertise and avoid in-person referrals unless necessary (Vimalananda et al. 2015). Evidence shows generally high provider and patient satisfaction with e-consult platforms; shorter wait times than for traditional in-person referrals; a reduction in face-to-face specialist appointments; and potential for reduced cost (Liddy et al. 2019). Rigorous evidence for the effect of e-consults on health outcomes is limited (Liddy et al. 2019).

Alternatively, telemedicine can allow patients to remotely access medical services and complete referrals from PHC providers—particularly for specialist services that may not otherwise be locally accessible. These initiatives are still largely underdeveloped within LMICs, with many nascent (often donor-funded) efforts but few sustained programs (Mars 2013). A rare scaled and sustained use of telemedicine is in Brazil, where some states have routinized remote electrocardiogram (ECG) testing, chest x-ray analysis, and ultrasounds as part of the national Family Health Program (Maldonado, Marques, and Cruz 2016). By end-2015, just one Brazilian state had performed almost 2.5 million remote ECGs and 74,000 teleconsultations. Over a five-year period, the state reported net US$11 million in cost savings (Scott and Mars 2015). In addition, a handful of telehealth networks in LMICs for humanitarian purposes have been sustained at least five years; in some cases, they have offered general remote consultation for all specialties, and in others, they have offered targeted support for dermatology, HIV, or trauma. However, evidence in support of these initiatives is limited. Elsewhere, feasibility studies suggest potential, although not scale or sustainability (Mars 2013).

Where routine care coordination processes are lacking, dedicated patient navigators can also help patients engage with a complex web of health services. A systematic review defines the patient navigation approach as "trained personnel"—potentially nurses, social workers, CHWs, or volunteers—"who help patients overcome modifiable barriers to care and achieve their care goals by providing a tailored approach to addressing individual needs" (McBrien et al. 2018). Patient navigation services can be quite wide in scope, encompassing all aspects of clinical, logistical, administrative, and emotional support, typically for chronic or life-threatening conditions like cancer.[3] The current evidence base is incomplete, but it generally suggests that patient navigators can be associated with more complete screening, faster diagnostic resolution, better mental health and quality of life among patients and their caregivers, lower A1C levels among diabetics, and higher clinical attendance and treatment adherence (Labrique et al. 2018).

Information technology (IT) and digital platforms for integrated care

More developed integrated care and payment models, including those from OECD countries, require interoperable data systems among specialists, hospitals, primary care settings, social service providers, and patients. These systems are often in their infancy in LMICs, with several limitations that prevent such platforms from realizing their full potential. First, fragmented donor-supported initiatives and vertical programs have driven a proliferation of health data systems and digital platforms, often with overlapping mandates or scope but limited interoperability and coverage, including for patients who seek care in the private sector. Second, health management information systems (HMIS) typically only capture service delivery data from patients who proactively seek care at a facility equipped to record and report the appropriate data. This limitation excludes individuals within the catchment area who do not visit such a health facility. Third, HMIS typically digitize health data at the district level and do not include patient-level electronic health records with unique patient identifiers, making it difficult to trace patients through the system and from facility to facility.

Although country information exchange policies can support or detract from system effectiveness (box 4.2), countries can take incremental data-informed approaches to more coordinated, transparent, and accountable primary health care, even where data are limited. Data management and storage, patient data security assurance, and reliable offline and back-up systems suited to LMICs all need to be considered during the design phase of a digital solution (Labrique et al. 2018).

BOX 4.2

HARNESSING TECHNOLOGY TO IMPROVE INFORMATION SHARING IN PRIMARY HEALTH CARE

A recent survey of 13,000 primary care providers across 11 high-income countries—Australia, Canada, France, Germany, the Netherlands, New Zealand, Norway, Sweden, Switzerland, the United Kingdom, and the United States—compares experiences in care coordination between providers and the use of health information technology. Seventy-four percent of physicians in Germany and 65 percent in the United Kingdom said they frequently coordinated patients with social services or other community providers. In contrast, only about 4 of 10 in Australia, Canada, and the United States reported the same. This is, in part, because, despite the presence of electronic information, primary care practices in the latter countries are not yet routinely exchanging information outside the practice; Germany, the United Kingdom, and other countries have higher levels of interoperability and a two-way exchange of information (Doty et al. 2020). Even countries that have improved their information-sharing capacities and practices still face challenges. In the United Kingdom, the lack of interoperability led to the National Health Service failing to invite 50,000 women for a cervical screening test (Iacobucci 2018). Additional promising innovations are underway. Estonia has introduced Blockchain for medical records, allowing patients to access their own medical records and to effectively become active agents in their own care (Vazirani et al. 2020). This application of Blockchain is still in its infancy, but the technology may help overcome problems of interoperability and better track health epidemics (PHCPI 2018).

Integrated data platforms are essential to improve care coherence and enhance patient experience; nevertheless, health data protections, and informed consent for the use of personal data are also important. Without strong protections in place, patients may not know how their data are used, the extent to which they are de-identified, who has access to their confidential clinical data, or how public and private providers share sensitive data. Under these conditions, patients are not in a position to determine how their data should be used and to refuse the use for purposes with which they are not comfortable. Appropriate regulations should include safeguards that limit how governments link and access clinical data from outside the health sector. Data protection regulations should guard against potential abuses with a clear mandate for an independent body to act as a data steward.

At the PHC facility level, data and measurement systems need to be part of a larger continuous quality-improvement process. Simply having data is not sufficient to improve performance. Team-based network managers must have the capacity to analyze the data, review performance regularly, and adapt care processes as needed (PHCPI 2018). Facility managers need to strike the right balance between collecting the appropriate data and avoiding the administrative burden on providers that can result from obligatory data reporting (OECD 2016a). Performance measurement and management requires establishing targets, monitoring performance against those targets, and implementing and adapting improvement efforts. Sharing data with staff as part of a continuous quality-improvement cycle allows countries to move away from inspection and punitive arrangements to a culture of problem solving and active collaboration among providers, supervisors, and team members (PHCPI 2018). A variety of performance measurement and management tools is available to help with this process (Hall 2019; Kane 2012; Necochea and Bossemeyer 2005).[4,5]

From inequities to fairness and accountability

Extending care into the community to address health disparities

With the support of CHWs, the PHC team offers care that extends beyond the static clinic into communities. Proactive frontline strategies can help address disparities in health outcomes by supporting basic health education and promotion; offering nutritional coaching and supplementation; identifying subclinical illness; and helping sustain adherence to treatment, among other strategies. In Brazil, community heath agents are each assigned about 150 households for monthly visits, during which they offer health promotion and support basic health care (Macinko and Harris 2015). In Costa Rica, CHWs within broader multidisciplinary teams calculate risk scores for individual households in their catchment areas; these scores are used to determine the frequency of future in-person visits (Pesec et al. 2017). South Africa's ward-based outreach teams (WBOTs) likewise consist of a nurse team manager and five to six CHWs, all linked to a fixed primary health center, who conduct health promotion, active case finding, and doorstep care within communities. Preliminary reviews of the program have shown significant increases in measles immunization coverage and reductions in severe diarrhea cases in regions served by outreach teams, although formal evaluations are still needed (Assegaai, Reagon, and Schneider 2018).[6] In an uncontrolled study in peri-urban Mali, daily door-to-door case detection by CHWs appeared to help double the early treatment of malaria, nearly halve the rate of febrile illnesses, and reduce under-five mortality (Johnson et al. 2018). Pilot studies also support the feasibility (although not necessarily cost-effectiveness) of proactive screening strategies for chronic and more complex diseases—for example, stroke detection in Karachi, Pakistan (Khan et al. 2015); cancer in New Delhi, India (Shridhar et al. 2015); and cardiovascular disease risk across four LMICs (Gaziano et al. 2015), often led by CHWs.

Increasingly, active outreach strategies can be supported by mobile health (mHealth) applications, helping identify chronic conditions even when qualified personnel are unavailable—and potentially helping increase the cost-effectiveness of active case finding strategies. In South Africa, for example, CHWs deployed a smartphone-based application (hearScreen™) to identify adults and children with hearing deficits, subsequently referring them for specialist attention (Hussein et al. 2016). In Madagascar, a cervical cancer screening program used smartphones to take snapshots of the cervix and email the images to remotely located specialists (Catarino et al. 2015). Such strategies have high upside potential in urbanizing centers, where mobile phones are common and network coverage is strong, but current evidence is largely limited to small-scale pilot and efficacy studies (Ettinger et al. 2016; Peiris et al. 2014).

Marginalized communities, or individuals facing potential diagnosis of a stigmatized disease, may be more likely to receive needed care when they can access health services directly within their communities, or even within their own homes. In Nigeria, for example, men who have sex with men (MSM) were nine times more likely to accept HIV testing and counseling if the service was directly offered by a member of the same community versus referral to a health center; the uptake was 21 times more likely among injection drug users (Adebajo et al. 2015). Even for the general population, systematic review evidence suggests that uptake of HIV testing and counseling services is far higher in community-based settings than within health facilities (Sulat et al. 2018). Increasingly, health services can also target the virtual communities where marginalized populations congregate. In urban China, for example, men who have sex with men volunteers identified members of the MSM community through their profiles on gay social networking sites and recruited them to testing and counseling services via chat rooms, instant messages, and emails (Zou et al. 2013). Internet-based outreach is still in its infancy within LMICS, and scale-up will require careful consideration of the privacy, rights, and safety of marginalized populations.

The COVID-19 pandemic has highlighted the importance of proactive community-based care and case management as a supplement to traditional, facility-based treatment, particularly in the context of limited inpatient capacity for COVID-19 patients and the importance of self-isolation to limit transmission potential. In the United States, the Cambridge Health Alliance (CHA) created multidisciplinary "community management teams" for the remote management of high-risk COVID-19 patients (in addition to primary care teams for patients at low or normal risk); the teams check in with the patients regularly by phone or teleconsultation "at points in the disease process associated with significant changes in clinical course, including four, seven, and 10 days after symptom onset. Patients at highest risk receive calls daily, sometimes multiple times a day. This triage process reserves the respiratory clinic for severely ill patients who have developed dyspnea, or shortness of breath, and enabled CHA to manage most patients without hospitalization" (Schweich 2020). In a small sample of patients, the model was estimated to avert almost one-half of hospitalizations (John, Zallman, and Blau 2020). In the Republic of Korea, where individuals who have been exposed to COVID-19 are asked to self-quarantine for two weeks, self-isolation is facilitated by deliveries of food and sanitation supplies, plus twice-daily check-ins from a dedicated case officer (Genries 2020). In Vietnam, whose successful COVID-19 response has been widely recognized, the local health station and village health workers played an essential role in raising community awareness about COVID-19 prevention; they also took on contact tracing and self-isolation monitoring on top of their routine responsibilities (Nguyen et al. 2020).

Empanelment and accountability

The empanelment process assigns a defined catchment population to a single, cohesive multidisciplinary care team. This process, in turn, creates a natural structure for accountability; the care team can be held accountable for the patient experience and health outcomes of the empaneled population. The focus on whole-population outcomes, versus patient experience among care seekers alone, reinforces an equity orientation; PHC teams are held accountable for their ability to engage, educate, and improve health outcomes, even among individuals or families who may feel reluctant or unempowered to seek care, including the poorest households and other marginalized populations. Care teams can be held accountable at all levels—by the populations they serve, by their peers and colleagues within the care team itself, and by payers and regulators at the regional or national level.

Within this general principle—that the care team should be accountable for the experience and outcomes of the empaneled populations—many different accountability mechanisms are available. These mechanisms can be modularly combined in various permutations to reinforce accountability at different levels and from different directions.

First, timely *data collection and benchmarking* can increase PHC professionals' and managers' awareness and understanding of their own performance, empowering them to make better decisions. Providing insights into peers' performance through benchmarking can further inspire emulation and positive reinforcement. In Costa Rica, for example, the Evaluación de la Prestación de Servicios de Salud (EPSS) offers a standardized benchmarking process across different health areas for dimensions of access, continuity, effectiveness, efficiency, and user satisfaction. PHC managers are assessed against targets and the performance of their peers, making them more accountable for their performance. To foster continuous quality improvements, performance targets are slightly increased each year, while health areas in the lowest quintile are required to develop remediation plans (PHCPI n.d.).

Second, *public reporting* on how different providers perform can help communities hold care teams accountable; they may also induce positive changes in health worker performance to protect their reputations or to attract additional patients (if empanelment is on a choice or opt-in basis). Rigorous studies of public reporting systems are mostly limited to high-income settings, but systematic review evidence suggests that they are associated with consistent and significant reductions in overall mortality (Campanella et al. 2016). With increasing mobile phone and internet access, web-based quality databases may be more applicable in middle-income countries; for a low-tech solution, performance data can also be posted on bulletin boards or in other public spaces. In China, such reporting has been shown to help reduce antibiotic prescriptions (Yang et al. 2014) and improve the rational use of medicines (Wang et al. 2014).

Community scorecards and citizen report cards are variants on public reporting that directly engage citizens to hold health organizations accountable for the services they provide. In Afghanistan, a community scorecard initiative based on stakeholders' discussions about performance scores and participatory action plans contributed to improvements in structural capacity indicators, such as water and power supply, availability of essential medicines and equipment, and number and cadres of service providers (Edward et al. 2015). In Uganda, report cards were shared with citizens and PHC staff through village meetings; PHC staff and citizen representatives worked together to identify strategies for improvement (PHCPI n.d.). The intervention led to a 13-percentage point reduction in absentee rates, 12-minute shorter waiting times, and a statistically significant reduction in the under-five mortality rates (Björkman and Svensson 2009). However, other evaluations on citizen report cards found partial or no results,[7] suggesting that the impact of this social accountability strategy depends on its implementation.

Finally, *financial accountability mechanisms* connect provider funding and remuneration to their performance. These mechanisms are considered in detail in *Priority Reform 3*.

From fragility to resilience

Preparedness, resilience, and the multidisciplinary platform

Integrated, multidisciplinary team-based PHC platforms also offer important benefits for preparedness, response, and resilience in emergencies—most recently, the COVID-19 pandemic. These benefits can be broadly segmented into three categories.

First, integrated and team-based PHC platforms can and should include explicit data collection, public health, and surveillance functions, integrated with national systems. Syndromic surveillance and close coordination with national public health authorities can help identify and contain nascent outbreaks before they spread more widely. Experiences from the severe acute respiratory syndrome (SARS) in east and southeast Asia, Zika in the Caribbean, and Ebola in West Africa, all showed that delayed detection and reporting of cases due to poor surveillance contributed to the escalation of these epidemics.[8] Many countries have relied on PHC for effective surveillance and contact tracing during the COVID-19 pandemic, especially coupled with CHWs; an integrated surveillance system appears to be the most important enabling factor. For example, Colombia, North Macedonia, and Vietnam have mobilized their information systems and integrated their COVID-19 surveillance systems with national information systems, with COVID-19 modules included and utilized for surveillance and in contact tracing in certain instances.

Second, established relationships and trust between the PHC team and community can enable effective communication and behavior change during an emergency. In Liberia, community education on preventive measures was among the most effective interventions to fight Ebola (Kirsch et al. 2017). During the Ebola and Zika epidemics, CHWs served as community-level communicators and educators, contributing to community health literacy in personal hygiene and other precautionary measures (Boyce and Katz 2019; CHIC 2020). Resilient PHC platforms can quickly adapt to increase the frequency of communication, ensuring clarity on emergency status and prevention and treatment recommendations. In partnership with central public health authorities, PHC teams' deep knowledge of their catchment communities can help tailor communication strategies and messaging to the population's specific concerns and preferences, building trust, for example, by highlighting facility and health worker adherence to safety standards and people-centered approaches to care. In Bangladesh, Colombia, Guinea-Bissau, Senegal, and Vietnam, PHC platforms, including CHWs, have helped inform communities about COVID-19 symptoms, transmission, and vulnerabilities; they have also helped to counteract social stigma. In Nigeria, 230,000 CHWs have been mobilized to deliver messaging and outreach. In Vietnam, community health stations and village health workers have played a crucial role in improving community awareness and enhancing trust. During an emergency recovery phase, resilient PHC facilities can progressively scale back communication efforts while ensuring continued clarity and transparency in communication about service procedures as the emergency subsides.

Third, team-based organizations may be better equipped than other organizational models to maintain essential services and prevent health system breakdowns during a crisis. Team-based approaches may more effectively sustain continuity of care; demonstrate greater agility in task shifting and alternative service delivery; and offer a first triage point to take stress off overburdened hospitals. Building on the strong foundation of a community-centric health system model to mount an effective response, Italy's Veneto region was able to prevent overcrowding in hospitals for COVID-19. Authorities required effective and proactive public health measures to be implemented in the earlier stages of the pandemic, including extensive testing of symptomatic and asymptomatic cases, proactive tracing of potential positives, a strong emphasis on home diagnosis and care, and priority for monitoring and protecting health care personnel and other essential workers. In North Macedonia, the family medicine system delivered most routine care, while hospitals focused on COVID-19, including care coordination (for example, electronic prescription refills). Team-based organizations, enabled by technology, may also be more agile in quickly transitioning to alternative service delivery models, such as telemedicine and home-based care.

Priority Reform 2: The fit-for-purpose multiprofessional health workforce

The first section of this chapter presented evidence on the benefits countries can expect if they implement multidisciplinary team-based care in PHC. We showed concrete steps that countries can follow to apply this model. Under this form of care organization, patients benefit from dedicated teams of health professionals that offer whole-of-person care in primary care facilities and extend that care into the community. Yet in many countries and communities, the PHC workforce remains insufficient—in headcount, deployment, competencies, orientation, and/or mandate—to make this vision a reality.

In poorer countries, absolute shortages of health workers are common; there are only 3 physicians and 11 nurses per 10,000 people in WHO's Africa region, compared to 34 doctors and 81 nurses per 10,000 in Europe (WHO 2019a). In wealthier countries, the health workforce is often rapidly expanding—yet primary care remains neglected, and the expansion has not been fast enough to effectively address the burden of chronic disease in aging populations. Further, day-to-day care for elderly people and people with disabilities has historically been provided by unpaid family members, often women (Hussein and Manthorpe 2005; Stone and Harahan 2010). Today, with greater female labor force participation, aging populations will require a larger cohort of home health care workers. Across all countries, inappropriate regulations and lack of training pathways limit task-shifting and scope of practice for non-physician health workers; where there are insufficient primary care doctors to meet patient need, such restrictions can create a significant impediment to access. Clinical staffing in rural communities poses a universal challenge; many health workers reject or leave underserved rural areas because of low pay, limited professional opportunities, poor working conditions, and quality-of-life concerns.

From dysfunctional gatekeeping to quality, comprehensive care for all

Universal coverage of comprehensive PHC is not possible without a fit-for-purpose workforce. Significant reforms to workforce training are needed to offer comprehensive PHC services in line with countries' universal health care (UHC) ambitions. Multiprofessional health education must be embedded within PHC settings; oriented to generalist practice; and focused on the unique knowledge, skills, and competencies required in a PHC setting. Further, universal provision of wide-ranging, high-quality PHC services requires the health workforce to be efficiently deployed (WHO 2018b). To achieve this, each cadre's specific scope of practice needs to be aligned with providers' comparative advantages within the multidisciplinary team unit. In mixed health systems, addressing workforce constraints to quality PHC may also require engaging and contracting private providers with public funds, while ensuring robust quality control.

A new paradigm for medical education

In addition to technical knowledge and skills, PHC team members need a range of nontechnical skills grounded in the patient-provider relationship and in the community context. A mutually trusting and respectful relationship is central to high-quality care, irrespective of the setting or discipline. Health workers require adaptive expertise, which involves innovation in addressing uncertain, complex, and novel situations, balanced with efficiency that draws on routine knowledge. Clinical decision-making requires skills different from those needed in most large hospitals. Geographic distance from tertiary care centers, inequities in the availability of human and institutional resources, and people's rising expectations for high-quality comprehensive care, even in economically constrained environments, create a new and challenging environment for PHC. These circumstances necessitate approaches to diagnosis and treatment that are grounded in clinical courage and are at once flexible and innovative, based on self-reliance, as well as efficient and effective use of resources.

The transition to community team-based care models therefore requires a reorientation of the medical education system, particularly for physicians. The culture, pedagogy, and incentive structure of most medical education often work against the development of a fit-for-purpose primary care workforce. In most countries, the bulk of medical education and training is conducted in hospitals and other specialized settings that do not reflect PHC realities and service conditions. Most undergraduate medical education programs begin with a classroom-based focus on basic science before progressing to clinical medicine at teaching/research hospitals. Following graduation, new doctors generally have little or no opportunity to work and train in rural and underserved clinical service settings because most first-year graduate positions are based in urban teaching hospitals.

Medical education reforms are required to embed education within community clinical settings and orient medical graduates to generalist/primary care specialization. Case-based learning allows students to explore case scenarios like those in which they will eventually practice, but students should also get direct exposure to community-based clinical settings early in their education. The longitudinal integrated clerkship, for example, is a well-established, year-long clinical education model whereby students learn their core clinical knowledge and skills in community settings with skilled PHC team members as their principal clinical teachers and role models, enhanced by integrated clinical learning. Through the program, students become members of the health team; the intense interaction with patients motivates student efforts and supports professional identity formation guided by social accountability.

Reorientation of medical education to community-based primary care is also predicated on professional respect, value, and prestige being afforded to local care providers, both as frontline providers of care and as local experts with knowledge and skills to justify academic appointments. Local PHC team members should be engaged as classroom teachers, including for small-group case-based learning, as well as for clinical training. Faculty status for community care providers demonstrates that the institution sees them as equal to campus and hospital-based faculty members, and it helps to counter the negative perception that community care providers are second class. This, in turn, raises their standing in the eyes of students, community members, and the providers themselves.

Training generalist physicians

Almost all wealthy countries have a "sufficient" number of health professionals—defined by the World Health Organization (WHO) as more than 10 medical doctors, 40 nurses/midwifery personnel, 5 dentists, and 5 pharmacists per 10,000 people (Roberts 1979). Nevertheless, physicians' reputational and financial incentives often favor specialization, which creates a scarcity of general practitioners. Generalists continue to decline as a share of all physicians, and in some countries, the number of geriatric trainees has stagnated (OECD 2020a). Medical students face strong financial incentives to avoid general practice or geriatrics in favor of more lucrative specialties. In the United States, doctor surveys show that primary care physicians earn more than $100,000 per year less than specialists (Kane 2018); in the United Kingdom, the salaries of physicians show more parity, but generalists still earn about 11 percent less than their specialist counterparts (Locke and Duquéroy 2018). Across the OECD, growth in specialist salaries almost always outpaces growth in generalist pay (OECD 2016b).

Many OECD countries have introduced initiatives to increase their rates of recruitment and training; however, generalists continue to decline as a proportion of physicians, with many fellowship slots remaining unfilled. The inadequacy of simply expanding generalist training demands alternative approaches to attract medical students to the field. Several incentive approaches can be used, including lower costs to obtain certification, subsidized medical education, or adjusted reimbursement rates from central payers to lower salary differentials.

In the United States, where medical school debts can be extremely high, loan forgiveness has been a popular approach, with mixed results. The US National Health Service Corps (NHSC) was first created in 1970 to address frontline shortages in rural and underserved areas; the program offers loan forgiveness to primary care clinicians with at least two to three years of service in underserved regions. NHSC has had some success in attracting physicians to underserved areas but fails to fill all available program slots, in part because of competition from other loan forgiveness programs without specialization or service requirements (Kamerow 2018). In 2005, South Carolina enacted legislation to create the first loan forgiveness program for trainees in geriatric medicine; in its first year, the program appeared to help attract more qualified applicants to the fellowship (Hirth, Eleazer, and Dever-Bumba 2008).

Payers—particularly national health insurance programs—can also use reimbursement rates as a lever to impact staffing levels and specialty choice. Although difficult to directly measure, choice of entry into primary care appears closely related to anticipated income (OECD 2016b). In the United States, historical rates of preference for family medicine closely mirror anticipated income vis-à-vis a specialist career path (Committee on the Governance and Financing of Graduate Medical Education and others 2014). This finding suggests that direct financial incentives can be a powerful means to encourage entry into frontline specialties. Economic research has found an association between higher Medicaid reimbursement rates and access to primary care (Alexander and Schnell 2017), while increases in Medicaid reimbursement rates have also been associated with better staffing levels at US nursing homes.

Efficient use of human resources

On its face, the team-based care model would appear to require an expansion of human resource capacity. However, team-based models join lay and CHWs, nurses, physicians, and potentially other health workers in a single unit. Doing this allows the efficient use of health workers for tasks appropriate for their skills and competencies—thereby avoiding over- or underqualification for the specific tasks undertaken and optimizing the use of higher-skilled cadres. This approach, where specific care tasks are delegated to nonphysician health workers under physician supervision, is known as "task shifting."

Evidence shows that CHWs and mid-level cadres can effectively deliver a range of health promotion and basic curative interventions: these include management of common childhood illnesses (Freeman et al. 2017; Gera et al. 2016; Global Health Workforce Alliance 1983); promotion of antenatal care and breastfeeding (Jennings et al. 2017; Lassi, Haider, and Bhutta 2010); and support for prevention and treatment of tuberculosis (Lewin et al. 2010), malaria, and HIV (Global Health Workforce Alliance 1983). Less clear is the ability of CHWs to manage more complex diseases or conduct skilled deliveries; their ability to safely perform these functions is likely to depend on CHW training and experience, which varies across settings (Dahn et al. 2015). For example, Ghana upskilled professional community nurses with midwifery skills to support skilled deliveries at rural health posts (Nyonator et al. 2005; Sakeah et al. 2014); elsewhere, some CHW cadres receive only weeks of training, which implies a clear lack of competence to assume such complex tasks (Dahn et al. 2015). CHWs should not be seen as a stopgap substitute for nurse- or physician-led care; instead, they should be embraced for their unique value-added as community links to health services and for their role in facilitating proactive health promotion and disease prevention within local communities.

Further evidence shows that nonphysician health care workers (NPHWs) can successfully screen individuals for asthma, cancer, diabetes, and hypertension; where NPHWs were also permitted to prescribe medicine, evidence further suggests they can do so effectively for patients with asthma, depression, epilepsy, and hypertension (Joshi et al. 2014). A study in Bangladesh, Guatemala, Mexico, and South Africa, for example, found that CHWs could effectively screen for cardiovascular disease (CVD) and refer people with a moderate to high risk to government clinics (Tsolekile, Abrahams-Gessel, and Puoane 2015). A separate systematic review also found evidence that adult diabetic patients who worked with a CHW knew more about their disease and had better self-care skills (Tsolekile, Abrahams-Gessel, and Puoane 2015).

Lay workers, including CHWs, have been used extensively to prescreen potential patients and support adherence to treatment regimes, with mixed results. VisionSpring, for example, trains people without a medical background to distribute oral contraceptives and conduct eye exams (Bhattacharyya et al. 2010). Alternatively, lay health workers can focus on nonmedical procedures, such as managing patient flow and recordkeeping, helping reduce the administrative burden on health workers. The Aravind Eye Care System in India, for example, trains high school graduates from rural areas to become patient flow managers (Bhattacharyya et al. 2010).

Telephone-based triage and advice services—wherein a patient can contact a health provider for basic diagnostic services, counseling, and medical advice—is also increasingly used as a substitute for face-to-face consultations, with call services now available in countries like Australia, Denmark, and the United Kingdom (Lake et al. 2017). Systematic reviews suggest that about one-half of the calls received by such hotlines can be addressed by telephone advice alone; however, there is still mixed evidence and many outstanding questions about their safety, cost-effectiveness, and overall impact on health service utilization and outcomes (Lake et al. 2017). The extreme ease of use for telephone consultations also presents an opportunity for overuse. Recent evidence shows that telephone consultations result in more frequent general practitioner-patient contacts than face-to-face consultations (Downes et al. 2017).

Leveraging and regulating the private sector workforce

High rates of private sector employment in the health field are a reality in many LMICs, especially when offering competitive salaries in the public sector would be prohibitively expensive (WHO 2013a). Recognizing this reality, some strategies—including private sector empanelment approaches described earlier—seek to address public sector workforce gaps by leveraging private sector health providers in the public interest. Some of the most effective policies use government-funded and administered insurance programs to contract private sector providers or encourage private providers to work with low-income patients through quotas or expanded coverage in health benefits plans. In the United Kingdom, for example, the government-funded National Health Service commissions privately run practices ("surgeries") to provide universal primary care; general practitioners are entirely funded by the public sector but often (co-)own and operate their own practices. Strategic purchasing approaches can enable public funds to purchase quality accredited PHC services across the public and private sectors, leveraging private sector capacity while avoiding common pitfalls, for example, quality gaps or impoverishing out-of-pocket expenditures.

A key challenge of private sector engagement is quality assurance. PHC purchasers can create incentives for incremental quality improvement and accreditation among private sector providers through "carrots," "sticks," or some combination of the two. "Carrots" could include access to prestigious or in-demand programs and responsibilities for graduates of accredited medical schools; financial bonuses for accredited providers; or the opportunity to participate in pay-for-performance or voucher schemes. In the Philippines, for example, special administrative and financial autonomy is restricted to accredited institutions (Cueto et al. 2006), while some Indian insurers offer higher reimbursement rates for accredited hospitals (Smits, Supachutikul, and Mate 2014). "Sticks" could include restrictions on the graduates from nonaccredited medical schools or on the eligibility of nonaccredited institutions to receive reimbursement through nationally funded universal health coverage or social health insurance programs. In Malaysia, for example, graduates of nonaccredited schools are not given licenses until they pass examinations at accredited schools (Cueto et al. 2006. In several LMICs—including Kenya, Nigeria, the Philippines, and Thailand—insurers require accreditation as a prerequisite for reimbursement (Smits, Supachutikul, and Mate 2014). In some countries where accreditation is not mandatory, the use of accreditation to select providers for empanelment-based national health plans can create exceptionally strong financial incentives for accreditation, essentially crowding out nonaccredited providers (Mate et al. 2014).

Tiered accreditation systems can also help incentivize incremental quality improvements in settings where achievement of the highest quality standards may seem too costly or unrealistic in the immediate future (Mate et al. 2014. In the United States, the National Committee for Quality Assurance offered new health maintenance organizations (HMOs) the option to pursue a separate accreditation on a pass/fail basis (Casey 2001); tiered accreditation in Lebanon offers accreditation for different time horizons and levels (3 years, 18 months, partially accredited, and failed), based on performance. However, few studies empirically evaluate the effects of switching accreditation systems (Ammar, Wakim, and Hajj 2007). In Brazil, a health insurance company paired incentives for achieving different tiers of accreditation with support to facilities in navigating the accreditation process. Hospitals received a 7 percent boost in per diem rates simply for beginning the accreditation process; incentives rose to 9 percent for achieving level 2 accreditation and 15 percent for achieving level 3 accreditation. By 2009, 19 out of 45 in-network hospitals had received accreditation, covering 69 percent of network hospital admissions (Borem et al. 2010).

Social franchising is an alternative approach to accreditation that allows in-network providers to adopt branding that identifies them as offering quality-assured services or commodities. An estimated 15,000–20,000 individual clinics in Africa, Asia, and Latin America now operate as part of social franchise networks (Montagu et al. 2016). The Janani franchise in Bihar, India, for example, repaints signs and wall advertisements for in-network providers on a yearly basis. Franchisees who are expelled or choose not to re-enroll do not get their signage repainted (Montagu 2002). Social franchising's emphasis on uniform care can also help introduce a common set of standards across multiple providers. The Greenstar Network in Pakistan provides monthly visits to in-network providers, during which they can discuss difficult cases, receive one-on-one training, and learn about new clinical practices (Montagu 2002). Similarly, the Planned Parenthood Federation of America independently evaluates and recertifies its local affiliates every four years (Montagu 2002). A systematic review of clinical social franchising in LMICs found that social franchising was associated with increased client satisfaction, but that its effects on health care utilization and outcomes relative to other models of care were mixed (Beyeler, York De La Cruz, and Montagu 2013).

Where human and financial resources to enforce quality standards are low, authorities can enlist professional medical groups as partners in the quality control process. In India, for example, professional councils have carried out awareness campaigns against the practice of medicine by unqualified practitioners, investigated complaints about unqualified practitioners, and reported such providers to government departments (Sheikh, Saligram, and Hort 2015). To ensure complaint mechanisms are used in the future and accountability is maintained, governments need to be prepared to follow up on any tips.

Alternatively, to maintain engagement in the public sector, several countries have allowed private sector providers to work in both the public and private sectors (dual practice). However, countries often impose restrictions on those who opt to do so. Costa Rica, for example, mandates that workers cannot engage in private practice during public working hours; Colombia stipulates that workers cannot have two-full time jobs for the same organization (Carpio and Bench 2015). Despite its widespread uptake, several concerns about dual practice remain. Many countries want to avoid a "revolving door," meaning that providers direct public sector patients to their own private enterprises, as well as burnout among health care workers. Additionally, long clinical and administrative hours have reportedly already started to lessen the appeal of dual practice in Latin America (Carpio and Bench 2015).

From fragmentation to people-centered integration

New provider competencies for people-centered, integrated care

Beyond clinical knowledge and skills, provision of community-oriented, people-centered integrated care requires a range of competencies for effective collaboration among the PHC team, the community, and other care providers. Access to care goes beyond physical or geographic and financial accessibility to include approachability, as well as acceptability for patients and communities to feel comfortable in seeking and obtaining health care (Levesque, Harris, and Russell 2013). Multidisciplinary teams will need to evaluate local health needs and acquire knowledge on communities' state of health and related influencing factors (Muldoon et al. 2010). They will also require strategic communications capacity to clearly communicate their vision of PHC and new ways of working, along with interpersonal skills and political savvy to build or strengthen their relationships with other stakeholders that are important for the health of their empaneled population (AAFP n.d.a; Fellows and Edwards 2016; Kumpunen et al. 2017). The team's population will likely have varying levels of health status, including healthy groups, patients who need specialist intervention, complex patients at risk of hospital admissions, and frail patients discharged from hospitals. Such a diverse spectrum of needs calls for professional management skills to stratify the patient population into risk groups and design targeted management interventions for each cohort (AAFP n.d.b; Hall 2011; Kumpunen et al. 2017).

At the intervention level, the PHC workforce must acquire new competencies to effectively work within a team-based model and ultimately help patients achieve their health goals. Ability to work and coordinate across boundaries is critical when providing care to an aging population with multimorbidities who must interact with multiple providers on a long-term basis. Case management is indispensable for improving quality and efficiency, considering that a small percentage of patients often accounts for the majority of total health spending (Conwell and Cohen 2005; Williams 2004; Wodchis, Austin, and Henry 2016). For conditions that involve self-management, the PHC workforce needs to engage and empower patients for joint planning and management around the patients' health goals (Global Health Workforce Alliance 1983; Raleigh et al. 2014).

The competencies discussed, in turn, highlight the importance of capacity to use and interpret data. The interactions between providers and patients generate an enormous amount of data that is then stored in various forms, including files in providers' cabinets, electronic health records, and registry systems. (Ideally, the PHC platform should benefit from a single interoperable digital platform with unique patient identifiers; see Priority Reform 1). Data about the empaneled population (demographic and socio-economic profiles, health service utilization, costs and outcomes, and other information) that are available to the PHC workforce, if properly applied, will be extremely useful for them as they evaluate community health needs, stratify risk groups, and provide integrated people-centered care. In Turkey, an enrollment database allows family physicians to identify individuals in a screening target group and enables community health centers to organize public campaigns and arrange transport for patients on the day of appointments. Close collaboration between family practices and the centers resulted in a significant increase in coverage rates for breast, cervical, and colorectal cancers between 2007 and 2014 (Jakab et al. 2018).

Finally, "soft skills" are needed to develop a trusting relationship between providers and patients, improving patient satisfaction and supporting positive health outcomes (Farmer 2015; Fellows and Edwards 2016; Heckman and Kautz 2012; Sills 2015). Such skills can be wide ranging, including responsiveness, empathy, adaptability, flexibility, time management, communication and teamwork, cultural sensitivity, collaboration, and brokering partnerships (AAPC Knowledge Center 2019; Feffer 2016). More importantly, in reimagined PHC settings, health workers need to develop the skills to act as partners and facilitators, rather than authorities, to empower patients and engage them in a shared decision-making process (Imison and Bohmer 2013).

Reorienting medical education and on-the-job training to better prepare the health workforce

Appropriate education is essential for ensuring that the PHC workforce has and can demonstrate the competencies necessary for delivering integrated people-centered care in the community and across the health system (Global Health Workforce Alliance 1983; WHO 2013b). Experts have called for a "third generation" of medical education reform to improve the performance of health systems by adapting core professional competencies to specific local contexts, while drawing on global knowledge. The proposed program emphasizes transformative learning that involves three fundamental shifts: from fact memorization to searching, analysis, and synthesis of information for decision-making; from seeking professional credentials to achieving core competencies for effective teamwork in health systems; and from noncritical adoption of educational models to creative adaptation of global resources to address local priorities (Frenck et al. 2010).

In alignment with this transformative vision for medical education, several shifts must take place in the orientation and culture of medical education and on-the-job training. Training for PHC should not be considered a "specialization," as this can reinforce health system silos. Interprofessional education (Interprofessional Educational Collaborative 2016) (box 4.3)—a pedagogical approach that engages two or more health care professions in an integrated learning environment (Gilbert, Yan, and Hoffman 2010)— has proved useful to ensure that professionals value one another's disciplines, increase providers' collaborative knowledge and skills, and improve their ability to manage people

---

BOX 4.3
CORE COMPETENCIES FOR INTERPROFESSIONAL COLLABORATIVE PRACTICE

The core competencies developed through interprofessional education feature the following desired principles: patient and family centered; community and population oriented; relationship focused; process oriented; linked to learning activities, educational strategies, and behavioral assessments that are developmentally appropriate for the learner; able to be integrated across the learning continuum; sensitive to the systems context and applicable across practice settings; applicable across professions; stated in language common and meaningful across the professions; and outcome driven.

+ **Competency 1**: Work with individuals of other professions to maintain a climate of mutual respect and shared values. (Values/Ethics for Interprofessional Practice)

+ **Competency 2**: Use the knowledge of one's own role and those of other professions to appropriately assess and address the health care needs of patients and to promote and advance the health of populations. (Roles/Responsibilities)

+ **Competency 3**: Communicate with patients, families, communities, and professionals in health and other fields in a responsive and responsible manner that supports a team approach to the promotion and maintenance of health and the prevention and treatment of disease. (Interprofessional Communication)

+ **Competency 4**: Apply relationship-building values and the principles of team dynamics to perform effectively in different team roles to plan, deliver, and evaluate patient/population-centered care and population health programs and policies that are safe, timely, efficient, effective, and equitable. (Teams and Teamwork)

Source: Interprofessional Education Collaborative 2016.

with chronic conditions (Cubic et al. 2012; Darlow et al. 2015; Hammick et al. 2007; Reeves et al. 2016). Creating shared values and common goals between primary care providers and other care providers helps trainees internalize integrated care precepts. The asymmetry of information between providers and patients has a long-standing presence in the health sector (Arrow 2001), but these patterns are changing rapidly, as technology enables patients to acquire knowledge more easily (Hardey 1999; Pandey et al 2013; Powell, Darvell, and Gray 2003). In this context, health workers at the PHC level may need to assume the role of advisers, guiding patients to reliable sources of information, rather than experts who consider themselves the sole authoritative sources of health information. Future PHC workers should be encouraged to take a participatory approach to promoting health and well-being in the communities they serve. Further, medical education and training need to prepare the PHC workforce to understand and apply evidence-based medicine principles to a rapidly expanding research and evidence base, for example, by learning how to follow new algorithms and protocols.

Health professionals will need education, training, and awareness of content not traditionally covered in the medical curriculum, such as community health needs assessment, risk stratification, coordination and case management, and personalized medicine, as well as their impact on practice. In Belgium, for example, one university's medical, nursing, and social work students undertake a "community diagnosis" exercise as part of the curriculum. The exercise involves analyzing relevant epidemiological, sociodemographic, and other population-based data on local communities, together with findings from visits to households and care providers, to arrive at a "community diagnosis" and draft an advocacy letter to local authorities recommending actions for improvement. Some countries (for example, Hungary and Kazakhstan) have also adjusted medical curricula for nurses to receive specific training in chronic diseases focused on patient education, prevention of complications, and chronic disease management (Jakab et al. 2018). In addition, coaching for frontline health care workers can also be provided to improve their soft skills, for example, via in-person and online training, role playing, case studies, guest speakers, and personality assessment tests (Conkey et al. 2013; Jünger and Köllner 2003; KICSS 2018).

Educational and accreditation standards should be adjusted and integrated into overall quality assurance mechanisms to support these pedagogical shifts, ensure adequate training in these competencies, and ensure consistency in quality standards from education through to practice (Bitton et al. 2019). Accreditation should also cover the competencies of educators and trainers and the adequacy of infrastructure, equipment, and clinical learning sites (Jakab et al. 2018).

PHC workforce policies for integrated, people-centered care

Collaborative practice and integrated care across the care continuum require a shared vision on the role of PHC. Mutually accepted interdisciplinary care protocols need to be established between PHC teams and providers or organizations from other settings and levels of care. Based on such protocols, consensus can be achieved on the content of care at each level of provision and on criteria for two-way referrals. Coordination, a key function that connects multiple providers under an integrated people-centered care model, should be included as part of the PHC work routine.

While providing integrated care in the community and across the health system, primary care teams need well-aligned quality measurement that promotes accountable performance by rewarding team members for managing complexity, solving problems, and thinking creatively when addressing the unique circumstances of patients with complex needs. Priorities for outcome and performance management include people-centered reporting and metrics that capture avoidance of inappropriate testing or treatment, while documenting attributes associated with better outcomes, lower costs, and improved patient experiences (Bitton et al. 2019; Bodenheimer et al. 2014).

PHC workforce performance can be improved through the increased use of tools for communication and management. People-centered care can be enhanced through communication tools such as integrated and individualized care plans, structured patient education, decision aids, outreach activities, lifestyle counseling, multidisciplinary assessments, and multidisciplinary treatment protocols. Similarly, care integration and population health management can be facilitated by patient registries, health registries, and risk stratification tools, building on health data generated via the empanelment process (Jakab et al. 2018).

Workforce planning and deployment should align with the reimagined PHC vision and performance management framework. Existing workforce skills and competencies should be carefully reviewed to identify any gaps and mismatches, as well as mitigation strategies. As previously discussed, repurposing the current workforce through task shifting is a commonly used strategy to engage existing health workers for new roles (Hoeft et al. 2018; Some et al. 2016; WHO 2008). When there is little scope to expand the roles of the existing workforce, creating new care professions/cadres is another option, although it often takes longer to show an impact. These new cadres can be created to fill new roles, as in the case of care coordinators, self-management counselors, and case managers (De Carvalho et al. 2017; Jakab et al. 2018). Alternatively, new cadres can take over some current activities from existing personnel, as with physician assistants and medical officers (Halter et al. 2013). In some cases, professional managers can be introduced to manage integrated multidisciplinary teams and coordinate services across the spectrum of prevention, promotion, care, and rehabilitation. Of course, creative workforce policies must still be compatible with the regulatory framework, for example, in terms of professional classification and licensing standards.

From inequities to fairness and accountability

Proactive polices for workforce development, deployment, and regulation can help address the maldistribution of health workers across countries and within national borders, creating conditions for more equitable service delivery to those most in need.

Engaging health professionals in rural service

Encouraging rural service requires changing the balance of incentives that pushes health workers toward urban centers in virtually all countries. One common approach is to offer financial or in-kind benefits to counterbalance health workers' quality-of-life concerns. Rural health workers receive housing benefits and electricity in Moldova, allowances in South Africa, and paid tuition fees for their children along with housing renovations in Zambia. Few studies have assessed interventions in LMICs empirically and individually (that is, not as part of a package of services). A Cochrane review found that the provision of bursaries or scholarships had variable success across countries, while increased financial compensation generated more consistently positive results, although with undetermined cost-effectiveness (Grobler et al. 2015). A review of systematic reviews similarly found that such policies were effective in attracting practitioners, but that few physicians stayed in rural areas long term (Chopra et al. 2008).

Rural service requirements may also help fill vacant postings, and several countries have made service in resource-constrained areas a prerequisite to graduation or certification. Japan and Lesotho exchange pregraduation financial aid for postgraduation rural service (Frehywot et al. 2010); other countries, such as Mongolia and Vietnam, have made rural service a prerequisite to certain career changes (for example, entering a postgraduate or specialization program) (Frehywot et al. 2010). Most of the existing research on compulsory service programs is descriptive and uses stakeholder interviews to document program effects. Anecdotal evidence suggests that participants in compulsory service programs often leave soon after the mandatory period ends. Such programs can also be difficult to enforce, particularly for wealthier individuals who can use their financial resources to bypass service requirements. Thailand imposes financial penalties on public medical school graduates who violate their rural service requirements—but many graduates choose to work in the private sector, quickly earning enough to offset the penalty (Wiwanitkit 2011).

Studies from high-income countries (HICs) and LMICs identify rural residence or upbringing as a consistent predictor of an applicant's eventual willingness to accept a postgraduation rural posting (Simoens 2004). Where sensible, medical schools can adjust admissions criteria to prioritize rural applicants, increasing the number of graduates who would be willing to accept rural positions. In addition, opening medical schools or other training facilities in rural areas could reduce the workforce gap via two channels. First, rural medical schools can offer continuing medical education and professional opportunities in rural areas, making rural service more attractive. Second, rural medical schools can attract more students from rural areas, who would be more inclined to remain in rural postings. In Japan, for example, almost 70 percent of graduates from a rurally located medical school remained in their home prefectures for at least six years after the end of their mandatory service periods (Dolea, Stormont, and Braichet 2010). In the Democratic Republic of the Congo, graduates from a rural medical school were almost four times as likely to practice in rural areas, compared to a cohort from an urban medical school (Longombe 2009); in China, a single rural medical school produced more rural doctors than 12 metropolitan schools combined (Wang 2002).

A specific medical education model to encourage rural community service is Community Engaged Medical Education (CEME), in which medical schools form an "interdependent and reciprocally beneficial partnership" with the communities they serve (Strasser et al. 2015), thereby creating opportunities for clinical learning in PHC services and other community clinical settings. CEME programs often recruit primarily local students through selection and admissions processes that value not only academic ability but also other characteristics important to local comprehensive PHC. Students support local PHC team members, who, in turn, serve as clinical teachers and role models. Trainees come to understand their rural/underserved setting as home base, preparing them to practice in the surrounding areas—with city rotations as a requirement to complete postgraduate training. Trainees undertake additional specific skills training relevant to their future practice, such as general surgery, anesthesia, procedural obstetrics, endoscopies, indigenous health, and geriatrics.

Examples of CEME programs illustrate the potential benefits. In the Philippines, a group of doctors in a highly rural and underserved region founded the Ateneo de Zamboanga University (ADZU) medical school in 1994. The school operates on an almost exclusively volunteer basis; most of its students are drawn from the local community, and the curriculum focuses on case-based learning, problem solving, and community health, in addition to clinical competency. As of 2011, 80 percent of its graduates were still practicing in the Zamboanga region, and 50 percent were practicing in rural areas (Cristobal and Worley 2012). Similarly, the Northern Ontario School of Medicine (NOSM) targets health improvement in northern Ontario, a vast and underserved region of Canada. NOSM's admissions process selects a student body that reflects the population distribution of northern Ontario; community members help with student selection, education, and support during community placements; 92 percent of NOSM-trained family physicians are practicing in northern Ontario; and many graduates now serve on faculty (Tesson et al. 2009; Strasser 2016a; Strasser et al. 2018).

Equitable mobility and cross-jurisdictional solutions

International recruitment has been a popular strategy for wealthier countries facing acute PHC workforce shortages, including expanding cohorts like home health care workers. However, outmigration of health workers from LMICs to high-income countries with far higher compensation can exacerbate existing international inequities in health workforce density and contribute to deepening human resource gaps in the origin country, particularly when the training slots for medical education are highly constrained.

Smarter processes can increase the benefits of health worker migration for all parties. A Global Skills Partnership (GSP) (Clemens 2015) consists of a bilateral agreement in which migrant-destination countries and migrant-origin countries share the benefits and costs of skilled migration. Responding to a nursing shortage in Germany combined with a surplus of recent graduates in China, one pilot program aimed to train and place 150 Chinese nurses within German nursing homes up to five years. Before their migration, the nurses received an eight-month intensive training course and language training to ease their entry into the German health system and society (Oelmaier 2012).

Accreditation and licensing differences between states or jurisdictions can make it challenging for health workers to move to areas of greater need or opportunity, even within the same country. In Canada, individual provinces set their own standards for licensure of foreign medical graduates, with widely varying processes (Nasmith 2000). A backlog of applications and bureaucratic processes can also make the licensure process very lengthy, and qualifying exams and supplemental education can be expensive and time consuming. In the United States, state-level licensing procedures can often take three to six months, with application fees typically totaling several hundred US dollars (Medicus Healthcare Solutions 2017).

Regulatory reforms can help increase health worker mobility. In the United States, the Interstate Medical Licensure Compact offers a voluntary state-based approach to reduce licensing barriers by introducing a common licensure application across 29 participating states (although the individual states still issue the licenses)[9] the Nurse Licensure Compact (NLC) likewise allows US nurses to obtain a single license for physical, telephone, and electronic practice across any of the participating states.[10] Regional efforts also include mutual recognition agreements for three types of health workers under the Association of Southeast Asian Nations Framework Agreement on Services (Forcier, Simoens, and Giuffrida 2004; Kanchanachitra et al. 2011).

Telehealth involves the use of telecommunications and virtual technology to deliver health care outside of traditional health care facilities (WHO 2018c). It includes virtual home health care, where patients can receive medical advice and guidance in their own homes, as well as virtual guidance for health workers in providing diagnosis, care, and referral of patients. Telehealth can connect health care providers with remote rural populations and mobility-constrained patients, and it offers more efficient routine care in non-emergency situations, for example, among patients with chronic conditions. Systematic reviews find that proactive telephone support or case management over the phone can improve clinical outcomes and reduce symptoms in people with heart disease, diabetes, or asthma (Barlow, Singh, and Bayer 2007), while regular phone calls from nurses can reduce hospital admissions and costs (Lake et al. 2017). A Cochrane review similarly concluded that 50 percent of calls taken by doctors or nurses could be handled over the phone without a subsequent hospital visit (Lake et al. 2017).

Regulatory reforms can also help enable telehealth's potential to at least partially break down geographical barriers to care and potentially address workforce shortages in specific regions, particularly underserved or remote rural areas. (However, internet access remains highly correlated with health worker density, limiting the applicability of telehealth in some of the most underserved regions and/or countries [Suzuki et al. 2020].) In some cases, onerous regulatory barriers can stymie efforts to provide telecare when the provider and patient are based in different jurisdictions. For example, for different US states or Canadian provinces, providers often must receive licensure in the jurisdiction in which their patient is based, limiting the potential for cross-jurisdiction practice. A few states have either established registries of qualified out-of-state telehealth providers or offer telemedicine-only medical licenses (Thomas and Capistrant 2017). The European Union takes a more flexible approach by defining the relevant jurisdiction as the one in which the provider is based, allowing a single provider to practice telemedicine with patients across the bloc (Hashiguchi 2020). Likewise, financing reforms can enable reimbursement of a broader range of telehealth services through public or private insurance packages, facilitating more equitable uptake.

COVID-19 has accelerated the relaxation of many regulatory and financing barriers to telehealth and restrictions regarding practice jurisdiction, at least temporarily. In the United States, the Department of Health and Human Services temporarily waived certain privacy requirements related to the choice of telehealth platform for the duration of the COVID-19 crisis (Department of Health and Human Services 2020). Several US states and the Center for Medicaid and Medicare Services (CMS) waived state-specific licensing requirements (Goodman and Ferrante 2020), and both the United States and France have expanded the range of reimbursable telehealth services (OECD 2020b; Ohannessian, Duong, and Odone 2020). In South Africa, an extraordinary policy decision authorized the broad use of telemedicine during the COVID-19 pandemic subject to consent and privacy guidance (AHPCSA 2020).

Beyond physical mobility, international or private sector collaborations can help expand countries' access to specific cadres of health care workers in high demand. Several public-private partnerships and regional coordination mechanisms already exist in East Africa. The East Africa Public Health Laboratory Networking Project (EAPHLNP) aims to establish a network of high-quality public-health laboratories in Burundi, Kenya, Rwanda, Tanzania, and Uganda; an evaluation of the network in Kenya documented improvements in client satisfaction, test accuracy, and scores on peer audits (Lehmann et al. 2018). Other initiatives include the Medical Education Training Partnership Initiative (MEPI), the Nursing Training Partnership Initiative (NEPI), and the Rwanda Human Resources for Health Program (HRH Program). Telemedicine approaches may also offer access to remote expertise for residents of rural villages. For example, in India's Aravind system, community members send photographs of patients' eyes and information about their symptoms to an Aravind doctor, who then assesses a patient's need for hospital care via a real-time chat (Bhattacharyya et al. 2010).

From fragility to resilience

Emergencies require health workers to take on tasks and competencies outside of their day-to-day routines; crises can also place enormous stress on health workers' physical welfare and mental health. Appropriate training, planning, psychosocial assistance, and practical support can ease the burden of crises on the health workforce and help sustain continuity of care.

Preparedness: Training and contingency planning

An adequate health workforce and appropriate training in outbreak prevention, detection, and response has been identified as a key characteristic of a health system prepared for emerging infectious diseases (Palagyi et al. 2019).

Even with the best planning, emergencies are by their nature unpredictable. Medical education—and training for nonphysician health workers—accordingly must emphasize agility and problem solving, helping prepare the health workforce to work confidently and capably in unusual conditions. This is consistent with the expectation that all health workers in PHC have a broad range of knowledge and skills as generalists within their disciplines, including technical capabilities and a range of nontechnical and leadership skills (Strasser et al. 2018).

Consequently, health workforce education and training should encompass mastering technical skills related to managing emergencies in the community, as well as nontechnical skills, including adaptive expertise and clinical courage. Adaptive expertise involves innovation in addressing uncertain, complex, and novel situations, balanced with efficiency that draws on routine knowledge (Croskerry 2018). Clinical courage balances probability and payoff to creatively manage problems in the moment at hand with whatever resources are available (McWhinney 1997). Leadership skills involve inspiring trust and respect, motivating action among team and community members, and allocating practical, achievable tasks (West et al. 1999). Learning in context through case-based learning (CBL) in the classroom and in community clinical settings is the most effective educational method for developing these generalist knowledge and skills (Strasser 2016b; Strasser et al. 2013). CBL encompasses learning the social and environmental determinants of health, including One Health (Rabinowitz et al. 2017) and integrating the individual and population health domains (Boelen and Berney 2000).

Immersive community-engaged education provides students and trainees with hands-on experience in interprofessional collaborative practice (Strasser et al. 2018). Integrated clinical learning (ICL) involves team teaching and team learning, whereby local health team members collaborate in teaching a mix of students of various health care disciplines (Pavelich and Berry 2009). ICL enriches the experience for all involved and embeds teamwork in the professional identity of future health workers. To consolidate their learning, it is important that students and trainees are involved in teams that undertake local contingency planning and practice exercises preparing for the management of crises, including infectious disease outbreaks.[11]

Agility, flexibility, and resilience in health emergencies

Some of the most effective workforce responses to the COVID-19 pandemic have required rapid task shifting, repurposing, or extraordinary deployment of existing health workers. The government of South Africa, for example, mobilized around 60,000 CHWs—half of whom were originally trained to trace/test for HIV—to support the COVID-19 response. In Bangladesh, Guinea-Bissau, Nigeria, and Senegal, CHWs and the PHC platform have been effectively deployed to conduct sample collection and case identification/isolation. In Guinea-Bissau, which has a strong community health workforce, CHWs work closely with dedicated contact tracing cadres, contributing their deep knowledge of community context. In Nigeria, over 30,000 PHC providers have been used to identify suspected COVID-19 cases, trace contacts, and conduct referrals.

Some countries (including the United Kingdom and the Netherlands) postponed re-registration and revalidation obligations for physicians. This measure reduced the administrative burden on practitioners and avoided potentially sidelining key professionals at the height of the crisis. Provisions have been made to recruit medical and nursing students to support health professionals, for example, by allowing final year students to graduate early and join the workforce or by offering them a gap semester to support practicing health professionals. Campaigns were launched in several countries (including Canada, Italy, and the United Kingdom) to bring retired or inactive health professionals and foreign-trained but unregistered professionals back into the workforce. Twinning individual facilities in hotspot areas with medical teams from other provinces also facilitated China's response to COVID-19. In the United Kingdom, the government brokered an agreement to take over private hospitals and their staffs for the duration of the crisis, resulting in tens of thousands of clinical staff provisionally moving to the public sector (Williams, Maier, and Scarpetti 2020).

The COVID-19 crisis has also led some countries to empower NPHWs with new responsibilities and authority. Pharmacists have received extraordinary authorization in several countries to assist in the COVID-19 response and relieve pressure on overburdened hospitals and physicians. Pharmacists have been allowed to issue and/or renew prescriptions (in Canada, France, and Poland); compound antiseptic solutions or hand sanitizers (in Belgium, the Czech Republic, Finland, Germany, and the Netherlands); and deliver prescriptions to patients' homes, sometimes including controlled substances, hospital-only drugs, and even oxygen (Canada, Croatia, Italy, and Portugal) (Merks et al. 2021).

To avoid saturating hospital capacities during the crisis, the broader health workforce, including community-based practitioners, can contribute to emergency-related service provision. Previous outbreaks suggest that task shifting, supported by adequate training, is necessary to cope with emergency challenges (Lee and Chuh 2010; Opstelten et al. 2009). One of the lessons learned from the SARS outbreak in Hong Kong SAR, China, concerns the need for a wider involvement of general practitioners, who could contribute to the response as educators, triage decision-makers, and vaccine administrators (Lee and Wong 2003). Patient management and triage strategies need to be adapted; health workers need to be trained in the specifics of the response and appropriate patient care; and heightened safety precautions need to be implemented. Maintaining routine or essential health services (for example, chronic disease management and antenatal care), while delivering emergency-related services requires the availability of inputs, such as health workers, medicines, and safety supplies. Management systems must be adjusted to ensure input availability and smooth patient flow. Crucially, public authorities need to provide clear guidelines and adequate financing. Shortages of personal protective equipment (PPE), insufficient allocation of PPE to PHC systems, and in particular, CHWs, have reduced PHC platforms' ability to sustain services during the COVID-19 pandemic (Nepomnyashchiy et al. 2020a; Nepomnyashchiy et al. 2020b).

Supplementary training during the crisis may also increase health workers' capacity, confidence, and morale in handling the outbreak. During the Ebola outbreak in Sierra Leone, health workers showed lower levels of fear and became more confident in providing care after safety training; tentative evidence suggests the trainings also prevented further infections among health workers (Bemah et al. 2019). In a Canadian hospital setting, group resilience training substantially increased health workers' self-reported confidence in dealing with the H1N1 virus (Aiello et al. 2011); less costly and more easily scaled computer-assisted training courses also demonstrated encouraging results in improving confidence and self-efficacy to manage the pandemic (Maunder et al. 2010). In contrast, some essential services were temporarily disrupted in Bangladesh because providers were unsure how to comply with social distancing requirements in their daily jobs (Islam et al. 2020).

Social and practical support for a resilient health workforce

Finally, health workers need significant social support—both during and in the aftermath of a crisis—to help mitigate resultant stress, exhaustion, and trauma. Burnout is common in health care professionals even during normal times, particularly among family doctors (Soler et al. 2008). The mental health toll of COVID-19 on frontline health providers has been extensively discussed and well-documented in media reports (Ellis 2020; Evelyn 2020; Hoffman 2020) and the academic literature (Islam et al. 2020). In Wuhan, China, for example, one-half of frontline nurses reported moderate or high levels of burnout; 91 percent reported moderate or high levels of fear; and almost all had at least one skin lesion caused by long hours in personal protective gear (Hu et al. 2020). Similarly high levels of stress and fear have been reported in previous viral outbreaks (Ricci-Cabello et al. 2020).

Comprehensive and agile psychosocial support to health workers is thus essential to prevent burnout and manage stress (Dutta 2020; Ihekweazu and Agogo 2020; Rangachari and Woods 2020; Santarone, McKenny, and Elkbuli 2020). Helplines, for example, can be established so frontline health and social workers can access psychological support from trained professionals and/or referrals to additional mental health services. Depending on the nature of the emergency and the country context, helplines can be set at national or local levels by professional associations or universities. In the digital era, more health workers can seek guidance and support through apps and online services. In addition to formal counseling sessions (in-person or remote) with psychiatrists or psychologists, many stress-reducing measures have been tried out during the COVID-19 pandemic. These include buddy systems, whereby health professionals can talk to matched peers (China, Norway), mindfulness sessions (Malta), and Zumba sessions (Kenya).

Practical support to frontline health workers during crises helps workers focus on patients and improve productivity. An important step is making childcare available where facilities would otherwise have been closed. A large number of countries have implemented measures in this area, including Austria, Belgium, Denmark, France, Germany, Malta, the Netherlands, Norway, Portugal, and the United Kingdom. Romania has paid health workers allowances for childcare, reducing health professionals' domestic work burdens. Free accommodation for health workers during a pandemic minimizes their commute times and risk of spreading disease if they become infected. Other practical forms of support can include free access to public transport (Hungary and some parts of the United Kingdom) and free parking at health facilities.

Finally, special compensation for health workers during emergencies can serve as an extrinsic motivation mechanism, recognizing their sacrifice and contribution. Following the outbreaks of several emerging infectious diseases (for example, Ebola, Middle East respiratory syndrome [MERS], and SARS), many countries have passed regulations to mandate hazard payment/compensation for overtime public health crises. This has supported health professionals' work in fighting COVID-19 in China and Vietnam, for instance. Several Eastern and Southern European countries also have also offered financial support to health workers in response to COVID-19, for example, one-time bonus payments (Bosnia and Herzegovina, Germany, Greece, Hungary, the Kyrgyz Republic, Romania, the Russian Federation), monthly bonus payments for the duration of the crisis (Albania, Bulgaria, Latvia), or temporary salary increases (Belarus and Lithuania). Meanwhile, in Denmark, COVID-19 has been recognized as a work-related injury for health care staff, enabling them to access associated benefits. In Africa, many governments have realized the need to improve hazard payments and provide insurance for staff on the front lines of the pandemic.

Priority Reform 3: Fit-for-purpose financing for public-health-enabled primary care

Financing has a critical role to play in facilitating the transition to high-performing PHC laid out in chapter 3 and elaborated in Priority Reforms 1 and 2 of this chapter. PHC investments yield high returns and promote sustainability, but achieving PHC goals requires substantial investment and careful planning across five key areas in health financing.

First, guaranteeing universal coverage of high quality, comprehensive PHC will require governments to raise adequate funding through prepaid, pooled financing, while making explicit efforts to remove financial barriers to care for the entire population. This investment must be guided by clear plans and explicitly defined PHC benefits packages that prioritize prevention and timely treatment at the appropriate level of care, thereby avoiding unnecessary hospitalizations or complications. Second, the shift to effective team-based care models requires innovations in the way providers are paid, accompanied by investments in data and information systems that facilitate closer coordination. Third, financing can address persistent inequities and facilitate accountability through inclusive decision-making processes, explicit removal of financial barriers on both the supply and demand sides, better measurement, and transparent planning and budgeting. Fourth, as demonstrated by COVID-19, countries require agile financing arrangements to adapt to shocks, build resilient systems, and protect spending on essential PHC services during emergencies. Finally, beyond direct health benefits, PHC also offers a best-buy to progress toward many nonhealth SDGs by targeting the social determinants of health across areas including education, housing, transport, and the environment (Anaf et al. 2014; Public Health Agency of Canada 2007; Public Health Agency of Canada and WHO 2008). However, leveraging these synergies will require new models of cross-sectoral prioritization and financing.

From dysfunctional gatekeeping to quality, comprehensive care for all

PHC investment should draw from general government revenues

Significant investments, not just adjustments at the margins, are needed to put PHC at the center of health systems. Substantial resources are required to finance a set of guaranteed services that gives adequate weight to health promotion and disease prevention and encompasses core public-health and health security functions, including disease surveillance, outbreak response, infection prevention and containment, and monitoring and evaluation. Modeling suggests that an estimated additional US$200 billion per year would be required from 2020 to 2030 for 67 LMICs to cover basic preventive and outpatient PHC services. Mobilizing these sums would require LMICs (in aggregate) to at least double their total health expenditure. The more ambitious vision described in this report, including a broad PHC package and cross-sectoral investments, would raise the overall price tag in these countries to some US$380 billion annually (Stenberg et al. 2019). These are averages and estimates: each country must identify its own locally relevant PHC policies, define a locally appropriate benefits package, and assess the costs and budgetary implications of its delivery. For the large majority of countries, a strong case can be made that these investments would pay large dividends—by improving population health (OECD 2020a), advancing economic inclusion, and improving countries' competitiveness.

The source of PHC resources has important implications for whether investment needs will be met. Universal coverage of high quality, comprehensive PHC first requires mobilizing adequate revenues for health overall through prepaid, pooled financing that eliminates out-of-pocket expenditures. Allocations from within the pot of pooled health resources must then adequately prioritize PHC. General government revenue is increasingly seen as the best mechanism for financing PHC, given the changing nature of work, the persistent informality in LMICs, and the public-good character of population-based public health services. Evidence also shows that financing through general government revenues facilitates access to health services and improves financial protection for the population (Jowett and Kutzin 2015; World Bank 2016). Additionally, many LMICs are still building health system foundations for quality PHC, including basic infrastructure (for example, running water and sanitation), human resources, and reliable supply chains for health products (Cotlear et al. 2015). Such fixed-cost investments cannot be readily financed through recurrent health insurance premiums or user fees. Box 4.4 lays out the case for PHC financing through general government revenue in detail.

BOX 4.4

WHY FINANCE PHC THROUGH GENERAL GOVERNMENT REVENUE?

General government revenue is increasingly seen as the best mechanism for financing universal health care (UCH)—and primary health care (PHC), specifically—for several reasons:

+ ***Changing nature of work****:* Demographic shifts and structural changes in employment are challenging the sustainability of employment-based resource mobilization models for the health sector, including labor taxes, employer-provided health insurance, and social health insurance (SHI). Particularly important shifts include population aging (and relatively fewer working-age adults relative to retirees), shrinking labor needs in some industries due to technological

(Continued)

BOX 4.4 *(continued)*

transformation (such as automation), and the recent rise of the gig economy (World Bank 2019a; World Bank 2019b). Roughly two-thirds of the countries with SHI now use government budget transfers, often on top of traditional employment-based resource mobilization, to at least partially finance their health systems (WHO 2019b). For example, Estonia and France, which once relied predominantly on labor taxes to finance their health systems, now use general government revenues to supplement SHI premiums (Habicht et al. 2018).

+ **Labor informality**: In low- and middle-income countries (LMICs), preexisting high levels of labor informality further complicate efforts to expand health coverage through employment-linked solutions. Some countries have extended SHI to the informal economy by offering the option to join SHI schemes voluntarily, for example, in Thailand through the earlier Voluntary Health Insurance Scheme (Tangcharoensathien et al. 2019), or through community-based health insurance. However, countries have been unable to achieve high levels of coverage without substantial government subsidies and compulsory enrollment, for example, in Rwanda (Ridde et al. 2018). High labor taxes to finance the health sector may even exacerbate the informality by creating an additional incentive to pay employees "off-book." Hungary, for example, used government financing to reduce employer payroll taxes and thereby reduce the incentive for informality (World Bank 2019b).

+ **Reducing financial barriers**: Suggestive evidence shows that removing user fees for primary health care in low-income countries (LICs) and LMICs results in higher utilization of services and better financial protection (Lagarde and Palmer 2008; Lagarde and Palmer 2011); some studies also suggest a link to better health outcomes (Qin et al. 2018). However, policies to remove user fees are only effective when backed by adequate levels of pooled financing from the government budget (WHO 2016).

+ **Financial crises**: During financial crises, high unemployment can result in health coverage losses and reduce the system's ability to mobilize and pool resources (Yazbeck et al. 2020). In Greece, the 2008 financial crisis resulted in extensive insurance coverage losses due to unemployment; the government subsequently passed legislation to guarantee all Greek citizens the right to primary health care (World Bank 2019a). Cumulative income shocks at the individual level can also limit the ability of families to pay out-of-pocket during a financial crisis, creating significant revenue losses for PHC facilities in systems reliant on out-of-pocket payments.

+ **Population-based common goods**: Public goods, including the public health and outbreak preparedness functions of PHC, are best financed through general government revenues (supplemented by development financing) to prevent fragmentation and adhere to international standards (Sparkes, Kutzin, and Earle 2019; Yazbeck and Soucat 2019).

Explicit PHC benefits packages for equitable and efficient resource allocation

Achieving an ambitious vision for PHC will require new investments, as well as the efficient and equitable allocation of all available health resources. All countries, at all levels of wealth, face resource constraints and trade-offs in the health sector. The best results come from prioritizing investment in the highest-impact health services within countries' budget constraints and ensuring that those services are delivered equitably to the whole population.

An explicitly defined and prioritized health benefits package for primary care—customized to local health care needs, burden of disease, citizen values and preferences, and aligned with local resource constraints—is essential for justifying allocation of limited resources for PHC and increasing accountability for its delivery (Glassman, Giedion, and Smith 2017). The *explicit* character of the benefits creates recognized entitlements for patients, empowers the poor to demand equitable access to services, helps to identify whether funds are being spent wisely on services that create the maximum benefit for society, and facilitates resource allocation decisions and orderly adherence to budget limits. Nationally agreed, prioritized PHC packages, combined with supply-side investments to ensure the package can be implemented, have been identified as a key enabling factor in child mortality reductions across 30 LMICs (Rohde et al. 2008).

Importantly, an *explicit* PHC benefits package is not necessarily a highly granular or prescriptive benefits package; it can also offer providers space for clinical judgment and "soft" engagement with patients and community members to build relationships and trust. (Too extensive granularity, particularly at the PHC level, risks inhibiting innovation and limiting clinicians' ability to tailor care to specific patient populations [Smith and Chalkidou 2017].) However, granularity is required in developing the list of drugs, devices, vaccines, and other health products and supplies that will be procured with public funds for use in PHC settings; patients can expect access at no cost at the PHC level.

Defining a benefits package requires a priority-setting process that is evidence based, fair, participatory, and inclusive, accounting for various perspectives (Kapiriri and Martin 2006) and competing values (for example, equity, cost-effectiveness, financial protection, scientific community opinion, and affordability). The process should promote transparency in decision-making; accountability of decision-makers to the public; and ownership among those participating (Glassman, Giedion, and Smith 2017). To the extent feasible, the process should evaluate potential services for inclusion in the benefits package according to consistent and transparent criteria that are aligned with a health system's objectives, which, in turn, make it possible to explain the reasons for adoption or rejection of specific products and services. Transparent criteria also facilitate governance and accountability, allowing proper debate about how priorities are to be set and how performance should be assessed. The process should include a diverse and representative group of stakeholders, including government, public and private sector health care providers, citizens, community representatives, patients, and others as necessary (Daniels 2000; Terwindt, Rajan, and Soucat 2016). Such an inclusive process can enhance procedural justice and lead to more sustainable and socially acceptable results.

Adaptation to local context, both during package definition and implementation, can increase the benefits-package impact, transparency, and acceptability. The Local Burden of Disease instrument from the Institute for Health Metrics and Evaluation (IHME), for example, aims to produce estimates of health outcomes and related measures at a granular, local resolution; these estimates will allow decision-makers to tailor policy decisions about benefits packages and resource allocation to local areas for maximum impact.[12] Likewise, the HIV mantra "Know your epidemic; know your response" promoted the use of geographical information systems (GIS) to map the "hot spots" and target the drivers of HIV infection in concentrated epidemics (Boyda et al. 2019; Wilson and Halperin 2008). Adapting to local context is also important for ensuring acceptance, ownership, and understanding of decision-making (Báscolo and Yavich 2009). In Kenya, Health Facility Management Committees representing communities were created to enhance community participation in managing funds received and prioritizing funding, based on needs, to implement the Essential Package of Health. In the United Kingdom, the participatory process led by the National Institute for Health and Clinical Excellence (NICE) has sensitized the public about the rationale for not including particular technologies (Glassman, Giedion, and Smith 2017).

Defining a benefits package should not be considered a one-off, static process; the benefits package should be a living document, continuously adjusted as resource availability changes; new data, evidence, and experience sharpen policy makers' understanding of local health needs and the value of specific services; the cost/price of specific health products or services change; and new health technologies or services become available. In countries with weak infrastructure and severe resource constraints, the essential packages should start with highly effective interventions that are cost-effective, in line with local health provider capacity, and that can be provided with available resources. Packages can be gradually expanded as resources increase, capacities improve, innovations emerge, prices fall, and/

or disease burdens shift (Glassman, Giedion, and Smith 2017). For instance, in the face of rapidly growing prevalence of hypertension and diabetes, China expanded the benefits package of its basic medical insurance scheme to cover prescription drugs related to these two conditions.[13]

Benefits package designers must also pay close attention to how the package affects those who are disadvantaged or vulnerable. For example, it is important to examine how the package may perpetuate or exacerbate existing health inequities across the population; whether certain key benefits for the most disadvantaged are excluded; and, in particular, whether the package incorporates adequate services for conditions typically affecting rural, poor, or otherwise marginalized groups. Doing this requires understanding patterns of local disease burden and service utilization derived from reliable data, as well as continuously monitoring the benefits distribution across the population over time.

Recognizing health system capacity and capabilities can help to effectively define benefits packages and link them explicitly to strategic purchasing and service delivery. In higher-income countries and many middle-income countries such as Thailand, actuarial analysis, costing and cost-effectiveness analysis, and a formal health technology assessment (HTA) process have proven useful for guiding evidence-based decision-making around benefits packages. The use of these techniques can lead to a more transparent, efficient system (Glassman, Giedion, and Smith 2017). HTA is most useful when making decisions about small expenditure changes that come on top of well-established existing service packages. For example, Thailand's Health Intervention and Technology Assessment Program (HITAP) initially opted against introduction of the HPV vaccine after its analysis showed it to be less cost-effective than screening (Teerawattananon and Tritasavit 2015); following a significant price reduction (Andrus and Walker 2015), the vaccine was later deemed cost-effective and subsequently introduced (*Nation-Thailand* 2017).

However, full HTA requires substantial expertise and capacities that are often absent in LMICs, where changes are often made at the margin and need to consider implementation factors (World Bank 2017a). In these settings, a reasonable option may be establishing a fully costed package that considers the burden of disease and cost-effectiveness, along with demand for services, while also setting priorities within the constraints of resource availability, human resources, and infrastructure capacity. This approach may be a practical alternative to HTA in the medium term, as countries build the capacity needed to take on more sophisticated approaches to priority setting. For example, Nigeria recently launched a reform to channel federal-level funding through a statutory transfer to finance a Basic Minimum Package of Health Services (BMPHS). The Federal Ministry of Health, with support from development partners, used detailed costing studies to agree on the composition of the benefits package. This costing informed the economic and financial costs of guaranteeing access for all Nigerians to the BMPHS in the long term; and it helped policy makers to build scenarios to consider options for the gradual expansion of the package, given the fiscal constraints in the medium term. The original package included 57 essential interventions covering 60 percent of the disease burden, which would be implemented in rural areas first and then gradually expanded in geography and scope. To set packages and roll-out plans, countries can adapt international estimates, for example, those provided by *Disease Control Priorities* (Horton 2017), introducing refinements as they strengthen their capacity to conduct more sophisticated analyses.

Financing upfront investments and routine operations

In addition to the direct, recurrent costs of service delivery, adequate financing of multidisciplinary PHC needs to account for upfront investment in system-wide overhead and routine operational costs. At the outset, the PHC system must be endowed with safe and sanitary facilities, equipment, digital platforms, and the drugs and consumables necessary to deliver the PHC package. Upfront investments are also needed for reform and expansion of health workforce training, as described in Priority Reform 2. Studies suggest that major investments need to go into system strengthening, with health workforce and infrastructure development jointly accounting for 53–66 percent of additional costs for strengthening PHC measures in LMICs (Stenberg et al. 2019). Gaps between the current state of PHC infrastructure and the required levels are likely to be larger in remote and marginalized areas. Brazil, Ethiopia, South Africa, Thailand, Turkey, and Ukraine have all recently increased funding for primary and community health services. These increases were accompanied by supply-side improvements to service quality and accessibility through improvements in infrastructure, staff training, management, provider-payment mechanisms to encourage quality, and governance (Patel et al. 2015; Wang et al. 2016).

Beyond upfront infrastructure investments, routine funding is required to cover facility overhead (for example, electricity, water, routine maintenance/cleaning, and similar inputs); staff salaries, including administrative support; and resupplies of pharmaceuticals and consumables. Input-based budgets must explicitly allocate line items for these anticipated recurrent costs; alternatively, strategic financing arrangements can bundle routine overhead costs into reimbursement or contracting. Shifts to PHC investment are often facilitated by strong public financial management (PFM) practices that reliably direct adequate funds to PHC facilities for routine operational costs, with sufficient resources for supervision to ensure appropriate use of funds.

How primary care is positioned in the government budget, and whether facilities can receive funds directly and exercise autonomy in shifting resources to new needs, play an important role in securing sufficient routine operational resources at the PHC level, particularly in LMICs (Piatti-Fünfkirchen and Schneider 2018). In many developing countries, administrative authorities (such as districts) act as agents for receiving and managing resources allocated to PHC together with resources for other purposes. Such arrangements have led to inadequate financing for PHC providers, in particular, inadequate resources for operational costs and hence missed opportunities to address community needs (Chansa et al. 2018). In some countries, a shift to a program-based budget classification system has helped to allocate resources to programs that are organized around policy goals, rather than along administrative and input lines, providing an opportunity to link spending to policy priorities (Jakab, Evetovits, and McDaid 2018). For example, the Primary Health Care Service Delivery Budget Program in the Kyrgyz Republic made the allocation for PHC at the facility level explicit, facilitating advocacy to increase this allocation (Gottret, Schieber, and Waters 2008). However, gains from such approaches are not automatic and often require institutional capacity strengthening to realize. When program-based budget classification is not feasible, facilities should be explicitly recognized in the budget such that budget provision can be made to primary care providers, enabling them to receive and spend funds.

The donor community has a crucial role

Rethinking development assistance can drive the investments and capacity building needed to deliver on the promise of a multisectoral, integrated, people-centered PHC system, while also addressing problems with lack of alignment and fragmentation. In LMICs, where the gap between health needs and current levels of service coverage is high, donor funding accounts for 20 percent of health spending in LICs and 3 percent in LMICs (WHO 2019b). Most donor funding is channeled to priority programs, such as immunization, HIV, tuberculosis (TB), malaria, and maternal and child health (MCH)—the very services that are core to PHC, although in the case of donor-supported programs, these are frequently delivered through vertical structures. A new era of development assistance will require shifting from investing in specific priority programs to investing in systems, including the capital investments and recurrent operational costs needed for a stronger PHC. Many donors, including Gavi, The Vaccine Alliance, and the Global Fund to Fight AIDS, TB, and Malaria, are signaling increased attention to investment in PHC systems and public financial management. Although fundraising through such global initiatives will likely remain disease specific, funding arrangements at the country level should not duplicate processes across specific programs. A further shift to financing *systems* rather than *programs* can lead to cross-programmatic efficiency gains and savings within primary health care (Sparkes, Durán, and Kutzin 2017).

Donors can also contribute to more resilient health systems by investing in surveillance and public health functions. The Global Action Plan Financing Accelerator highlights several critical features of a next generation of development assistance for health (DAH) (Yazbeck et al. 2020), including enhanced support for fiscal, public financial management, and efficiency reforms, as well as advocacy platforms. The COVID-19 epidemic has already forced donors to become more flexible, for example, by allowing reallocations of their investments to address the COVID-19 response, granting flexibilities in donor policies, and looking for opportunities to build on existing programmatic infrastructure to address COVID-19 and protect essential services. For example, in LMICs, Gavi has invested heavily in cold chain infrastructure; the cold chain can be used for diagnostic testing and delivery of COVID-19 vaccines.

The alignment of donor financing and concessional lending behind government reforms can strengthen the infrastructure and institutions needed for stronger PHC systems. For example, in the Lao People's Democratic Republic, the government's Health Sector Reform Strategy (HSRS) focuses on building a people-centered health system that provides equitable access to a prioritized set of essential health services, backed by increases in domestic financing and delivered through an improved service delivery model that includes strengthening the integrated outreach model for the most remote populations. The World Bank's Health and Nutrition Services Access Project (HANSA) is designed to strengthen subnational financing, governance, and service delivery at the PHC level. It serves as a platform for the alignment of development partners in support of sustainable financing for UHC, whereby the Global Fund and Australia's Department of Foreign Affairs and Trade provide joint financing of US$36 million through mainstreamed government systems (World Bank 2017b).

From fragmentation to people-centered integration

Paying providers for care coordination and integration

Traditional fee-for-service (FFS), line-item budgets, or capitation on its own are increasingly seen as poorly aligned with team-based, integrated care models (table 4.3) (OECD 2016a). Many countries have adopted financing

Table 4.3 Misalignments between traditional payment mechanisms and team-based care models

	IDEAL APPROACH FOR TEAM-BASED CARE MODELS	FEE-FOR-SERVICE	INPUT-BASED FINANCING	CAPITATION
Payment Recipient	A team of providers or an integrated unit	Individual provider or unit	Individual unit	Individual provider or unit
Payment Criteria	Based on health outcomes, value of health care	Predefined fee schedule for specific items (inputs, procedures, and so on)	Prices of inputs	Fixed amount per enrolled patient (sometimes risk adjusted), not always linked to explicit performance standards
Relevant Time Horizon	An extended period of time (often multiple years)	A visit or an encounter	Periodic lump sum (monthly or annual)	Periodic (often annual)
Beneficiary Population	A defined population group assigned to providers (that is, empanelment)	Anyone visiting the concerned providers	Anyone visiting the concerned providers	A defined population group assigned to providers (that is, empanelment)
Incentives for...	Health promotion and preventive care	Weak; encourages increased activity	Weak; incentivizes low transaction costs; incentivizes reduced quality when demand is high	Can encourage prevention/promotion depending on the payment agreement but can also lead to avoidance of high-risk patients
	Retaining patients at the PHC level where appropriate	Strong but can create supplier-induced demand and unnecessary care	Weak; encourages unnecessary referrals to higher levels	Can incentivize improved quality of care and healthier behaviors but can also lead to under-provision of services
	Close coordination across providers	Weak; discourages referrals to higher levels	Weak; does not reward good performance or coordination	Can incentivize unnecessary referral to higher levels

Source: Original table for this publication.

Note: PHC = primary health care.

innovations to foster team-based care; promote coordination and integration; and improve quality, outcomes, and efficiency (OECD 2016a). These emerging models, sometimes referred to as "value-based" payments, shift clinical and financial accountability to providers by adjusting and conditioning reimbursement based on certain cost, quality, and patient experience metrics. Providers are incentivized through these models to innovate and provide high-quality care while minimizing costs (McClellan et al. 2019). Providers are also financially incentivized to work with a defined population group so that they can reap the benefits of preventive services and investment in high-quality services.

Different payment mechanisms are often blended together to drive transformations to a set of policy objectives, as each method may have its own pros and cons (Langenbrunner, Cashin, and O'Dougherty 2009). The negative effects of a given payment type may be neutralized when blended with other payment methods. For example, FFS payments can encourage the increased use of preventive services (for example, vaccinations, mammograms, and screening); they can also encourage the safe delivery of some services at the primary care level that otherwise might be referred to specialists (for example, for wound care or drainage of abscesses) (Robinson 2001). Fee-for-service for preventive care, in combination with capitation payments for everything else, can effectively increase the provision of preventive care while maintaining an incentive for efficiency and cost savings (Langenbrunner and Somanathan 2011; Langenbrunner and Wiley 2002). As of 2016, 25 of 34 OECD countries use some form of blending, while the other 9 use a single payment mechanism for primary health care (either fee-for-service, capitation, or global) (OECD 2016a). Many LMICs also use blended payments to align incentives against competing policy objectives, including Kazakhstan and Myanmar. For example, a capitation payment combined with a small proportion of fee-for-service payment for priority preventive services (such as prenatal care and immunization in Estonia) can be adopted to incentivize health promotion (Results for Development Institute 2017).

Team-based care and coordination with other care providers can be explicitly incentivized through direct payment linked to such activities. Pay-for-coordination, for example, offers a lump sum to a given provider, per chronic patient, to coordinate care across a team of professionals working at different levels—for example, primary care, secondary care, public health, prevention, and health education (OECD 2016a). The first country to use this payment method was France, where primary care centers (not health care workers specifically) received payment for the coordination of noncommunicable disease prevention and care, with the flexibility to allocate the additional payment as they see fit. The payment represents, on average, 5 percent of providers' income and is paid by the social health insurance agency (CNAMTS) (Afrite et al. 2013; Tandon and Dozol 2019). Austria, France, Germany, Hungary, and other countries have since adopted this model (Jakab, Evetovits, and McDaid 2018). The Comprehensive Primary Care Plus (CPC+) model in the United States also has an element of care management fee, which is non-visit-based and paid per beneficiary per month.[14]

Alternatively, several payment models can indirectly incentivize or facilitate care coordination and integration—both horizontally and vertically:

+ ***Bundled payments*** provide a single payment for an entire episode of care across multiple types of providers in different settings. This model extends the logic of diagnosis-related group (DRG) payments, which offer a single payment for an acute episode to a single provider, to reimbursing costs related to an entire clinical pathway of care for select conditions—including primary health care, specialists, hospitalization, rehabilitation, and any other care needed during a defined "episode," that is, over a specified time period for a given disease/condition. The provider delivery group assumes the financial risk for the cost of services and costs associated with preventable complications. By design, bundled payments encourage coordination and integration of care across diverse providers and institutions, remove the incentives for cost shifting to other providers, and encourage implementation of evidence-based clinical pathways (Blumenthal and Squires 2016). For example, the Netherlands and Portugal both use bundled payments for the care of chronic conditions such as HIV/AIDS and diabetes, with quality requirements across service delivery settings (OECD 2016a).

+ ***Population-based payments*** are paid per person and cover a wide range of services by various providers, who are, in turn, encouraged to control costs and meet quality standards (for example, in Germany, Spain, and the United States). Such population-based payments create a strong financial incentive to integrate a functional network of providers in conjunction with effective health promotion. In Germany, for example, two statutory health insurance funds have contracted a private joint venture, "Gesundes Kinzigtal GmbH" (GK), to run a population-based integrated care model for their insured population; the program is financed by cost savings realized from better prevention and improved efficiency (Hildebrandt et al. 2010). Members of the program are also offered vouchers to be used for participating in health promotion programs. An evaluation shows that the program has improved overall patient experience, quality of care, and population health, while reducing health care costs and emergency hospital admissions (Hildebrandt et al. 2015).

+ ***Pay-for-performance (P4P)*** provides financial incentives for achieving specific objectives, which can either directly or indirectly promote care coordination and integration, depending on the performance indicators selected. Like pay-for-coordination, it can be used to promote specific functions, such as the management of a chronic disease like diabetes. It can also be based on patient experience measures, clinical quality measures, and utilization measures that drive down cost—all of which are facilitated by better coordination and integration. Pay-for-performance is used extensively in OECD countries; in middle-income countries like Brazil, China, and India; and in lower-income countries like Rwanda (Cashin et al. 2014). A review of experiences from 10 OECD countries found that P4P has helped clarify the provider goals, improve the processes for purchasing health services, and improve the measurement of provider activity and performance; it has also created a more informed dialogue between purchasers and providers—although it has not significantly improved overall health outcomes (Cashin et al. 2014).

+ ***A shared savings*** approach, often applied in combination with the methods described, can promote both care integration and strengthen empanelment. Under a shared savings approach, providers bear financial risks subject to their performance in meeting predefined quality standards for the patient population. Providers can be initially paid through FFS or capitation, but payments are eventually adjusted based on performance against quality and patient experience metrics. The approach promotes the collective accountability of various providers, encourages investment in high-quality and efficient services including PHC, and fosters a long-term relationship between providers and patients. For example, United States Accountable Care Organizations (ACOs) consist of voluntary networks of providers, including primary health care, hospitals, and sometimes specialists and others, who assume financial responsibility and clinical accountability for a defined patient population (Barnes et al. 2014). ACOs typically serve at least 5,000 beneficiaries assigned for at least three years. They are primarily paid based on traditional FFS; however, they receive a supplemental reward or penalty, based on how their total costs per patient compare with historical references. If costs fall below budgeted targets, ACOs are permitted to keep the partial savings, conditional on having met quality targets. These more refined approaches require a threshold capacity of human resource skills (including purchaser and provider administrators), institutional capacity (for correct pricing and negotiating), and governance arrangements.

Such payment approaches can act as powerful levers for transforming PHC in more developed economies, but low-income countries will require a more gradual process, given the high administrative workload and extensive capacity required to effectively execute payment functions. Payment mechanism discussions are highly political and require consultation with a range of stakeholders to prevent unintended effects. Investment in infrastructure (for example, interoperable data platforms collecting information on care for empaneled populations) and the health workforce (recruitment and training) will be critical for implementation. Public financial management rules must also be aligned with strategic purchasing goals. For example, providers need sufficient managerial and financial autonomy and capacity to respond to financial incentives (Piatti-Fünfkirchen and Schneider 2018; WHO 2018d). In many LMICs, districts or related government administrative levels are often allocated a budget for various purposes, including supervision, public health services, and primary care; the funds are not disbursed directly to facilities. PFM rules often need to be adjusted to allow providers to change the mix of inputs so that efficiency gains can be realized (WHO 2018d).

Other recent innovations are also changing the way PHC providers can receive funds. Mobile money payments, or e-payments, reduce the dependence on physical financial interactions and the need for cash; they can provide a secure way for providers to both receive and use funds quickly and efficiently, without compromising accountability. This is important, given that primary care facilities often lack access to bank accounts even when they are registered as spending units, allowing them to receive a budget allocation. Mobile money transactions allow a balance to be sent from central-level or district administrations to mobile wallets at remote primary care facilities to be used as part of the operational budget. Through such innovations, primary care provider payment reforms can be operationalized and have the potential for efficiency gains, accountability, transparency, and financial inclusion. Zambia is currently in the process of pursuing such a reform (Piatti-Funfkirchen, Hashim, and Farooq 2019).

Integrated payment models are facilitated by integrated data platforms. These platforms are at various stages of maturity, but all countries can embark on a strengthening initiative and adapt payment models as more information becomes available and policy makers improve their capacity to generate, analyze, and use data for decision-making (Mathauer et al. 2019). For example, the verification of claims data and health outcomes can inform a dialogue between purchasers and providers regarding the current performance, opportunities, barriers to improvement, and mechanisms to overcome these barriers, which might include financial incentives.

From inequities to fairness and accountability

When well designed and sufficiently resourced, PHC financing mechanisms play an essential role in promoting and reinforcing values of fairness, equity, and accountability within the overall healthcare system. Value-based payment mechanisms, for example, reinforce provider accountability for population-wide health outcomes, including for poor and vulnerable people. Sufficient pooled resource mobilization plays a redistributive role, leveraging social resources for equitable service coverage. Likewise, fair, inclusive, and transparent design of explicit health benefits packages creates an equitable entitlement across the entire population; providers and the government, in turn, can be held accountable for ensuring this package is, in fact, delivered.

In this section, we consider four elements of PHC financing for fairness and accountability that this report has not previously discussed:

+ Financing to break down demand-side access barriers

+ Pro-equity and accountability in intergovernmental transfers

+ Transparency and accountability in planning and budgeting

+ Community engagement in resource allocation.

Financing to break down demand-side access barriers

For truly equitable access and utilization, all PHC services must be free at the point of service. There is broad consensus that financial barriers to PHC services in LMICs (such as user fees) should be removed (WHO 2016). Nevertheless, financing reforms that are not backed by mobilization of additional resources and careful planning to compensate for simultaneous revenue loss and costs associated with increased utilization can cause their own problems, for example, a shift to informal payments, patients' forgoing services altogether, or ad hoc or implicit rationing (McPake et al. 2011). This further highlights the importance of defining an explicit benefits package, as well as a fair and inclusive priority-setting process appropriate for the local context.

Even when PHC is free at the point of service, some populations may still face financial or nonfinancial barriers to access services. These barriers could include migrants or refugees who fall between the cracks of empanelment strategies; marginalized populations who are socially stigmatized or fear judgment or abuse from health care providers; rural populations geographically distant even from outlying PHC facilities; or groups where the opportunity cost of accessing services (for example, missed work and wages) may discourage utilization. Understanding the drivers of the nonutilization of PHC services is critical for developing targeted interventions to improve equity and fill gaps in financial protection (Amurao 2016).

Financing mechanisms are not a panacea, but some approaches can ease these broader inequities and demand-side access barriers. Conditional cash transfers, often targeting poorer groups, can improve financial access to care even when the conditions are not explicitly tied to health. Transfer payments are often used for out-of-pocket payments (where they exist), travel costs, or childcare (Lagarde, Haines, and Palmer 2014). Voucher programs, especially common for antenatal care or delivery, can also help vulnerable groups to receive free care. Evidence shows they are associated with positive impact on the use of maternal and child health services (De Brauw and Peterman 2020; Hunter et al. 2017; Lagarde, Haines, and Palmer 2009) and nutritional status (De Groot et al. 2017). However, it is hard to attribute positive effects to these incentives alone, since other components may also contribute (Glassman et al. 2013; Lagarde, Haines, and Palmer 2009).

Accountability through intergovernmental transfers

In highly decentralized contexts, conditions on intergovernmental transfers can help create accountability for sufficient financing and/or quality delivery of PHC at subnational levels. In Kenya, for example, the share of the national government budget allocated to health was greatly reduced after the devolution of health care responsibility to the county level. To restore priority for health in country budgets, the central government established a UHC conditional grant; local authorities (counties) must direct at least 30 percent of the budget to health to receive the grant (Cotlear, Alawode, and Muchiri 2020). In Nigeria, a recent reform through the BHCPF finances PHC from the federal government through a statutory transfer, moving away from unconditional block grants that had left PHC underprioritized and facilities with little operational funding. The statutory transfer protects funding for PHC by transferring funds to facilities for a basic package of essential PHC services. The statutory transfer also overcomes the common problem of funds budgeted but not disbursed; subsidization of enrollment aims to reduce the financial barriers for the most vulnerable in a country where 70 percent of total health spending comes from out-of-pocket payments (Cotlear, Alawode, and Muchiri 2020; Hafez 2018). The disbursement of funds is subject to receiving financial reports showing the source and use of funds in alignment with the agreed purpose, improvements in monitoring, and quality assurance criteria.

Similarly, specific financing mechanisms can ensure equitable nationwide resources for PHC, given regional variations in wealth or other relevant population characteristics. Italy, for example, earmarks 38.5 percent of the value added tax (VAT) for a national equalization fund to help regions with lower revenue-raising ability provide the core benefits package (Cashin, Sparkes, and Bloom 2017). The Philippines uses an earmark on the Sin Tax levied on alcohol and tobacco to fully subsidize the enrollment of the poorest 40 percent of the population in the National Health Insurance Scheme (Kaiser, Bredenkamp, and Iglesias 2016), which includes a benefits package for primary health care.

Transparent, participatory, and accountable planning and budgeting

Improving the allocation of resources will require strong measurement and an understanding of existing performance challenges. Improved budget transparency and better expenditure data can provide a picture of country performance and identify necessary financing reforms. Data on the current level and distribution of health spending are most useful when combined with data on health outcomes, service coverage data, and financial protection, disaggregated across gender and equity markers, where possible (WHO 2019b). Recent global efforts have sought to measure PHC expenditure in a comparative and standardized manner, but implementation and capacity for a standardized methodology is still advancing. One limitation is that the current approach covers only a narrow definition of recurrent expenditure for PHC (WHO 2019b). Accordingly, continuous investment in data systems, by governments and donors, will be essential to guide PHC reforms.

A robust strategic planning process for PHC (articulating a vision and charting a plan for achieving that vision through measurable goals), coupled with strong government leadership, can help shift resource usage to PHC. For example, Turkey's Health Transformation Program, launched in 2003, aimed to develop a universal PHC-based delivery system funded through a unified social insurance system. In addition to strong economic growth, a key contributor to success was the iterative planning, implementation, monitoring and evaluation, and refinement of the reform, which drove more spending to health generally and PHC specifically (Johanson 2015). This process allowed the country to adapt to common pitfalls; policies are not always implemented as planned and strategic plans are often wish lists. Over the course of a decade, the program led to improved health outcomes, increased health service utilization (for example, increased per capita outpatient physician visits from 3.1 in 2002 to 8.2 in 2013), and a reduction by 47 percent in out-of-pocket financing between 1999 and 2012 (World Bank 2018a). Box 4.5 provides additional examples of how a key donor facility is supporting countries' strategic planning processes in health.

BOX 4.5

GLOBAL FINANCING FACILITY AND THE WORLD BANK: A PARTNERSHIP TO SUPPORT PRIMARY HEALTH CARE

The Global Financing Facility for Women, Children and Adolescents (GFF)—a country-led partnership between country governments, development partners, the private sector, and civil society organizations—supports 36 low-income and lower-middle-income countries. Hosted at the World Bank, the partnership focuses on catalyzing high-impact investments for reproductive, maternal, newborn, child, and adolescent health and nutrition improve RMNCAH-N in the world's most vulnerable countries, while also strengthening the wider health systems needed to deliver at scale and sustain impact. The GFF has pioneered a shift from traditional development approaches to a more sustainable way forward where governments lead and bring their global partners together to support prioritized, costed national plans with evidence-driven investments to improve RMNCAH-N through targeted strengthening of service delivery systems, particularly primary health care—to save lives. By facilitating multistakeholder country platforms, the GFF supports its partner governments to mobilize and align both domestic and external funding behind national priorities.

As of June 2020, the GFF has directly invested about US$602 million in grants linked to approximately US$4.7 billion of World Bank International Development Association (IDA/IBRD) financing and helped align much larger volumes of domestic public and private resources, as well as external financing in support of GFF partner country investment cases. In line with GFF's new strategy, it also provides critical technical assistance and support in key areas such as country leadership and alignment of partners, gender equality, health system redesign, health financing, and results.

The GFF's collaborative, country-led approach has already yielded significant results in improving access to PHC-related services by drawing attention to the front lines and community-level delivery, as well as by funding health system reforms. For example, in Côte d'Ivoire, the country's investment case that focused on strengthening primary health care has resulted in the prime minister's decision to increase the health budget by at least 15 percent annually. In Cambodia and Tanzania, the GFF country-driven processes led to the integration of nutrition into the full continuum of essential health services for maternal and child health.

Other investment cases in Burkina Faso, Cameroon, Ethiopia, Guinea-Bissau, Liberia, Mozambique, and Niger have focused funding on a prioritized set of high-impact services delivered at the primary care level and have designed reforms to increase the share of funds that flow to, and are managed by, frontline service providers.

Source: Global Financing Facility for Women, Children and Adolescents, https://www.globalfinancingfacility.org.

Engaging communities in resource allocation decisions

Empowering PHC teams and communities helps to improve participation in decision-making with respect to how resources are allocated to respond to population health needs (WHO 2018d). Transferring decision-making to local governments can enable better alignment between resource allocation and community needs (WHO 2018d). For example, some countries have moved to "participatory budgeting," which allows communities to have direct decision-making powers over the allocation of public resources in their area (Campbell et al. 2018). The model, which requires formal evaluations to understand its impact, is gaining popularity as a means of empowering communities to adequately fund local priorities. In Brazil, for example, the wide adoption of this approach across municipalities has led to increased expenditure on basic sanitation and primary health care services, which were previously underfinanced. An evaluation study also found a significant reduction in infant mortality rates among municipalities that adopted participatory budgeting (Gonçalves 2014). In Nigeria, ward development committees (WDCs) were established by volunteer community members to advocate for the health and social needs of their communities and give them autonomy over the utilization of funds for PHC improvements and outreach activities. A functioning and responsive complaints mechanism was also established. Five percent of the BHCPF was set aside specifically for fund administration, including setting up this robust mechanism to receive and respond to community complaints (Hafez 2018).

From fragility to resilience

As COVID-19 has made clear, shocks like global pandemics may require considerable additional health service spending, while severely reducing government capacity to raise revenues. Flexible financing systems can enable more resilient systems that can adapt to shocks with appropriate response measures, maintain essential PHC services during a crisis, and rapidly disburse sufficient financial protection to citizens.

Surging resources to the front lines

Unpredictable crises typically require extraordinary resource mobilization and deployment. Experience in past public health emergencies suggests that additional health sector funding is often needed for the following:

+   Core population-based functions essential for responding to shocks, including comprehensive surveillance, data and information systems; regulation; and communication and information campaigns

+ Adaptations to sustain essential routine health services, including the use of alternative care models (for example, telehealth and home-based care), reductions in/removal of copayments or user charges, expansion of coverage to previously uncovered populations (for example, migrants), investment in information and communications technology (ICT) capacity, facility reconfiguration and equipment, hazard pay for health workers, and financial support for facilities to survive through the crisis

+ Clinical and psychosocial care for patients directly affected by the crisis, for example, COVID-19 or Ebola patients or persons injured in a natural disaster.

The ability to surge the required funding to the front lines must be supported by country legal frameworks. Options can include contingency appropriations within the approved budget, emergency spending provisions that allow for spending in excess of budgeted amounts, expenditure reprioritization through reallocations and transfers, supplementary budgets, and external grants/loans. COVID-19 experiences have shown that countries with well-defined and flexible budgetary programs in health are more likely to have flexible and effective responses, compared with countries with rigid line-item budgets. France, New Zealand, and to some extent, South Africa offer positive examples. Uganda ensures sufficient funding for core population-based functions through a ring-fenced surveillance budget that includes a contingency fund to release money during an outbreak, with distinct funding for routine surveillance and response activities. At the district level, there is also a protected budget from which funding is released when a district officer finds a suspected case of concern. Many countries have also injected additional funding to the health sector during the COVID-19 pandemic by drawing on national reserves, health insurance reserves, or social insurance reserves.

Further, rapid deployment of additional funding to the front lines may require adjustments to typical payment mechanisms. For example, several countries are channeling additional COVID-19 response funds through purchasing agencies, including Austria, Croatia, Estonia, Latvia, Poland, Romania, and Serbia. Frontline providers can also be granted greater flexibility and spending authority so that they can respond more rapidly to key supply shortages or stock-outs, for example, concerning soap, medicines, or other materials. Some countries may need to activate exceptional spending procedures during the first phase of a crisis and then formalize these procedures using supplementary budget laws. In some cases, declaring a state of emergency can facilitate the release of new funds and speed up public procurement by enabling simplified procedures for trusted suppliers. In response to COVID-19, Italy passed a law ("Cure Italy") to enable sole-source procurement; Lithuania plans to simplify public health procurement rules.

Advance payments can also help bring financial resources to frontline workers quickly. PHC facilities can be adversely impacted as a result of additional expenses that are not part of routine budgeting/purchasing arrangements. Interruptions in routine service demand may worsen facilities' financial situation due to crisis management measures or public fear; this negative effect may be exacerbated if case-based or volume-linked payment methods are used. This situation has occurred in PHC facilities of Columbia, North Macedonia, and the United States during the COVID-19 pandemic. Advance payments may be in the form of front-loading budgets or capitation payments, or by "prefunding" payments that would otherwise come through retrospective reimbursement of claims. For long-term resilience, past public health emergency experience calls for prospective payment mechanisms and delinking payment from service volume with a larger focus instead on service value.

Purchasing arrangement flexibility assures that frontline providers receive the required resources promptly. Flexibility can be applied to "who provides services," "what services to provide," and "to whom to provide services." For example, some countries established rules to pay for services provided by noncontracted providers during COVID-19: Cyprus and Georgia paid private providers to fill service delivery gaps; Switzerland mandated service delivery for designated patient groups by acute hospitals that are normally not included in cantonal hospital plans and are not reimbursed through DRG-based payments. In Britain, an agreement has also been brokered for the government to take over private hospitals and their staff for the duration of the crisis, resulting in tens of thousands of clinical staff at the disposal of the public sector (Maier, Scarpetti, and Williams 2020).

Resilience and the benefits package

An explicit health benefits package, defined during a period of relative calm, may need to be rapidly amended so the health system can respond to a crisis. Rules and mechanisms that allow for timely benefits package adjustments can enable provider reimbursement for new or different types of services; remove financial barriers to patient service utilization; and ensure vulnerable groups receive necessary care.

During the COVID-19 crisis, many countries have expanded the scope of benefits packages, ensuring access for and financial protection from the costs of COVID-19 diagnosis and care; offering coverage for and incentivizing use of "touchless" teleconsultations or home-based care; and compensating health workers for the costs of providing these adapted services. For example, the health insurance department in China included eligible online-based medical service expenditure for primary health care in its package during COVID-19, thereby ensuring continuity of service for chronic disease patients (China National Healthcare Security Administration 2020). In settings where telehealth was already covered by insurance, efforts were made to minimize or eliminate disparity in reimbursement value between in-person and virtual visits. Such efforts were seen across Europe (Belgium, Czech Republic, Germany, Luxembourg, the Netherlands, Sweden, and Switzerland), as well as Canada and the United States). In some contexts, free access to health services was provided to vulnerable groups, including migrants in Belgium, France, and Portugal. In Belgium and Ireland, user charges were removed for teleconsultations in primary care, including for suspected COVID-19 cases.

Countries are also making modifications to their governance arrangements to adopt new testing and treatments as they become available, thereby ensuring no payment is required by their populations. For example, in China, the drugs and treatments that were listed in the COVID-19 clinical treatment protocol developed by the National Health Commission were added to the health insurance benefits package on a temporary basis. If other types of services need to be put on hold to finance the new interventions, it is critical to anticipate the implications in terms of health impact (current and future), equity, effects on financial protection, and possible implications for public confidence in government (Chalkidou et al. 2020). In some cases, building out models for countries to rapidly evaluate newly available technologies may help countries to better use scarce resources for shock responses without compromising essential services or other priorities (Hatswell 2020; Lorgelly and Adler 2020; Painter et al. 2020).

Enabling multisectoral engagement through PHC reform

Chapter 3 discussed multisectoral action for health as a cross-cutting agenda that can accelerate structural shifts toward stronger PHC. This chapter has shown how reforms in care organization, workforce development, and health financing can directly support those shifts. These priority reforms can also contribute to improving PHC through other channels, for example, by creating new openings and incentives for multisectoral collaboration. In closing this chapter, we look at specific opportunities and barriers to multisectoral working that are associated with the three priority reforms.

Linking clinical care and action on health determinants

A fundamental condition for effective multisectoral engagement is strong intersectoral stewardship at the policy level (WHO 2013). This central stewardship function then supports the development of needed skills and competencies at the level of community-based PHC delivery. When appropriately staffed, trained, equipped, and compensated, frontline PHC teams can plan and provide primary care and public health services; they can also ensure local coordination for intersectoral interventions (UN 2019).

Implementation barriers and the scarcity of good evidence on intersectoral actions are widely acknowledged. Compelling evidence exists that the availability of quality PHC services is associated with reduced disparities in health across socioeconomic and ethnic groups in many countries, but whether and how multisectoral strategies have contributed to these results is often unclear (Starfield, Shi, and Macinko 2005). There is abundant literature on integrating primary care with public or population health (Levesque et al. 2013; Martin-Misener et al. 2012; White 2015), and some on integrating PHC with the rest of the health system (Frenk 2009), but evidence is generally much thinner on how to connect PHC with other sectors of government in pursuing health for all (PAHO 2019).

However, recent work has begun to strengthen the evidence base supporting some intersectoral policies and interventions as cost-effective means to improve population health. In the third edition of *Disease Control Priorities (DCP3)*, Jamison and collaborators identify 71 proven intersectoral policies, which they divide into (1) financial/fiscal (such as excise taxes on tobacco and other harmful products); (2) regulatory (such as ambient and indoor air pollution and inadequate or excessive nutrient intakes); (3) built environment (such as road traffic injuries, water supply and sanitation); and (4) informational (such as consumer education). These policies are aimed at reducing or eliminating behavioral and environmental risk factors. The effectiveness of these policies is solidly backed by evidence. However, they are by definition developed at the central political level rather than the local political level. That said, successful implementation of many of these policies must be tailored to local conditions. This process especially concerns measures related to personal and group behaviors, such as tobacco and alcohol use, salt intake, micronutrient deficiencies, and unsafe sexual behavior. Local PHC teams are well placed to participate in implementing such policies, using socio-culturally acceptable approaches (Jamison et al. 2018).

One approach that has been widely applied over the past two decades, especially in LMICs, involves linking health and social protection agendas to facilitate communities' expression of their health and health care needs and to increase their uptake of some services. Many programs have chosen conditional cash transfers (CCTs) as their main vehicle. CCTs provide cash benefits to households, contingent on their use of essential health services at the PHC level, such as maternal and child health services and immunizations. Some program models engage a widening spectrum of determinants of health, including education, water supply and sanitation, food security, and nutrition (Lagarde, Haines, and Palmer 2014; Levy 2006). Experts have cautioned that, while CCTs may cushion the health consequences of poverty and reduce certain health inequalities, by themselves, these programs are not able to tackle the structural socio-cultural and economic inequities that are the root causes of inequities in health (Cruz, De Moura, and Neto 2017). However, when their strengths and limitations are understood, CCTs can work as complementary intersectoral interventions in support of people-centered primary health care. Key concerns in effective CCT design, such as proper targeting, coverage, scale-up, and longer-term sustainability (Ladhani and Sitter 2020) involve skill sets that are not generally present at the PHC level. However, local implementation and adaptation of these programs also require specific skills that need to be deliberately instilled in PHC teams. These encompass not only technical skills but also communications, administrative, managerial, and advocacy capacities. The best-prepared teams will develop capacities to secure appropriate funding and remove bureaucratic hurdles for intersectoral action.

Another area of increasing interest is "convergence." This refers to a strategy of zeroing in on the poorest communities in a given country for simultaneous technical and financial support; the process often involves international finance institutions and their development partners. Support is delivered across several sectors concomitantly, mainly health, education, nutrition, agriculture, and water and sanitation.[15] Although it is too early to fully assess their effectiveness, such intersectoral interventions—if designed and executed with the full participation of local communities and local government support—could address key social determinants of health while boosting PHC capacities at the local level.

In upper-middle-income countries with full population coverage of essential health services, current challenges for PHC are related to noncommunicable diseases, multiple morbidities, and behavioral determinants of healthier living and aging. Special concerns arise in low-income and/or low-growth "lagging" regions (World Bank 2018b), which are often rural. People in these regions often have limited access to comprehensive, quality health care. Indeed, several European countries, as well as Brazil, China, Colombia, and Turkey, use metrics or indexes to define lagging areas that include health and healthy living and aging.

Not surprisingly, these same countries emphasize community- or people-centered health care, with PHC at the center. Their different approaches all highlight the importance of integration across sectors and levels of care, communications strategies, stakeholder engagement, and continuous performance monitoring. All have undertaken or are considering regulatory reforms and workforce measures to facilitate the introduction of multidisciplinary teams (Somanathan, Finkel, and Arur 2019; Sumer, Shear, and Yener 2019; World Bank and WHO 2019a).

Building skills for multisectoral action among PHC practitioners

Training in advocacy, communication, and resource generation for multisectoral action

Chapter 3 identifies proper undergraduate, graduate, and in-service training as essential to building health workers' skills and competencies for multisectoral engagement (Rechel 2020). PHC professionals need to expand their skills in preparation for a range of newer interdisciplinary roles across the care spectrum—from health promotion, disease prevention, and management of chronic diseases to palliation and social care. Equally important for PHC professionals is acquiring leadership/stewardship, management, and communication skills to be able to confidently advocate for healthier living in the communities they serve. Such advocacy has many facets. It can include reaching out to local practitioners in other sectors whose activities influence health outcomes in the community and with whom opportunities for productive intersectoral partnerships may exist. It also involves sustained dialogue with communities themselves, to strengthen health literacy, encourage healthy lifestyle choices, and promote greater community agency and self-reliance in health, often across diverse socio-cultural contexts.

Achieving this is easier said than done, in a context of rapidly shifting disease burdens and demographics, as well as technological change and evolving social expectations that challenge health professionals' traditional status in many settings. Policy makers may encounter substantial opposition to reforms of curriculum and pedagogy in undergraduate medical training, especially if the reforms propose to expand already-packed academic programs with new material, such as management or advocacy skills that may be perceived as peripheral to many future physicians' career plans. As countries weigh possible changes to health worker education and training, factors such as the chronic shortages of properly trained health workers, the difficulty of deploying them to underserved areas, the migration of health professionals within and across national borders, and the long delays in recouping public investment in the training of health professionals must also be considered.

Recognizing these challenges, there are at least three ways in which countries can address the shortage of skills and competencies in multisectoral engagement.

+ First, in the shorter run, countries can leverage the continuous on-the-job learning that is already part of many PHC professionals' routine experience, especially in LMICs. Conscientious PHC practitioners, whether CHWs or PHC doctors and nurses, already participate in such learning as an integral part of their polyvalent vocation (UN 2019). Indeed, PHC professionals themselves increasingly perceive advocacy and communication skills as a key competency in daily PHC practice, as well as a foundation for more ambitious multisectoral engagement at the program-design and policy levels. Action to reinforce their capacities could include not only short-term on-the-job training but also "embedded PHC research" (AlKhaldi, Meghari, and Ahmed 2020) to systematically document local health and health care needs and preferences, as well as the broader socio-cultural and economic determinants of health. Front-line PHC workers will be most motivated to build such competencies when they can apply them in the day-to-day practice of their jobs and be recognized and rewarded for doing so.

+ A second, longer-run agenda, is to instill flexibility in existing undergraduate and graduate training courses to encourage the pursuit of joint degrees in areas like business administration (MBA), health or medical administration (MHA, MA), or public health (MPH). The United States has seen a recent very rapid increase in joint degree programs linking an MD degree with a PhD, MPH, or MA qualification. The number of MD/MBA programs in the United States alone now exceeds 60, including online training; many of them have started since 2000 (Viswanathan 2014).[16] Similar dual programs are also becoming more common in Canada (Canadian-universities.net 2021). While many of these programs are more attuned to the business side of health care in high-income settings, some prepare students for other vocations, including community-based primary care.[17] Such dual programs will eventually be more widely offered in other countries and to other health professionals. A fundamental concern is to customize them to local needs and ensure their accessibility and relevance to people who work in PHC or who aspire to do so. Available tools include tuition support, options for on-the-job and on-line degree acquisition, and tangible benefits in compensation and career advancement.

+ Last and perhaps most important, countries need to build capacities for multisectoral stewardship at the highest policy level. This first involves understanding the training and other requirements for doing so effectively, a question that remains unresolved, despite recurrent efforts in many countries with varied approaches and uneven results. Top-level multisectoral stewardship also needs to be mirrored through the successive levels of the health system down to the local administrative level and the PHC front lines. Relevant skills—including intersectoral dialogue, advocacy, and communication—must be embedded within health worker training curricula.

The current context may provide an opportunity to launch ambitious reforms in this respect. Along with the global systemic disruption caused by COVID-19, the era of the Sustainable Development Goals (SDGs) is one in which the complex interplay between health and development progress in other sectors has again come to the fore. There is growing acknowledgment of how action in other sectors influences health, and now there is an acute awareness that what happens in health can swiftly and overwhelmingly affect countries' economic performance and every other part of life (Bennett et al. 2020; Hussain et al. 2020).

Financing multisectoral engagement

Valuing multisectoral benefits in resource allocation

The case for multisectoral action to strengthen PHC is clear. Only through multisectoral action can the PHC platform cohesively target the social determinants of health across sectors like education, nutrition, agriculture, housing, transport, and environment (Anaf et al. 2014; Public Health Agency of Canada 2007; Public Health Agency of Canada and WHO 2008). Capitalizing on the synergies across health and other sectors, however, will require governments to use new ways of promoting and financing win-win measures that can spur progress on multiple development goals at once (Marmot et al. 2008). A growing body of literature on frameworks can be used to guide governments on multisectoral investment in health to support stronger PHC platforms (De Leeuw 2017; Glandon et al. 2018; McGuire et al. 2019; Rasanathan et al. 2017; Rasanathan et al. 2018).

Win-win taxes, such as those on products that harm health (notably tobacco, alcohol, sugary drinks, and salt in processed food), offer a clear example of an effective multisectoral investment. Such taxes provide one of the most cost-effective (and often cost-saving) approaches to reduce health-damaging product consumption, improve population health and individual productivity, and lower future medical treatment costs. These measures complement the promotive/preventive aspects of the PHC platform while making medium-term health financing more sustainable (Bloomberg Philanthropies 2019). Although earmarking funds on the expenditure side requires careful consideration of the trade-offs (Cashin, Sparkes, and Bloom 2017; World Bank 2017c) in some countries, these taxes have contributed directly to PHC. For example, the Philippines' influential Sin Tax on alcohol and tobacco uses an earmark to fully subsidize the enrollment of the poorest 40 percent of the population and senior citizens in the National Health Insurance Scheme (Kaiser, Bredenkamp, and Iglesias 2016), which includes a benefits package for primary health care. In the first three years of earmark tax implementation, the budget for the Department of Health tripled (Kaiser, Bredenkamp, and Iglesias 2016).

Countries can also consider joint financing of specific interventions that further the PHC agenda: this modality typically involves one or more non-health sectors investing in health, based on evidence that the investment will also benefit its own sector. This financing model tends to be intervention specific. For example, a randomized controlled trial of school-based deworming treatment, partially supported by the education budget, reduced school absenteeism by one-fourth and was far more cost-effective than alternative mechanisms to boost school attendance (McGuire et al. 2019).

Similarly, voluntary, school-located programs, which often involve a partnership that includes joint financing between a local school system and a health department, have successfully increased the uptake for several vaccines (Cawley, Hull, and Rousculp 2010; Lindley et al. 2008).

Governments can also explore integrative financing by pooling or aligning resources across sectors to better link PHC coordination and other service provision. For example, Canada and New Zealand have implemented various jointly financed integrated health and social care sector models for older adults with complex health needs who live in community settings.

The evidence suggests that these programs have several positive multisectoral outcomes: they meet the elderly population's social and health needs, lead to better health outcomes, and reduce costly and often inappropriate hospital and long-term residential care (Béland et al. 2006; Parsons et al. 2012). Joint financing can take place at various levels (national, regional, local) when two or more budget holders contribute to a single pool for spending on preagreed services or interventions, or by aligning resources to ensure joint monitoring of spending and performance but separate management of resources (McGuire et al. 2019).

Ministers of health can be at the center of the intersectoral dialogue, together with the ministry of finance, as they work together to identify and finance such interventions, breaking down the silos typical of more traditional decision-making on resource allocation. In LMICs, this approach marks a departure from a situation where the health sector often struggles to make the case for investing in health, sometimes because of a failure to highlight nonhealth benefits that might raise other sectors' interest in health gains (De Leeuw 2017; Rasanathan et al. 2017). Cost-benefit analysis captures human welfare improvement benefits across all sectors in monetary terms. Thus, it may help make a more effective case for intersectoral partnership than cost-effectiveness analysis, which is conducted in individual sectors and can undervalue benefits beyond the health sector (Angevine and Berven 2014). Intersectoral priority setting can also increase the quality and quantity of public spending and ensure both value for money and equity (Dercon and O'Connell 2018).

Finally, with strong ministry of finance leadership, governments can facilitate a whole-of-government approach to proactively tackle the structural, social, and behavioral determinants of health (Davies et al. 2014; Stubbs et al. 2014; World Bank 2019a). This approach can make traditional governmental decision-making mechanisms more reflective of social diversity by promoting greater engagement of the private sector, civil society, communities, and individuals in health-related actions (WHO 2018e). The World Bank's Human Capital Project consistently highlights the potential benefits of the whole-of-government approach (box 4.6).

New Zealand offers an illustrative example of an operationalized whole-of-government approach. The country passed a "Well-being Budget" in 2019, whereby all ministries were asked to frame their funding requests based on how that funding would help improve intergenerational well-being. In addition, the budget statement explicitly recognizes that, while Maori and Pacific peoples account for only 22 percent of the population, they make up over 60 percent of avoidable hospitalizations; many admissions could

BOX 4.6

A WHOLE-OF-GOVERNMENT APPROACH TO STRENGTHEN HUMAN CAPITAL

The World Bank's Human Capital Project (HCP) is a global, multisectoral effort to accelerate more and better investments in people for greater equity and economic growth. The HCP contributes to a whole-of-government approach in three ways: by sustaining efforts across political cycles; by linking different sectoral programs; and by expanding the policy design evidence base (World Bank 2018c). This approach recognizes that getting children into school, reducing child mortality, tackling communicable diseases, increasing life expectancy, and expanding social safety nets in low- and middle-income countries are not simply moral imperatives; they are also economic imperatives, as they will allow people to compete and thrive in a rapidly-changing environment (World Bank 2018c). While technology brings opportunity, paving the way to create new jobs, increase productivity and deliver effective public services, it also changes the skills that employers seek; workers need to be better at complex problem solving, teamwork, and adaptability (World Bank 2019b). The HCP therefore encourages and supports countries to spend on health, education, and social protection programs, in addition to sectors beyond human development. For example, in Nepal, investments in sanitation are contributing significantly to preventing anemia (World Bank 2018c).

be prevented by making PHC work better for these minority populations, including by tackling language and cultural barriers (New Zealand Treasury 2019). Other whole-of-government models target a specific problem. Peru used such an approach to reduce its chronic child malnutrition rate from 28 percent to 13 percent between 2005 and 2016. This success can be largely attributed to strong leadership by the Ministry of Economy and Finance, which lasted through successive changes of political administration. The approach encouraged multilevel, cross-government coordination and used a results-based approach to allocate resources only to evidence-based interventions across sectors. It incorporated a communications strategy, education, and demand-side incentives provided through a conditional cash transfer program.

Strong leadership is needed at the national level to ensure effectiveness, but whole-of-government PHC strengthening approaches must be supported by bottom-up participation, reliable funding, and a strong accountability structure. Even well-organized efforts at the national level may be limited in their capacity to influence social determinants of health, if they are not aligned with local initiatives that express communities' concerns, priorities, and preferred solutions (Marmot et al. 2008; Public Health Agency of Canada and WHO 2008).

Conclusions

This chapter has described three priority reform agendas that can enable countries to improve the performance of their PHC networks. These reforms will prepare PHC to work catalytically in strengthening effectiveness, efficiency, equity, and crisis resilience across the broader health system.

The reforms outlined are technically demanding. They require sustained effort, substantial investment, and determined leadership. However, a fundamental lesson from this analysis is that progress toward fit-for-purpose PHC is feasible in virtually all countries. The evidence presented here shows that many economies—including some facing chronic financial challenges and institutional fragility—have already taken impressive strides along the road. The changes needed to get the best from PHC can be achieved, even where resources are highly constrained.

The health and economic context shaped by COVID-19 will complicate these efforts. The pandemic, however, has generated exceptional political and public support for health system change. COVID-19 has taught bitter lessons about how important strong health systems are and what happens when they fail. Today, the wounds of the pandemic are still raw. That is why this is the time to act.

Implementing fit-for-purpose PHC demands political endurance, but measurable health and economic benefits from pro-PHC reforms can emerge in a relatively short timeframe. PHC-level interventions with an intersectoral character, such as school-based deworming programs, can boost school attendance and create conditions for better learning in a matter of weeks (World Bank 2019b). Improvements in adult health through PHC-driven interventions in nutrition, malaria treatment, and smoking cessation can spur worker productivity gains within months (World Bank 2020). LMICs implementing strategies comparable to some described in this chapter have registered impressive gains in child survival and stunting rates in less than five years, saving lives now and laying strong foundations for future human capital and economic growth (World Bank 2020). Community-based mental health delivered through PHC holds promise to reduce a disease burden that weighs heavily on economic performance in virtually all countries. While much remains to be learned, early studies of community-based mental health programs in some LMICs have shown promising results in politically acceptable timeframes (Marquez and Garcia 2019). As the PHC evidence base improves, more examples of health and economic "quick wins" from PHC reforms will emerge.

Today, countries are working to recover from COVID-19, rekindle economic growth, and get back on the path of progress to their most important development goals, including poverty eradication and UHC. Fit-for-purpose primary health care is a powerful resource for this work. As countries continue to walk the talk on PHC reform, their rewards will grow through reduced health care costs, more resilient health systems, stronger human capital, higher productivity—and above all, longer, healthier, more satisfying lives for people.

Notes

1. For each of the three reform axes, that reform's impacts on each of the four PHC shifts is discussed in turn. While points of overlap exist among some of the 12 matrix cells, this structure has important advantages of clarity and usability. It allows readers interested in a specific reform axis (for example, financing) to easily follow out its implications for each of the PHC change outcomes. Meanwhile, readers primarily interested in policy and practice solutions supporting one particular outcome (for example, crisis resilience in PHC systems) can quickly find the subsections where the impacts of each main reform thrust on this outcome are discussed.

2. Centers for Medicare & Medicaid Services (CMS). "Shared Savings Program," CMS, n.d.

3. National Cancer Institute (NCI). n.d. "NCI Dictionary of Cancer Terms: Patient Navigator," n.d.

4. Institute for Healthcare Improvement (IHI). n.d. "SBAR Tool: Situation-Background-Assessment-Recommendation," n.d.

5. Institute for Healthcare Improvement (IHI). n.d. "5 Whys: Finding the Root Cause," n.d.

6. Alliance for Health Policy and Systems Research. n.d.

7. Great Barrier Reef and World Migratory Bird. 2020. "Transparency for Development Proposals," no. January: 4–5.

8. World Bank. n.d. "The World Bank Group's Response to the COVID-19 Pandemic."

9. Physician Licensure, n.d. "Interstate Medical Licensure Compact."

10. NCSBN, "Nurse Licensure Compact (CLC)."

11. Our Impact. n.d. "THEnet: The Training for Health Equity Network."

12. Institute for Health Metrics and Evaluation, https://vizhub.healthdata.org/lbd/under5. See also Golding et al. 2017.

13. Southern Metropolis Daily Client. "Outpatient Drugs for Hypertension and Diabetes Are Included in Medical Insurance, and the Reimbursement Ratio Is at Least 50%, Benefiting 300 Million People," n.d.

14. CMS Innovation Center, "Comprehensive Primary Care Plus," n.d.

15. See, for instance, Lao PDR WSS Multisectoral Convergence Project for Nutrition and Health and Nutrition Service Access Project (HANSA) https://www.worldbank.org/en/news/loans-credits/2020/03/12/lao-pdr-health-and-nutrition-services-access-project.

16. http://www.mdmbaprograms.Org/Md-Mba-Programs/ Accessed July 7, 2020, n.d.

17. Primary Care Progress. "Strengthening the Community at the Heart of Care," n.d.

References

AAFP (American Academy of Family Physicians). n.d. a. "The Key Functions of a Medical Home: Comprehensiveness and Coordination." AAFP, Leawood, Kansas.

AAFP (American Academy of Family Physicians). n.d. b. "Practice Management." *High Impact Changes for Practice Transformation*. AAFP, Leawood, Kansas.

AAPC (American Academy of Professional Coders). 2019. "Realize the Value of Soft Skills in Healthcare." Blog, August. https://www.aapc.com/blog/48405-realize -the-value-of-soft-skills-in-healthcare.

Adebajo, Sylvia, Jean Njab, Ayodeji Oginni, Francis Ukwuije, Babatunde A. O. Ahonsi, and. Theo Lorenc. 2015. "Evaluating the Effect of HIV Prevention Strategies on Uptake of HIV Counselling and Testing among Male Most-at-Risk-Populations in Nigeria: A Cross-Sectional Analysis." *Sexually Transmitted Infections* 91 (8): 555–60, https://doi.org/10.1136/sextrans-2014-051659.

Afrite, Anissa, Yann Bourgueil, Fabien Daniel, Julien Mousquèsa (Irdes), Pierre-Emmanuel Couralet, and Guillaume Chevillard. 2013. "The Impact of Multi-Professional Group Practices. Evaluation Aims and Methods for 'Maisons', 'Pôles de Santé,' and 'Centres de Santé' within the Framework of Experiments with New Mechanisms of Remuneration." *Questions d'économie de La Santé* 189: 1–6.

AHPCSA (Africa Allied Health Professions Council of South Africa). 2020. "Extraordinary AHPCSA Policy Decision: Telehealth and Telemedicine as a Result of South African State of Disaster." Board Notice, March 25, Pretoria, South Africa.

Aiello, Andria, Michelle Young-Eun Khayeri, S. Raja, N. Peladeau, D. Romano, M. Leszcz, et al. 2011. "Resilience Training for Hospital Workers in Anticipation of an Influenza Pandemic." *Journal of Continuing Education in the Health Professions* 31 (1): 15–20, https://doi.org/10.1002/chp.20096.

Aiyenigba, Emmanuel, Jeffrey Arias, Tricia Bolender, Donika Dimovska, Gina Lagomarsino, and Ola Soyinka. 2016. "Intermediaries: The Missing Link in Improving Mixed Market Health Systems?" Results for Development, Washington, DC.

Alexander, Diane, and Molly Schnell. 2017. "Closing the Gap: The Impact of the Medicaid Primary Care Rate Increase on Access and Health." Working Paper No. 2017-10, Federal Reserve Bank of Chicago, Chicago, IL.

AlKhaldi, Mohammed, Hamza Meghari, and Sara Ahmed. 2020. "A New Era for Health Policy and Systems Research." *Think Global Health*." July, https://www.thinkglobalhealth.org/article/new-era-health-policy-and -systems-research.

Alliance for Health Policy and Systems Research. n.d. "Primary Health Care Systems (PRIMASYS): New Case Studies Available." World Health Organization, Geneva.

Alliance for Health Policy and Systems Research and Bill & Melinda Gates Foundation. 2015. "Report of the Expert Consultation on Primary Care Systems Priorities and Performance (PRIMASYS)." Report, Alliance for Health Policy and Systems Research, Geneva.

Ammar, W., R. Wakim, and I. Hajj. 2007. "Accreditation of Hospitals in Lebanon: A Challenging Experience." *Eastern Mediterranean Health Journal* 13 (1): 138–49.

Amurao, Cristine Villena. 2016. "Closing the Gap." *Fuels and Lubes International* 22 (4): 16–19.

Anaf, Julia, Fran Baum, Toby Freeman, Ron Labonte, Sara Javanparast, Gwyn Jolley, Angela Lawless, and Michael Bentley. 2014. "Factors Shaping Intersectoral Action in Primary Health Care Services." *Australian and New Zealand Journal of Public Health* 38 (6): 553–59, https://doi.org/10.1111/1753-6405.12284.

Andrus, Jon Kim, and Damian G. Walker. 2015. "Perspectives on Expanding the Evidence Base to Inform Vaccine Introduction: Program Costing and Cost-Effectiveness Analyses." *Vaccine* 33 (S1): A2–3, https://doi.org/10.1016/j.vaccine.2015.01.001.

Angevine, Peter D., and Sigurd Berven. 2014. "Health Economic Studies: An Introduction to Cost-Benefit, Cost-Effectiveness, and Cost-Utility Analyses." *Spine* 39 (22 Suppl 1): S9–15, https://doi.org/10.1097/BRS.0000000000000576.

Aquino, Rosana, Nelson F. De Oliveira, and Mauricio L. Barreto. 2009. "Impact of the Family Health Program on Infant Mortality in Brazilian Municipalities." *American Journal of Public Health* 99 (1): 87–93, https://doi.org/10.2105/AJPH.2007.127480.

Aravind Eye Care System. 2015. "A Trip to an Eye Camp: Aravind Eye Care System." Aravind Eye Care System, Tamil Nadu, India.

Arrow, Kenneth J. 2001. "Uncertainty and the Welfare Economics of Medical Care." *Journal of Health Politics, Policy and Law* 26 (5): 851–83, https://doi.org/10.1215/03616878-26-5-851.

Assegaai, T., G. Reagon, and H. Schneider. 2018. "Evaluating the Effect of Ward-Based Outreach Teams on Primary Healthcare Performance in North West Province, South Africa: A Plausibility Design Using Routine Data." *South African Medical Journal* 108 (4): 329, https://doi.org/10.7196/samj.2017.v108i4.12755.

Atim, Chris, Koku Awoonor, and Elizabeth Hammah. 2019. "UHC through PHC: Piloting Preferred Primary Care Provider Networks in Ghana." Abstract for the Fifth African Health Economics and Policy Association Conference on Securing PHC for All: The Foundation for Making Progress on UHC in Africa, March 11–14, Accra Ghana.

Barlow, James, Debbie Singh, and Steffen Bayer. 2007. "A Systematic Review of the Benefits of Home Telecare for Frail Elderly People and Those with Long-Term Conditions." *Journal of Telemedicine and Telecare* 13 (4), https://doi.org/10.1258/135763307780908058.

Barnes, Andrew J., Lynn Unruh, Askar Chukmaitov, and Ewout van Ginneken. 2014. "Accountable Care Organizations in the USA: Types, Developments and Challenges." *Health Policy* 118 (1): 1–7, https://doi.org/10.1016/j.healthpol.2014.07.019.

Báscolo, Ernesto, and Natalia Yavich. 2009. "Governance and the Effectiveness of the Buenos Aires Public Health Insurance Implementation Process." *Journal of Ambulatory Care Management* 32 (2): 91–102, https://doi.org/10.1097/JAC.0b013e31819941bb.

Bastos, Mayara Lisboa, Dick Menzies, Thomas Hone, Kainsoh Dehghani, and Annete Trajman. 2017. "The Impact of the Brazilian Family Health on Selected Primary Care Sensitive Conditions: A Systematic Review." *PLoS ONE* 12 (8): e0182336, https://doi.org/10.1371/journal.pone.0182336.

Bearden, Trudy, Hannah L. Ratcliffe, Jonathan R. Sugarman, Asaf Bitton, Leonard Abbam Anaman, Gilbert Buckle, Momodou Cham, et al. 2019. "Empanelment: A Foundational Component of Primary Health Care." Gates Open Research 3:1654.

Béland, François, Howard Bergman, Paule Lebel, A. Mark Clarfield, Pierre Tousignant, André-Pierre Contandriopoulos, and Luc Dallaire. 2006. "A System of Integrated Care for Older Persons with Disabilities in Canada: Results from a Randomized Controlled Trial." *Journals of Gerontology*. Series A, Biological Sciences and Medical Sciences 61 (4): 367–73, https://doi.org/10.1093/gerona/61.4.367.

Bemah, Philip, April Baller, Catherine Cooper, Moses Massaquoi, Laura Skrip, Julius Monday Rude, Anthony Twyman, et al. 2019. "Strengthening Healthcare Workforce Capacity during and Post Ebola Outbreaks in Liberia: An Innovative and Effective Approach to Epidemic Preparedness and Response." *Pan African Medical Journal* 33 (Suppl 2): 9, https://doi.org/10.11604/pamj.supp.2019.33.2.17619.

Bennett, Sara, Nasreen Jessani, Douglas Glandon, Mary Qui, Kerry Scott, Ankita Meghani, et al. 2020. "Understanding the Implications of the Sustainable Development Goals for Health Policy and Systems Research: Results of a Research Priority Setting Exercise." *Globalization and Health* 16 (1): 1–13, https://doi.org/10.1186/s12992-019-0534-2.

Beyeler, Naomi, Anna York De La Cruz, and Dominic Montagu. 2013. "The Impact of Clinical Social Franchising on Health Services in Low- and Middle-Income Countries: A Systematic Review." *PLoS ONE* 8 (4): 1–9, https://doi.org/10.1371/journal.pone.0060669.

Bhattacharyya, Onil, Sara Khor, Anita McGahan, David Dunne, Abdallah S. Daar, and Peter A. Singer. 2010. "Innovative Health Service Delivery Models in Low and Middle Income Countries: What Can We Learn from the Private Sector?" *Health Research Policy and System* 8 (24), https://doi.org/10.1186/1478-4505-8-24.

Bitton, Asaf, Jocelyn Fifield, Hannah Ratcliffe, Ami Karlage, Hong Wang, Jeremy H. Veillard, Dan Schwartz, and Lisa R. Hirschhorn. 2019. "Primary Healthcare System Performance in Low-Income and Middle-Income Countries: A Scoping Review of the Evidence from 2010 to 2017." *BMJ Global Health* 4 (Suppl 8): e001551, https://doi.org/10.1136/bmjgh-2019-001551.

Björkman, Martina, and Jakob Svensson. 2009. "Power to the People: Evidence from a Randomized Field Experiment on Community-Based Monitoring in Uganda." *Quarterly Journal of Economics* 124 (2): 735–69, https://doi.org/10.1162/qjec.2009.124.2.735.

Bloomberg Philanthropies. 2019. "Task Force on Fiscal Policy for Health." Bloomberg Philanthropies, New York, NY. https://www.commonwealthfund.org/blog/2016/promise-and-pitfalls-bundled-payments.

Blumenthal, David, and David Squires. 2016. "The Promise and Pitfalls of Bundled Payments." *Achieving Universal Coverage* (blog), The Commonwealth Fund, New York, NY, September 7.

Bodenheimer, Thomas, Amireh Ghorob, Rachel Willard-Grace, and Kevin Grumbach. 2014. "The 10 Building Blocks of High-Performing Primary Care." *Annals of Family Medicine* 12 (2): 166–71, https://doi.org/10.1370/afm.1616.

Boelen, C., and B. Berney. 2000. "Challenges and Opportunities for Partnership in Health Development: A Working Paper." World Health Organization, Geneva.

Bonciani, M., W. Schäfer, S. Barsanti, S. Heinemann, and P. P. Groenewegen. 2018. "The Benefits of Co-Location in Primary Care Practices: The Perspectives of General Practitioners and Patients in 34 Countries." *BMC Health Services Research* 18: 132, https://doi.org/10.1186/s12913-018-2913-4.

Borem, Paulo, Estevao Alves Valle, Monica Silva Monteiro De Castro, Ronaldo Kenzou Fujii, Ana Luiza de Oliveira Farias, Fabio Leite Gastal, and Catherine Connor. 2010. "Pay-for-Performance in Brazil: UNIMED-Belo Horizonte Physician Cooperative." Health Systems 20/20 Case Studies Series, Abt Associates Inc., Bethesda, Maryland.

Boyce, Matthew R., and Rebecca Katz. 2019. "Community Health Workers and Pandemic Preparedness: Current and Prospective Roles." *Frontiers in Public Health* 7: 62, https://doi.org/10.3389/fpubh.2019.00062.

Boyda, Danielle C., Samuel B. Holzman, Amanda Berman, M. Kathryn Grabowski, and Larry W. Chang. 2019. "Geographic Information Systems, Spatial Analysis, and HIV in Africa: A Scoping Review." *PLoS ONE* 14 (5): 1–22, https://doi.org/10.1371/JOURNAL.PONE.0216388.

Boyle, Theresa. 2019. "Ontario Family Doctors Average $400,000-plus for Part-Time Hours. Province Wants to Claw Back Pay." TheSpec.com, January 28.

Busse, Reinhard, and Juliane Stahl. 2014. "Integrated Care Experiences and Outcomes in Germany, the Netherlands, and England." *Health Affairs* 33 (9): 1549–58, https://doi.org/10.1377/hlthaff.2014.0419.

Campanella, Paolo, Vladimir Vukovic, Paolo Parente, Adela Sulejmani, Walter Ricciardi, and Maria Lucia Specchia. 2016. "The Impact of Public Reporting on Clinical Outcomes: A Systematic Review and Meta-Analysis." *BMC Health Services Research* 16 (1), https://doi.org/10.1186/s12913-016-1543-y.

Campbell, Mhairi, Oliver Escobar, Candida Fenton, and Peter Craig. 2018. "The Impact of Participatory Budgeting on Health and Wellbeing: A Scoping Review of Evaluations." *BMC Public Health* 18 (1): 1–11, https://doi.org/10.1186/s12889-018-5735-8.

Canadian-universities.net. 2021. "Health and Medical MBA Degree Programs in Canada," accessed May 28, 2021, http://www.canadian-universities.net/MBA/Health_and_Medical_MBA.html.

Carpio, Carmen, and Natalia Santiago Bench. 2015. *The Health Workforce in Latin America and the Caribbean: An Analysis of Colombia, Costa Rica, Jamaica, Panama, Peru, and Uruguay.* Directions in Development. Washington, DC: World Bank. https://doi.org/10.1596/978-1-4648-0594-3.

Carter, Renee, Bruno Riverlin, Jean-Frederic Levesque, Genevieve Gariepy, and Amelie Quesnel-Vallee. 2016. "The Impact of Primary Care Reform on Health System Performance in Canada: A Systematic Review." *BMC Health Services Research* 16 (1), https://doi.org/10.1186/s12913-016-1571-7.

Casey, M. 2001. "State HMO Accreditation and External Quality Review Requirements: Implications for HMOs Serving Rural Areas." *Journal of Rural Health* 17 (1): 40–52, https://doi.org/10.1111/j.1748-0361.2001.tb00253.x.

Cashin, Cheryl, Y-Ling Chi, Peter Smith, Michael Borowitz, and Sarah Thomson. 2014. *Paying for Performance in Health Care Implications for Health System Performance and Accountability European Observatory on Health Systems and Policies Series.* Maidenhead: Open University Press.

Cashin, Cheryl, Susan Sparkes, and Danielle Bloom. 2017. "Earmarking for Health: From Theory to Practice." Health Finance Working Paper No. 5, World Health Organization. Geneva, http://apps.who.int/iris/bitstream/10665/255004/1/9789241512206-eng.pdf?ua=1.

Catarino, Rosa, Pierre Vassilakos, Stefano Scaringella, Manuela Undurraga-Malinverno, Ulrike Meyer-Hamme, Dominique Ricard-Gauthier, Juan Carlos Matute, and Patrick Petignat. 2015. "Smartphone Use for Cervical Cancer Screening in Low-Resource Countries: A Pilot Study Conducted in Madagascar." *PLoS ONE* 10 (7): e0134309, https://doi.org/10.1371/journal.pone.0134309.

Cawley, John, Harry F. Hull, and Matthew D. Rousculp. 2010. "Strategies for Implementing School-Located Influenza Vaccination of Children: A Systematic Literature Review." *Journal of School Health* 80 (4): 167–75, https://doi.org/10.1111/j.1746-1561.2009.00482.x.

Chalkidou, Kalipso, Damian Walker, Richard Sullivan, Edwine Barasa, Dalia Dawoud, Francis Ruiz, et al. 2020. "Healthcare Technologies and COVID-19: Speed Is Not Always a Good Thing." Blog, Center for Global Development, June 29, https:// www.cgdev.org/blog/healthcare-technologies-and-covid-19-speed-not-always -good-thing.

Chansa, Collins, Netsanet Walelign Workie, Moritz Piatti, Thulani Matsebula, and Katelyn Jison Yoo. 2018. "Zambia Health Sector Public Expenditure Review." *Zambia Health Sector Public Expenditure Review*, https://doi.org/10.1596/31784.

CHIC (Community Health Impact Coalition). 2020. "Priorities for the Global COVID-19 Response," April.

China National Healthcare Security Administration. 2020. "Centering on People to Ensure Financial Protection of Patients."

Chopra, Mickey, Salla Munro, John N. Lavis, Gunn Vist, and Sara Bennett. 2008. "Effects of Policy Options for Human Resources for Health: An Analysis of Systematic Reviews." *The Lancet* 371 (9613): 668–74, https://doi.org/10.1016 /S0140-6736(08)60305-0.

Clemens, Michael A. 2015. "Global Skill Partnerships: A Proposal for Technical Training in a Mobile World." *IZA Journal of Labor Policy* 4 (1): 10–12, https://doi .org/10.1186/s40173-014-0028-z.

Conwell, Leslie J., and Joel W. Cohen. 2005. "Characteristics of Persons with High Medical Expenditures in the U.S. Civilian Noninstitutionalized Population, 2002." Statistical Brief 73: 6. Agency for Healthcare Research and Quality, Rockville, Maryland.

Cotlear, D., G. Alawode, and S. Muchiri. 2020. "Bridging the Gap Between the Ministries of Finance and Health in Decentralized Health Care Systems: A Comparison of Nigeria and Kenya," http://www.healthpolicyplus.com /DecentralizedHealth.cfm.

Cotlear, Daniel, Daniel Cotlear, Somil Nagpal, Owen Smith, Ajay Tandon, and Rafael Cortez. 2015. *Going Universal: How 24 Developing Countries Are Implementing Universal Health Coverage Reforms from the Bottom Up*. Washington, DC: World Bank, https://doi.org/10.1596/978-1-4648-0610-0.

Council on Graduate Medical Education. 2013. "Improving Value in Graduate Medical Education." Twenty-First Report, Rockville, Maryland.

Cristobal, F., and P. Worley. 2012. "Can Medical Education in Poor Rural Areas Be Cost-Effective and Sustainable?: The Case of the Ateneo de Zamboanga University School of Medicine." *Rural and Remote Health* 12 (1): 1–7, https://doi .org/10.22605/rrh1835.

Croskerry, Pat. 2018. "Adaptive Expertise in Medical Decision Making." *Medical Teacher* 40 (8): 803–08, https://doi.org/10.1080/0142159X.2018.1484898.

Cruz, Rebeca Carmo De Souza, Leides Barroso Azevedo De Moura, and Joaquim José Soares Neto. 2017. "Conditional Cash Transfers and the Creation of Equal Opportunities of Health for Children in Low and Middle-Income Countries: A Literature Review." *International Journal for Equity in Health* 16 (1): 1–12, https://doi.org/10.1186/s12939-017-0647-2.

Cubic, Barbara, Janette Mance, Jeri N. Turgesen, and Jennifer D. Lamanna. 2012. "Interprofessional Education: Preparing Psychologists for Success in Integrated Primary Care." *Journal of Clinical Psychology in Medical Settings* 19 (1): 84–92, https://doi.org/10.1007/s10880-011-9291-y.

Cueto, Jose, et al. 2006. "Accreditation of Undergraduate Medical Training Programs: Practices in Nine Developing Countries as Compared with the United States." *Education for Health: Change in Learning and Practice* 19 (2): 207–22.

Dahn, Bernice, Addis Tamire Woldemariam, Henry Perry, Akiki Maeda, Drew von Glahn, et al. 2015. "Strengthening Primary Health Care through Community Health Workers: Investment Case and Financing Recommendations." Report. https://www.who.int/hrh/news/2015/CHW-Financing-FINAL-July-15-2015.pdf.

Daniels, N. 2000. "Accountability for Reasonableness." *British Medical Journal* 321: 1300, https://doi.org/10.1136/bmj.321.7272.1300.

Darlow, Ben, Karen Coleman, Eileen McKinlay, Sarah Donovan, Louise Beckingsale, Ben Gray, Hazel Neser, Meredith Perry, James Stanley, and Sue Pullon. 2015. "The Positive Impact of Interprofessional Education: A Controlled Trial to Evaluate a Programme for Health Professional Students." *BMC Medical Education* 15 (1): 1–9, https://doi.org/10.1186/s12909-015-0385-3.

Davies, Sally C., Eleanor Winpenny, Sarah Ball, Tom Fowler, Jennifer Rubin, and Ellen Nolte. 2014. "For Debate: A New Wave in Public Health Improvement." *The Lancet* 384 (99957): P1889–95, https://doi.org/10.1016/S0140-6736(13)62341-7.

De Brauw, Alan, and Amber Peterman. 2020. "Can Conditional Cash Transfers Improve Maternal Health Care? Evidence from El Salvador's Comunidades Solidarias Rurales Program." *Health Economics* 29 (6): 700–15, https://doi.org/10.1002/hec.4012.

De Carvalho, Islene Araujo, JoAnne Epping-Jordan, Anne Margriet Pot, Edward Kelley, Nuria Toro, Jotheeswaran A. Thiyagarajana, and John R. Beard. 2017. "Organizing Integrated Health-Care Services to Meet Older People's Needs." *Bulletin of the World Health Organization* 95 (11): 756–63, https://doi.org/10.2471/BLT.16.187617.

De Groot, Richard, Tia Palermo, Sudhanshu Handa, Luigi Peter Ragno, and Amber Peterman. 2017. "Cash Transfers and Child Nutrition: Pathways and Impacts." *Development Policy Review* 35 (5): 621–43, https://doi.org/10.1111/dpr.12255.

De Leeuw, Evelyne. 2017. "Engagement of Sectors Other than Health in Integrated Health Governance, Policy, and Action." *Annual Review of Public Health* 38: 329–49, https://doi.org/10.1146/annurev-publhealth-031816-044309.

Department of Health and Human Services. 2020. "OCR Announces Notification of Enforcement Discretion for Telehealth Remote Communications during the COVID-19 Nationwide Public Health Emergency." Department of Health and Human Services, Washington, DC.

Dercon, S., and Stephen A. O'Connell. 2018. "Foreword: Why Measurement of Costs and Benefits Matters for the SDG Campaign." In *Prioritizing Development*, ed. B. Lomborg, https://doi.org/10.1017/9781108233767.001.

Dolea, Carmen, Laura Stormont, and Jean Marc Braichet. 2010. "Evaluated Strategies to Increase Attraction and Retention of Health Workers in Remote and Rural Areas." *Bulletin of the World Health Organization* 88: 379–85, https://doi.org/10.2471/BLT.09.070607.

Doty, Michelle M., Roosa Tikkanen, Arnav Shah, and Eric C. Schneider. 2020. "Primary Care Physicians' Role in Coordinating Medical and Health-Related Social Needs in Eleven Countries." *Health Affairs* 39 (1): 115–23, https://doi.org/10.1377/hlthaff.2019.01088.

Dourado, Inês, Maria Guadalupe Medina, and Rosana Aquino. 2013. "The Effect of the Family Health Strategy on Usual Source of Care in Brazil: Data from the 2013 National Health Survey (PNS 2013)." *International Journal for Equity in Health* 15, https://doi.org/10.1186/s12939-016-0440-7.

Downes, Martin J., Merehau C. Mervin, Joshua M. Byrnes, and Paul A. Scuffman. 2017. "Telephone Consultations for General Practice: A Systematic Review." *Systematic Reviews* 6 (1): 1–6, https://doi.org/10.1186/s13643-017-0529-0.

Dutta, Sheila. 2020. "Supporting Mental Health and Resilience in Frontline COVID-19 (Coronavirus) Health Care Workers." Investing in Health, blog, World Bank, Washington, DC.

Edward, Anbrasi, Kojo Osei-Bonsu, Casey Branchini, Temor shah Yargal, Said Habib Arwal, Ahmad Jan Naeeem. 2015. "Enhancing Governance and Health System Accountability for People Centered Healthcare: An Exploratory Study of Community Scorecards in Afghanistan." *BMC Health Services Research* 15 (1): 1–15, https://doi.org/10.1186/s12913-015-0946-5.

Ellis, Emma Grey. 2020. "How Health Care Workers Avoid Bringing Covid-19 Home." Blog, WIRED.

Ettinger, Kate Michi, Hamilton Pharaoh, Reymound Yaw Buckman, and Hoffie Conradie. 2016. "Building Quality MHealth for Low Resource Settings." *Journal of Medical Engineering and Technology* 40 (7-8): 1–16. https://doi.org/10.1080/0309 1902.2016.1213906.

Evelyn, Kenya. 2020. "New York ER Doctor Who Treated Coronavirus Patients Dies by Suicide." *The Guardian,* April 28.

Farmer, Diana L. 2015. "Soft Skills Matter." *JAMA Surgery* 150 (3): 207. https://doi .org/10.1001/jamasurg.2014.2250.

Feffer, Mark. 2016. "HR's Hard Challenge: When Employees Lack Soft Skills." Blog, SHRM, April 1, https://www.shrm.org/hr-today/news/hr-magazine/0416/pages /hrs-hard-challenge-when-employees-lack-soft-skills.aspx.

Fellows and Edwards. 2016. "Future Skills and Competences of the Health Workforce in Europe." Centre for Workforce Intelligence, United Kingdom.

Forcier, Mélanie Bourassa, Steven Simoens, and Antonio Giuffrida. 2004. "Impact, Regulation and Health Policy Implications of Physician Migration in OECD Countries." *Human Resources for Health* 2: 1–11, https://doi.org/10.1186/1478 -4491-2-12.

Frandsen, Brigham R., Karen E. Joynt, James B. Rebitzer, and Ashish K. Jha. 2015. "Care Fragmentation, Quality, and Costs among Chronically Ill Patients." *American Journal of Managed Care* 21 (5): 355–62.

Freeman, Paul A., Meike Schleiff, Emma Sacks, Bahie M. Rassekh, Sundeep Gupta, and Henry B. Perry. 2017. "Comprehensive Review of the Evidence Regarding the Effectiveness of Community-Based Primary Health Care in Improving Maternal, Neonatal and Child Health: 4. Child Health Findings." *Journal of Global Health* 7 (1), https://doi.org/10.7189/jogh.07.010904.

Frehywot, Seble, Fitzhugh Mullan, Perry W. Payne, and Heather Ross. 2010. "Compulsory Service Programmes for Recruiting Health Workers in Remote and Rural Areas: Do They Work?" *Bulletin of the World Health Organization* 88 (5): 364–70, https://doi.org/10.2471/BLT.09.071605.

Frenk, Julio. 2009. "Reinventing Primary Health Care: The Need for Systems Integration." *The Lancet* 374 (9684): 170–73, https://doi.org/10.1016/S0140 -6736(09)60693-0: 1923-58.

Frenk, Julio, Lincoln Chen, Zulfiqar A. Bhutta, Jordan Cohen, Nigel Crisp, Timothy Evans, Harvey Fineberg, et al. 2010. "Health Professionals for a New Century: Transforming Education to Strengthen Health Systems in an Interdependent World." *The Lancet* 376 (9756): 1923–58.

Gandhi, Tejal K., Allen Kachalia, Eric J. Thomas, Ann Louise Puopolo, Catherine Yoon, Troyen A. Brennan, and David M. Studdert. 2006. "Missed and Delayed Diagnoses in the Ambulatory Setting: A Study of Closed Malpractice Claims." *Annals of Internal Medicine* 145 (7): 488–96**.**

Gaziano, Thomas A., Shafika Abrahams-Gessel, Catalina A. Denman, Carlos Mendoze Montano, Masuma Khanam, Thandi Puoane, and Naomi S. Levitt. 2015. "An Assessment of Community Health Workers' Ability to Screen for Cardiovascular Disease Risk with a Simple, Non-Invasive Risk Assessment Instrument in Bangladesh, Guatemala, Mexico, and South Africa: An Observational Study." *The Lancet Global Health* 3 (9): e556–63, https://doi .org/10.1016/S2214-109X(15)00143-6.

Genries, Marie. 2020. "Food, Water and Masks: South Korea's COVID-19 Quarantine Kits." The Observers, France 24, May 3.

Gera, Tarun, Dheeraj Shah, Paul Garner, Marty Richardson, and Harshpal S. Sachdev. 2016. "Integrated Management of Childhood Illness (IMCI) Strategy for Children under Five." *Cochrane Database of Systematic Reviews* 6: CD010123, https://doi.org/10.1002/14651858.CD010123.pub2.

Gilbert, John H.V., Jean Yan, and Steven J. Hoffman. 2010. "A WHO Report: Framework for Action on Interprofessional Education and Collaborative Practice." *Journal of Allied Health* 39 (Suppl. 1): 196–97.

Glandon, Douglas, Ankita Meghani, Nasreen Jesani, Mary Qui, and Sara Bennett. 2018. "Identifying Health Policy and Systems Research Priorities on Multisectoral Collaboration for Health in Low-Income and Middle-Income Countries." *BMJ Global Health* 3: https://doi.org/10.1136/bmjgh-2018-000970.

Glassman, Amanda, Denishan Duran, Lisa Fleisher, Daniel Singer, Rachel Sturke, Gustavo Angeles, Jodi Charles, et al. 2013. "Impact of Conditional Cash Transfers on Maternal and Newborn Health." *Journal of Health, Population, and Nutrition* 31 (4): S48–S66.

Glassman, Amanda, Ursula Giedion, and Peter C. Smith. 2017. *What's In, What's Out: Designing Benefits for Universal Health Coverage.* Washington, DC: Center for Global Development.

Global Health Workforce Alliance (the Alliance) et al. "Global Experience of Community Health Workers for Delivery of Health Related Millennium Development Goals: A Systematic Review, Country Case Studies, and Recommendations for Integration into National Health Systems." *Annual Review of Medicine* 34 (1983): 413–27.

Golding, Nick, Roy Burstein, Joshua Longbottom, Annie J. Browne, Nancy Fullman, Aaron Osgood-Zimmerman, Lucas Earl, and others. 2017. "Mapping Under-5 and Neonatal Mortality in Africa, 2000–15: A Baseline Analysis for the Sustainable Development Goals." *The Lancet* 390 (10108): 2171–82.

Gonçalves, Sónia. 2014. "The Effects of Participatory Budgeting on Municipal Expenditures and Infant Mortality in Brazil." *World Development* 53: 94–110, https://doi.org/10.1016/j.worlddev.2013.01.009.

Goodman, Rachel B., and Thomas B. Ferrante. 2020. "COVID-19: States Waive In-State Licensing Requirements for Health Care Providers." *Insights* (blog), March 17, https://www.foley.com/en/insights/publications/2020/03/covid-19 -states-waive-licensing-requirements.

Gottret, P., G. J. Schieber, and H. R. Waters. 2008. *Good Practices in Health Financing: Lessons from Reforms in Low- and Middle-Income Countries.* Washington, DC: World Bank.

Grobler, Liesl, Be J. Marais, S. A. Mabunda, P. N. Marindi, Helmuth Reuter, and Jimmy Volmink. 2015. "Interventions for Increasing the Proportion of Health Professionals Practising in Rural and Other Underserved Areas." Cochrane Database of Systematic Reviews 30: 6: CD005314.

Habicht, Triin, Marge Reinap, Kaija Kasekamp, Riina Sikkut, Laura Aaben, and Ewout van Ginneken. 2018. "Estonia: Health System Review." *Health Systems in Transition* 20 (1): 1–189.

Hafez, Reem. 2018. "Nigeria Health Financing System Assessment." Health, Nutrition and Population Discussion Paper, World Bank, Washington, DC. https://doi .org/10.1596/30174.

Haggerty, Jeannie L., Robert J. Reid, George K. Freeman, Barbara H. Starfield, Carol E. Adair, and Rachael McKendry. 2003. "Continuity of Care: A Multidisciplinary Review." *British Medical Journal* 327(7425):1219–21, https://doi.org/10.1136 /bmj.327.7425.1219.

Hall, Laura Lee. 2019. "Plan-Do-Study-Act (PDSA): Four STEPS to Using PDSA within Your Practice." 1–11. American Medical Association, Chicago, Illinois.

Hall, Mark A. 2011. "Risk Adjustment under the Affordable Care Act: A Guide for Federal and State Regulators." Issue Brief, The Commonwealth Fund 7: 1–12.

Halter, Mary, Vari Drennan, Kaushik Chattopadhyay, Wilfred Carneiro, Jennnifer Yiallouros, Simon de Lusignan, Heather Gage, Jonathan Gabe, and Robert Grant. 2013. "The Contribution of Physician Assistants in Primary Care: A Systematic Review." *BMC Health Services Research 13* (223), https://doi .org/10.1186/1472-6963-13-223.

Hammick, M. D. Freeth, I. Koppel, S. Reeves, and H. Barr. 2007. "A Best Evidence Systematic Review of Interprofessional Education: BEME Guide No. 9." *Medical Teacher*, 735–51, https://doi.org/10.1080/01421590701682576.

Hardey, Michael. 1999. "Doctor in the House: The Internet as a Source of Lay Health Knowledge and the Challenge to Expertise." *Sociology of Health and Illness* 21 (6): 820–35, https://doi.org/10.1111/1467-9566.00185.

Hashiguchi, Tiago Cravo Oliveira. 2020. "Bringing Health Care to the Patient: An Overview of the Use of Telemedicine in OECD Countries." OECD Health Working Papers 116. OECD Publishing, Paris. https://www.oecd-ilibrary.org/social-issues -migration-health/bringing-health-care-to-the-patient_8e56ede7-en.

Hatswell, Anthony J. 2020. "Learnings for Health Economics from the Early Stages of the COVID-19 Pandemic." *PharmacoEconomics Open* 4: 203–5, https://doi .org/10.1007/s41669-020-00216-9.

Heckman, James J., and Tim Kautz. 2012. "Hard Evidence on Soft Skills." *Labour Economics* 19 (4): 451–64, https://doi.org/10.1016/j.labeco.2012.05.014.

Hildebrandt, Helmut, C. Hermann, R. Knittel, M. Ricjter-Reichhelm, A. Siegel, and W. Witzenrath. 2010. "Gesundes Kinzigtal Integrated Care: Improving Population Health by a Shared Health Gain Approach and a Shared Savings Contract." *International Journal of Integrated Care* 10, no. 2, https://doi.org/10.5334/ijic.539.

Hildebrandt, Helmut, Alexander Pimperl, Timo Schulte, Christopher Hermann, Harald Riedel, Ingrid Schubert, et al. 2015. "Pursuing the Triple Aim: Evaluation of the Integrated Care System Gesundes Kinzigtal: Population Health, Patient Experience and Cost-Effectiveness." *Bundesgesundheitsblatt - Gesundheitsforschung - Gesundheitsschutz* 58 (4–5): 383–92.

Hirth, Victor A., G. Paul Eleazer, and Maureen Dever-Bumba. 2008. "A Step toward Solving the Geriatrician Shortage." *American Journal of Medicine* 121 (3): 247–51, https://doi.org/10.1016/j.amjmed.2007.10.030.

Hoeft, Theresa J., John C. Fortnoy, Vikram Patel, and Jürgen Unützer. 2018. "Task-Sharing Approaches to Improve Mental Health Care in Rural and Other Low-Resource Settings: A Systematic Review." *Journal of Rural Health* 34, no. 1: 48–62, https://doi.org/10.1111/jrh.12229.

Hoffman, Jan. 2020. "'I Can't Turn My Brain Off': PTSD and Burnout Threaten Medical Workers." *New York Times,* https://www.nytimes.com/2020/05/16/health /coronavirus-ptsd-medical-workers.html.

Horberg, Michael A., Leo B. Hurley, William James Towner, Michael W. Allerton, Beth Ting-Ting Tang, Sheryl Lynn Catz, et al. 2012. "Determination of Optimized Multidisciplinary Care Team for Maximal Antiretroviral Therapy Adherence." *Journal of Acquired Immune Deficiency Syndrome* 60 (2): 183–90, https://doi .org/10.1097/QAI.0b013e31824bd605.

Horton, Susan. 2017. "Cost-Effectiveness Analysis in Disease Control Priorities, Third Edition." In *Disease Control Priorities, Third Edition* (Volume 9*): Improving Health and Reducing Poverty,* 145–56. Washington, DC: World Bank, https://doi .org/10.1596/978-1-4648-0527-1_ch7.

Hu, Deying, Yue Kong, Wengang Li, Quiying Han, Xin Zhang, Li Xia Zhu, Su Wei Wan, Qu Shen, et al. 2020. "Frontline Nurses' Burnout, Anxiety, Depression, and Fear Statuses and Their Associated Factors during the COVID-19 Outbreak in Wuhan, China: A Large-Scale Cross-Sectional Study." *EClinicalMedicine* 24: 100424, https://doi.org/10.1016/j.eclinm.2020.100424.

Hunter, Benjamin M., Sean Harrison, Anayda Portela, and Debra Bick. 2017. "The Effects of Cash Transfers and Vouchers on the Use and Quality of Maternity Care Services: A Systematic Review." *PLoS ONE* 12, https://doi.org/10.1371 /journal.pone.0173068.

Hussain, Sameera, Dena Javadi, Jean Andrey, Abdul Ghaffer, and Roger Labonté. 2020. "Health Intersectoralism in the Sustainable Development Goal Era: From Theory to Practice." *Globalization and Health* 16 (15), https://doi.org/10.1186 /s12992-020-0543-1.

Hussein, Shereen, and Jill Manthorpe. 2005. "An International Review of the Long-Term Care Workforce: Policies and Shortages." *Journal of Aging and Social Policy* 17 (4): 75–94, https://doi.org/10.1300/J031v17n04_05.

Hussein, Shouneez Yousuf, De Wet Swanepoel, Leigh Biagio de Jager, Hermanus C. Myburgh, Robert H. Eikelboom, and Jannie Hugo. 2016. "Smartphone Hearing Screening in MHealth Assisted Community-Based Primary Care." *Journal of Telemedicine and Telecare* 22 (7): 405–12, https://doi .org/10.1177/1357633X15610721.

Hussey, Peter S.Eric C. Schneider, Robert S. Rudin, et al. 2014. "Continuity and the Costs of Care for Chronic Disease." *JAMA Internal Medicine* 174 (5): 742–48, https://doi.org/10.1001/jamainternmed.2014.245.

Iacobucci, Gareth. 2018. "Cervical Screening: GP Leaders Slam Capita over Failure to Send Up to 48,500 Letters." *BMJ* 363: k4832, https://doi.org/10.1136/bmj.k4832.

Ihekweazu, Chikwe, and Emmanuel Agogo. 2020. "Africa's Response to COVID-19." 1 *BMC Med* 18 (151). https://doi.org/10.1186/s12916-020-01622-w.

Imison, Candace, and Richard Bohmer. 2013. "NHS and Social Care Workforce: Meeting Our Needs Now and in the Future?" *Time to Think Differently: Perspectives*, The King's Fund, London.

Interprofessional Educational Collaborative. 2016. "Core Competencies for Interprofessional Collaborative Practice: 2016 Update." Interprofessional Education Collaborative, Washington, DC. https://hsc.unm.edu/ipe/resources /ipec-2016-core-competencies.pdf.

Islam, Sufia, Rizwanul Islam, Fouzia Mannan, Sabera Rahman, and Tahiva Islam. 2020. "COVID-19 Pandemic: An Analysis of the Healthcare, Social and Economic Challenges in Bangladesh." *Progress in Disaster Science* 8: 100135, https://doi .org/10.1016/j.pdisas.2020.100135.

Jackson, George L., Benjamin J. Powers, Ranee Chatterjee, Janet Prvu Bettger, Alex R. Kemper, Vic Hasselblad, Rowena J. Dolor, et al. 2013. "The Patient-Centered Medical Home: A Systematic Review." *Annals of Internal Medicine* 158 (3): 169–78, https://doi.org/10.7326/0003-4819-158-3-201302050-00579.

Jakab, Melitta, Tamas Evetovits, and David McDaid. 2018. "Health Financing Strategies to Support Scale-up of Core Noncommunicable Disease Interventions and Services," World Health Organization Regional Office for Europe, Copenhagen, http://eprints.lse.ac.uk/90269/.

Jakab, Melitta, Jill Farrington, Liesbeth Borgermans, and Frederiek Mantingh, eds. 2018. *Health Systems Respond to Noncommunicable Diseases: Time for Ambition.* Copenhagen: WHO Regional Office for Europe, https://www.euro.who.int/__data/assets/pdf_file/0009/380997/Book-NCD-HS.pdf.

Jamison, Dean T., Ala Alwan, Charles Mock, Rachel Nugent, David Watkins, et al. 2018. "Universal Health Coverage and Intersectoral Action for Health: Key Messages from Disease Control Priorities, 3rd Edition." *The Lancet* 391 (10125), 1108–20, https://doi.org/10.1016/S0140-6736(17)32906-9.

Jennings, Mary Carol, Subarna Pradhan, Meike Schleiff, Emma Sacks, Paul A. Freeman, Sundeep Gupta, et al. 2017. "A Comprehensive Review of the Evidence Regarding the Effectiveness of Community-Based Primary Health Care in Improving Maternal, Neonatal and Child Health: 2. Maternal Health Findings." *Journal of Global Health* 7 (1): 010902 https://doi.org/10.7189/jogh.07.010902.

Johanson, Anne S. 2015. "Strategic Planning for Health: A Case Study from Turkey." https://apps.who.int/iris/handle/10665/154199.

John, James Rufus, Hir Jani, Kath Peters, Kingsley Agho, and W. Kathy Tannous. 2020. "The Effectiveness of Patient-Centred Medical Home-Based Models of Care versus Standard Primary Care in Chronic Disease Management: A Systematic Review and Meta-Analysis of Randomised and Non-Randomised Controlled Trials." *International Journal of Environmental Research and Public Health* 17 (18): 1–50, https://doi.org/10.3390/ijerph17186886.

John, Janice, Leah Zallman, and Jessamyn Blau. 2020. "Our Hospital's Community Management Strategy for Covid-19 Works—Yours Can, Too." *STAT,* https://www.statnews.com/2020/04/23/community-management-strategy-for-covid-19-works/.

Johnson, Ari D., Oumar Thiero, Caroline Whidden, Belco Poudiougou, Djoumé Diakité, Fousséni Traoré, Salif Samaké, Diakalia Koné, Ibrahim Cissé, and Kassoum Kayentao. 2018. "Proactive Community Case Management and Child Survival in Periurban Mali." *BMJ Global Health* 3 (2): 1–10, https://doi.org/10.1136/bmjgh-2017-000634.

Joshi, Rohina, Mohammed Alim, Andre-Pascal Kengne, Stephen Jan, Pallab K. Maulik, David Peoiris, and Anushka A. Patel. 2014. "Task Shifting for Non-Communicable Disease Management in Low and Middle Income Countries: A Systematic Review." *PLoS ONE* (August) https://doi.org/10.1371/journal.pone.0103754.

Jowett, Matthew, and Joe Kutzin. 2015. "Raising Revenues for Health in Support of UHC: Strategic Issues for Policy Makers." Health Financing Policy Brief No. 1, Health Systems Governance and Financing, World Health Organization.

Juliani, Carmen, Maura MacPhee, and Wilza Spiri. 2017. "Brazilian Specialists' Perspectives on the Patient Referral Process." *Healthcare* 5 (1): 4, https://doi.org/10.3390/healthcare5010004.

Jünger, Jana, and Volker Köllner. 2003. "Integration Eines Kommunikationstrainings in Die Klinische Lehre - Beispiele Aus Den Reformstudiengängen Der Universitäten Heidelberg Und Dresden - [Integration of a Doctor/Patient-Communication-Training into Clinical Teaching. Examples from the Reform-Cu]."

Psychotherapie Psychosomatik Medizinische Psychologie, 53 (2), 56–64, https://doi.org/10.1055/s-2003-36962.

Kaiser, Kai, Caryn Bredenkamp, and Roberto Iglesias. 2016. S*in Tax Reform in the Philippines : Transforming Public Finance, Health, and Governance for More Inclusive Development.* Directions in Development–Countries and Regions. Washington, DC: World Bank, http://hdl.handle.net/10986/24617.

Kamerow, Douglas B. 2018. "Is the National Health Service Corps the Answer? (For Placing Family Doctors in Underserved Areas)." *Journal of the American Board of Family Medicine* 31 (4): 499–500, https://doi.org/10.3122/jabfm .2018.04.180153.

Kanchanachitra, Churnrurtai, Magnus Lindelow, Timothy Johnston, Piya Havnoravongchai, Fely Marilyn Lorenzo, Nguyen Lan Huong, Siswanto Agus Wilopo, and Jennifer Frances dela Rosa. 2011. "Human Resources for Health in Southeast Asia: Shortages, Distributional Challenges, and International Trade in Health Services." *The Lancet* 377 (3767): 769–81, https://doi.org/10.1016/S0140 -6736(10)62035-1.

Kane, Leslie. 2018. "Medscape Physician Compensation Report 2018." *Medscape.*

Kane, Robert. 2012. "How to Use the Fishbone Tool for Root Cause Analysis." CMS QAPI.

Kapiriri, Lydia, and Douglas K. Martin. 2006. "Priority Setting in Developing Countries Health Care Institutions: The Case of a Ugandan Hospital." *BMC Health Services Research* 6 (127), https://doi.org/10.1186/1472-6963-6-127.

Khan, Maria, Aueesha Kamran Kamal, Muhammad Islam, Minaz Mawani, Junaid Abdul Razzak, and Omrana Pasha. 2015. "Can Trained Field Community Workers Identify Stroke Using a Stroke Symptom Questionnaire as Well as Neurologists? Adaptation and Validation of a Community Worker Administered Stroke Symptom Questionnaire in a Peri-Urban Pakistani Community." *Journal of Stroke and Cerebrovascular Diseases* 24 (1): 91–99, https://doi.org/10.1016/j .jstrokecerebrovasdis.2014.07.030.

KICSS 2018. The 13th International Conference on Knowledge, Information and Creativity Support Systems, Pattaya, Thailand.

Kirsch, Thomas D., Heidi Mosesnon, Moses Moassaquoi, Tolbert G. Nyenswah, Rachel Goodermote, et al. 2017. "Impact of Interventions and the Incidence of Ebola Virus Disease in Liberia–Implications for Future Epidemics." *Health Policy and Planning* 32 (2): 205–14, https://doi.org/10.1093/heapol/czw113.

Kripalani, Sunil, Frank LeFevre, Christopher O. Phillips, et al. 2007. "Deficits in Communication and Information Transfer Between Hospital-Based and Primary Care Physicians: Implications for Patient Safety and Continuity of Care." *Journal of the American Medical Association* 297 (8): 831–41, https://doi.org/10.1001 /jama.297.8.831.

Kumpunen, Stephanie, Rebecca Rosen, Lucia Kossarova, and Chris Sherlaw-Johnson. 2017. "Primary Care Home: Evaluating a New Model of Primary Care." Nuffield Trust, https://www.nuffieldtrust.org.uk/files/2017-08/pch-report-final.pdf.

Kunckler, Margot, et al. 2017. "Cervical Cancer Screening in a Low-Resource Setting: A Pilot Study on an HPV-Based Screen-and-Treat Approach." *Cancer Medicine* 6 (7): 1752–61, https://doi.org/10.1002/cam4.1089.

Labrique, Alain B., et al. 2018. "Best Practices in Scaling Digital Health in Low and Middle Income Countries." *Globalization and Health* 14 (103), https://doi .org/10.1186/s12992-018-0424-z.

Ladhani, Sheliza, and Kathleen C. Sitter. 2020. "Conditional Cash Transfers: A Critical Review." *Development Policy Review* 38, no. 1: 28–41, https://doi.org/10.1111 /dpr.12416.

Lagarde, Mylene, Andy Haines, and Natasha Palmer. 2009. "The Impact of Conditional Cash Transfers on Health Outcomes and Use of Health Services in Low and Middle Income Countries." *Cochrane Database of Systematic Reviews* 4 (8137), https://doi.org/10.1002/14651858.CD008137.

Lagarde, Mylene, Andy Haines, and Natasha Palmer. 2014. "Conditional Cash Transfers for Improving Uptake of Health Interventions in Low- and Middle-Income Countries." *Journal of the American Medical Association* 298 (16): 1900–1910.

Lagarde, Mylene, and Natasha Palmer. 2008. "The Impact of User Fees on Health Service Utilization in Low- and Middle-Income Countries: How Strong Is the Evidence?" *Bulletin of the World Health Organization* 86 (11), https://doi.org/10.2471/BLT.07.049197.

Lagarde, Mylene, and Natasha Palmer. 2011. "The Impact of User Fees on Access to Health Services in Low- and Middle-Income Countries," *Cochrane Database of Systematic Reviews* 4 (9094), https://doi.org/10.1002/14651858.cd009094.

Lake, Rebecca, Andrew Georgiou, Julie li, Mary Byrne, Maureen Robinson, and Johanna I. Westbrook. 2017. "The Quality, Safety and Governance of Telephone Triage and Advice Services—An Overview of Evidence from Systematic Reviews." *BMC Health Services Research* 17: 614, https://doi.org/10.1186/s12913-017-2564-x.

Langenbrunner, John C., Cheryl Cashin, and Sheila O'Dougherty. 2009. *Designing and Implementing Health Care Provider Payment Systems: How-to Manuals.* Washington, DC: World Bank, https://openknowledge.worldbank.org/handle/10986/13806.

Langenbrunner, John C., and Aparnaa Somanathan. 2011. "Financing Health Care in East Asia and the Pacific: Best Practices and Remaining Challenges Human Development." *Directions in Development: Human Development.* Washington, DC: World Bank, https://openknowledge.worldbank.org/handle/10986/2321.

Langenbrunner, John C., and M. M. Wiley. 2002. "Hospital Payment Mechanisms: Theory and Practice in Transition Countries." In *Hospitals in a Changing Europe,* ed. by M. McKee and J. Healy. Buckingham, UK: Open University Press.

Lassi, Zohra S., Batool A. Haider, and Zulfiqar A. Bhutta. 2010. "Community-Based Intervention Packages for Reducing Maternal and Neonatal Morbidity and Mortality and Improving Neonatal Outcomes," *Cochrane Database of Systematic Reviews* 11 (7754), https://doi.org/10.1002/14651858.cd007754.pub2.

Lee, Albert, and Antonio AT Chuh. 2010. "Facing the Threat of Influenza Pandemic: Roles of and Implications to General Practitioners." *BMC Public Health* 10 (661), https://doi.org/10.1186/1471-2458-10-661.

Lee, Albert, and Wiliam Wong. 2003. "Primary Care during the SARS Outbreak." *British Journal of General Practice* 53 (494): 733, https://bjgp.org/content/53/494/733.

Lehmann, Joel, Bernard Muture, Martin Matu, and Miriam Schneidman. 2018. "Performance Evaluation of Public Health Laboratories in Kenya." Health, Nutrition and Population Discussion Paper, World Bank, Washington, DC. https://openknowledge.worldbank.org/handle/10986/29781.

Levesque, Jean Frédéric, Mylaine Breton, Nicolas Senn, Pascale Levesque, Pierre Bergeron, and Denis A. Roy. 2013. "The Interaction of Public Health and Primary Care: Functional Roles and Organizational Models that Bridge Individual and Population Perspectives." *Public Health Reviews* 35 (14), https://doi.org/10.1007/bf03391699.

Levesque, Jean Frédéric, Mark F. Harris, and Grant Russell. 2013. "Patient-Centred Access to Health Care: Conceptualising Access at the Interface of Health Systems

and Populations." *International Journal for Equity in Health* 12 (18), https://doi
.org/10.1186/1475-9276-12-18.

Levy, Santiago. 2006. *Progress Against Poverty: Sustaining Mexico's Progresa-
Oportunidades Program on JSTOR*. Washington, DC: Brookings Institution
Press.

Lewin, Simon, Susan Munabi-Babigumira, Claire Glenton, Karen Daniels, Xavier
Bosch-Capblanch, et al. 2010. "Lay Health Workers in Primary and Community
Health Care for Maternal and Child Health and the Management of Infectious
Diseases." *Cochrane Database of Systematic Reviews* 3 (4015), https://doi
.org/10.1002/14651858.CD004015.pub3.

Liddy, Clare, et al. 2019. "A Systematic Review of Asynchronous, Provider-to-Provider,
Electronic Consultation Services to Improve Access to Specialty Care Available
Worldwide," *Telemedicine and E-Health* 25 (3): 184–98, https://doi.org/10.1089
/tmj.2018.0005.

Lindley, Megan C., et al. 2008. "The Role of Schools in Strengthening Delivery of
New Adolescent Vaccinations." *Pediatrics* 121 (Supp. 1): S46–S54, https://doi
.org/10.1542/peds.2007-1115F.

Locke, Tim, and Véronique Duquéroy. 2018. "UK Doctors' Salary Report." Medscape.

Longombe, Ahuka O. 2009. "Medical Schools in Rural Areas: Necessity or
Aberration?" *Rural and Remote Health* 9 (3): 1131, https://www.rrh.org.au
/journal/article/1131.

Lorgelly, Paula K., and Amanda Adler. 2020. "Impact of a Global Pandemic on Health
Technology Assessment." *Applied Health Economics and Health Policy* 18 (3):
339–43, https://doi.org/10.1007/s40258-020-00590-9.

Lutfiyya, May Nawal, et al. 2019. "The State of the Science of Interprofessional
Collaborative Practice: A Scoping Review of the Patient Health-Related
Outcomes Based Literature Published between 2010 and 2018." *PLoS ONE* 14 (6):
1–18, https://doi.org/10.1371/journal.pone.0218578.

Macinko, James, et al. 2010. "Major Expansion of Primary Care in Brazil Linked
to Decline in Unnecessary Hospitalization." *Health Affairs* 29 (12): 2149–60,
https://doi.org/10.1377/hlthaff.2010.0251.

Macinko, James, and Matthew J. Harris. 2015. "Brazil's Family Health Strategy:
Delivering Community-Based Primary Care in a Universal Health System."
New England Journal of Medicine 372 (2): 2177–81, https://doi.org/10.1056
/nejmp1501140.

Macinko, James, Matthew J. Harris, and Marcia Gomes Rocha. 2017. "Brazil's
National Program for Improving Primary Care Access and Quality (PMAQ):
Fulfilling the Potential of the World's Largest Payment for Performance System
in Primary Care." *Journal of Ambulatory Care Management* 40 (2): S4–11,
https://doi.org/10.1097/JAC.0000000000000189.

Maldonado, Jose Manuel Santos de Varge, Alexandre Barbosa Marques, and
Antonio Cruz. 2016. "Telemedicine: Challenges to Dissemination in Brazil."
Cadernos de Saude Publica 32, https://doi.org/10.1590/0102-311X00155615.

Marmot, Michael, et al. 2008. "Closing the Gap in a Generation: Health Equity
Through Action on the Social Determinants of Health." *The Lancet* 372 (9650):
1661–69, https://doi.org/10.1016/S0140-6736(08)61690-6.

Marquez, Patricio V., and Jaime Nicolas Bayona Garcia. 2019. "Paradigm Shift: Peru
Leading the Way in Reforming Mental Health Services," World Bank Blogs,
March 25, https://blogs.worldbank.org/health/paradigm-shift-peru-leading
-way-reforming-mental-health-services.

Mars, Maurice. 2013. "Telemedicine and Advances in Urban and Rural Healthcare Delivery in Africa." *Progress in Cardiovascular Diseases* 56 (3): 326–35, https://doi.org/10.1016/j.pcad.2013.10.006.

Martin-Misener, Ruth, et al. 2012. "A Scoping Literature Review of Collaboration Between Primary Care and Public Health." *Primary Health Care Research and Development* 13 (4): 327–46, https://doi.org/10.1017/S1463423611000491.

Mate, Kedar S., et al. 2014. "Accreditation as a Path to Achieving Universal Quality Health Coverage," *Globalization and Health* 10: 68, https://doi.org/10.1186/s12992-014-0068-6.

Mathauer, Inka, Elina Dale, Matthew Jowett, and Joe Kutzin. 2019. "Purchasing Health Services for Universal Health Coverage: How to Make It More Strategic?" Health Financing Policy Brief No. 6, World Health Organization, Geneva.

Maunder, Robert G., et al. 2010. "Computer-Assisted Resilience Training to Prepare Healthcare Workers for Pandemic Influenza: A Randomized Trial of the Optimal Dose of Training." *BMC Health Services Research* 10: 72, https://doi.org/10.1186/1472-6963-10-72.

McBrien, Kerry A., et al. 2018. "Patient Navigators for People with Chronic Disease: A Systematic Review." *PLoS ONE* 13 (2), https://doi.org/10.1371/journal.pone.0191980.

McClellan, Mark, et al. 2019. "Achieving Universal Health Coverage through Value-Based Care and Public-Private Collaboration." Brookings, Washington, DC, https://www.brookings.edu/blog/future-development/2019/09/20/achieving-universal-health-coverage-through-value-based-care-and-public-private-collaboration/.

McGuire, Finn, Lavanya Vijayashingham, Anna Vassall, Roy Small, Douglas Webb, Teresa Guthrie, and Michelle Remme. 2019. "Financing Intersectoral Action for Health: A Systematic Review of Co-Financing Models," *Globalization and Health* 15: 86, https://doi.org/10.1186/s12992-019-0513-7.

McPake, Barbara, Nouria Brikci, Giorgio Cometto, Alice Schmidt, and Edson Araujo. 2011. "Removing User Fees: Learning from International Experience to Support the Process," *Health Policy and Planning* 26 (Supp. 2): 104–17, https://doi.org/10.1093/heapol/czr064.

McWhinney, Ian R. 1997. *A Textbook of Family Medicine*. New York: Oxford University Press.

Medicus Healthcare Solutions. 2017. "Physician Licensure Application Fees and Timelines by State." Medicus Healthcare Solutions, Windham, New Hampshire.

Merks, Piotr, et al. 2021. "The Legal Extension of the Role of Pharmacists in Light of the COVID-19 Global Pandemic." *Research in Social and Administrative Pharmacy* 17 (1): 1807–12, https://doi.org/10.1016/j.sapharm.2020.05.033.

MOHLTC (Ministry of Health and Long-Term Care). n.d. "Q&A : Understanding Family Health Teams," Family Health Teams, Ontario MOHLTC, https://www.health.gov.on.ca/en/pro/programs/fht/fht_understanding.aspx.

Montagu, Dominic. 2002. "Franchising of Health Services in Low-Income Countries," *Health Policy and Planning* 17 (2): 121–30, https://doi.org/10.1093/heapol/17.2.121.

Montagu, Dominic, and Catherine Goodman. 2016. "Prohibit, Constrain, Encourage, or Purchase: How Should We Engage with the Private Health-Care Sector?" *The Lancet* 388, (10044): 613–21, https://doi.org/10.1016/S0140-6736(16)30242-2.

Montagu, Dominic, et al. 2016. "Recent Trends in Working with the Private Sector to Improve Basic Healthcare: A Review of Evidence and Interventions." *Health Policy and Planning* 31 (8), 1117–32, https://doi.org/10.1093/heapol/czw018.

Muldoon, Laura, et al. 2010. "Community Orientation in Primary Care Practices: Results from the Comparison of Models of Primary Health Care in Ontario Study." *Canadian Family Physician* 56 (7): 676–83.

Naledi, Tracey, Peter Barron, and Helen Schneider. 2011. "Primary Health Care in SA since 1994 and Implications of the New Vision for PHC Re-Engineering." *South African Health Review* (1), 17–28.

Nasmith, Louise. 2000. "Licence Requirements for International Medical Graduates: Should National Standards Be Adopted?" *Canadian Medical Association Journal* 162 (6): 795–96.

Necochea, Edgar, and Débora Bossemeyer. 2005. *Standards-Based Management and Recognition: A Field Guide*, Jhpiego.

Nepomnyashchiy, Lyudmila, et al. 2020a. "COVID-19: Africa Needs Unprecedented Attention to Strengthen Community Health Systems." *The Lancet* 396 (10245): 150–52, https://doi.org/10.1016/S0140-6736(20)31532-4.

Nepomnyashchiy, Lyudmila, et al. 2020b. "Protecting Community Health Workers PPE Needs and Recommendations for Policy Action." Center for Global Development, https://www.cgdev.org/publication/protecting-community-health-workers-ppe-needs-and-recommendations-policy-action.

New Zealand Treasury. 2019. *The Wellbeing Budget 2019*, https://www.treasury.govt.nz/sites/default/files/2019-05/b19-wellbeing-budget.pdf.

Nguyen, Nhan Phuc Thanh, et al. 2020. "Preventive Behavior of Vietnamese People in Response to the COVID-19 Pandemic." *PLoS ONE* 15 (9): e0238830, https://doi.org/10.1371/journal.pone.0238830.

Nnko, Soori, et al. 2016. "Perceptions, Attitude and Uptake of Rapid Syphilis Testing Services in Antenatal Clinics in North-Western Tanzania." *Health Policy and Planning* 31 (5): 667–73, https://doi.org/10.1093/heapol/czv116.

Nyonator, Frank K., et al. 2005. "The Ghana Community-Based Health Planning and Services Initiative for Scaling up Service Delivery Innovation." *Health Policy and Planning* 20, (1): 25–34, https://doi.org/10.1093/heapol/czi003.

Nyweide, David J., et al. 2013. "Continuity of Care and the Risk of Preventable Hospitalization in Older Adults." *Journal of the American Medical Association–Internal Medicine* 173 (20): 1879–85, https://doi.org/10.1001/jamainternmed.2013.10059.

OECD (Organisation for Economic Co-operation and Development). 2016a. "Better Ways to Pay for Health Care." OECD Publishing, https://www.oecd-ilibrary.org/social-issues-migration-health/better-ways-to-pay-for-health-care_9789264258211-en.

OECD (Organisation for Economic Co-operation and Development). 2016b. "Health Workforce Policies in OECD Countries: Right Jobs, Right Skills, Right Place." OECD Publishing, https://www.oecd.org/publications/health-workforce-policies-in-oecd-countries-9789264239517-en.htm.

OECD (Organisation for Economic Co-operation and Development). 2020a. *Realising the Potential of Primary Health Care*. OECD Health Policy Studies, OECD Publishing, https://doi.org/10.1787/a92adee4-en.

OECD (Organisation for Economic Co-operation and Development). 2020b. "Beyond Containment: Health Systems Responses to Covid-19 in the OECD." *Tackling Coronavirus (COVID-19): Contributing to a Global Effort*, OECD Publishing, Paris.

Oelmaier, Tobias. 2012. "Germany Looks to China for Nursing Support." *Deutsche Welle (DW)*, https://www.dw.com/en/germany-looks-to-china-for-nursing -support/a-16310640.

Ohannessian, Robin, Tu Anh Duong, and Anna Odone. 2020. "Global Telemedicine Implementation and Integration within Health Systems to Fight the COVID-19 Pandemic: A Call to Action." *JMIR Public Health and Surveillance* 6 (2), https://doi .org/10.2196/18810.

Opstelten, Wim, et al. 2009. "BMC Family Practice Threat of an Influenza Pandemic: Family Physicians in the Front Line." *BMC Family Practice* 10 (11), https://doi .org/10.1186/1471-2296-10-11.

PAHO (Pan American Health Organization). 2019. *Universal Health in the 21st Century: 40 Years of Alma-Ata: Report of the High-Level Commission*. Washington, DC: PAHO, https://www.paho.org/en/documents/universal-health -21st-century-40-years-alma-ata-report-high-level-commission-revised.

Painter, Christopher, et al. 2020. "Early Health Technology Assessment for a COVID-19 Vaccine." Center for Global Development, https://www.cgdev.org /blog/early-health-technology-assessment-covid-19-vaccine.

Palagyi, Anna, et al. 2019. "Health System Preparedness for Emerging Infectious Diseases: A Synthesis of the Literature." *Global Public Health* 14 (12): 1847–68, https://doi.org/10.1080/17441692.2019.1614645.

Pandey, Ambarish, et al. 2013. "Smartphone Apps as a Source of Cancer Information: Changing Trends in Health Information-Seeking Behavior." *Journal of Cancer Education* 28 (1): 138–42, https://doi.org/10.1007/s13187-012-0446-9.

Parsons, Matthew, et al. 2012. "Should Care Managers for Older Adults Be Located in Primary Care? A Randomized Controlled Trial." *Journal of the American Geriatrics Society* 60 (1): 86–92, https://doi.org/10.1111/j.1532-5415.2011.03763.x.

Patel, Vikram, et al. 2015. "Assuring Health Coverage for All in India." *The Lancet* 386 (10011): 2422–35, https://doi.org/10.1016/S0140-6736(15)00955-1.

Pavelich, Kirsten, and Sue Berry. 2009. "Realizing the Potential of Integrated Clinical Learning." *Northern Ontario School of Medicine*, https://www.nosm.ca /wp-content/uploads/2018/06/ICL-Report_no-Appendix_for-web.pdf.

Peiris, David, et al. 2014. "Use of MHealth Systems and Tools for Non-Communicable Diseases in Low- and Middle-Income Countries: A Systematic Review." *Journal of Cardiovascular Translational Research* 7 (8): 677–91, https://doi.org/10.1007 /s12265-014-9581-5.

Pesec, Madeline, et al. 2017. "Primary Health Care That Works: The Costa Rican Experience." *Health Affairs* 36 (3:) 531–38, https://doi.org/10.1377 /hlthaff.2016.1319.

PHCPI (Primary Health Care Performance Initiative). 2018. "Improvement Strategies Model: Facility Organization and Management: Team-Based," 13.

PHCPI (Primary Health Care Performance Initiative). 2019. "Improvement Strategies Model: Population Health Management: Community Engagement," Version 1.

Piatti-Fünfkirchen, Moritz, Ali Hashim, and Khuram Farooq. 2019. "Balancing Control and Flexibility in Public Expenditure Management: Using Banking Sector Innovations for Improved Expenditure Control and Effective Service Delivery." Policy Research Working Paper 9029, World Bank, Washington, DC, https://doi .org/10.1596/1813-9450-9029.

Piatti-Fünfkirchen, Moritz, and Pia Schneider. 2018. "From Stumbling Block to Enabler: The Role of Public Financial Management in Health Service Delivery in Tanzania and Zambia." *Health Systems and Reform* 4 (4): 336–45, https://doi.org/10.1080/23288604.2018.1513266.

Pimperl, Alexander, Helmut Hildebrandt, Oliver Groene, Krishna Udayakumar, Jonathan Gonzalez-Smith, Kushal Kadakia, and Andrea Thoumi. 2017. "Case Study: Gesundes Kinzigtal, Germany: Accountable Care in Practice: Global Perspectives." Duke-Margolis Center for Health Policy, Washington, DC.

Pourat, Nadereh, et al. 2015. "In California, Primary Care Continuity Was Associated with Reduced Emergency Department Use and Fewer Hospitalizations." *Health Affairs* 34 (7): 1113–20, https://doi.org/10.1377/hlthaff.2014.1165.

Powell, John A., M. Darvell, and J. A.M. Gray. 2003. "The Doctor, the Patient and the World-Wide Web: How the Internet Is Changing Healthcare." *Journal of the Royal Society of Medicine* 96 (2): 74–76, https://www.ncbi.nlm.nih.gov/pmc/articles/PMC539397/.

Primary Health Care Performance Initiative (PHCPI). n.d. "Improvement Strategies Model: Adjustment to Population Health Management: Innovation & Learning."

Public Health Agency of Canada. 2007. *Crossing Sectors: Experiences in Intersectoral Action, Public Policy and Health*. Ottawa, Canada, https://www.who.int/social_determinants/links/events/crossing_sectors_2007.pdf.

Public Health Agency of Canada and World Health Organization. 2008. *Health Equity Through Intersectoral Action: An Analysis of 18 Country Case Studies*. Ottawa, Canada, and Geneva, Switzerland, http://www.who.int/social_determinants/resources/health_equity_isa_2008_en.pdf.

Qin, Vicky Mengqi, et al. 2018. "The Impact of User Charges on Health Outcomes in Low-Income and Middle-Income Countries: A Systematic Review." *BMJ Global Health* 3: 1–12, https://doi.org/10.1136/bmjgh-2018-001087.

Rabinowitz, Peter M., et al. 2017. "Incorporating One Health into Medical Education," *BMC Medical Education* 17: 45, https://doi.org/10.1186/s12909-017-0883-6.

Raleigh, Veena, et al. 2014. "Integrated Care and Support Pioneers: Indicators for Measuring the Quality of Integrated Care," *Policy Research Innovation Unit*, https://piru.ac.uk/assets/files/IC_and_support_Pioneers-Indicators.pdf.

Rangachari, Pavani, and Jacquelynn L. Woods. 2020. "Preserving Organizational Resilience, Patient Safety, and Staff Retention during COVID-19 Requires a Holistic Consideration of the Psychological Safety of Healthcare Workers." *International Journal of Environmental Research and Public Health* 17 (12): 1–12, https://doi.org/10.3390/ijerph17124267.

Rasanathan, Kumanan, et al. 2017. "Governing Multisectoral Action for Health in Low- and Middle-Income Countries," *PLoS Medicine* 14 (4): 1–9, https://doi.org/10.1371/journal.pmed.1002285.

Rasanathan, Kumanan, et al. 2018. "Governing Multisectoral Action for Health in Low-Income and Middle-Income Countries: An Agenda for the Way Forward," *BMJ Global Health* 3: 1–6, https://doi.org/10.1136/bmjgh-2018-000890.

Rasella, Davide, et al. 2014. "Impact of Primary Health Care on Mortality from Heart and Cerebrovascular Diseases in Brazil: A Nationwide Analysis of Longitudinal Data." *BMJ (Online)* 349, https://doi.org/10.1136/bmj.g4014.

Rechel, Bernd. 2020. "How to Enhance the Integration of Primary Care and Public Health? Approaches, Facilitating Factors and Policy Options." Health Systems and Policy Analysis, Policy Brief 34, ed. World Health Organization. Copenhagen, Denmark, https://apps.who.int/iris/bitstream/handle/10665/330491/Policy-brief-34-1997-8073-eng.pdf.

Reddy, Ashok, et al. 2015. "The Effect of Primary Care Provider Turnover on Patient Experience of Care and Ambulatory Quality of Care," *JAMA Internal Medicine* 175 (7): 1157–62, https://doi.org/10.1001/jamainternmed.2015.1853.

Reeves, Scott, Simon Fletcher, Hugh Barr, Ivan Birch, Sylvain Boet, Nigel Davis, Angus McFadyen, Josette Rivera, and Somon Kitto. 2016. "A BEME Systematic Review of the Effects of Interprofessional Education: BEME Guide No. 39," *Medical Teacher* 38, 7: 656–68 https://doi.org/10.3109/0142159X.2016.1173663.

Results for Development Institute. 2017. "Financing and Payment Models for Primary Health Care: Six Lessons from JLN Country Implementation Experience." Joint Learning Network, Arlington, Virginia.

Ricci-Cabello, Ignacio, et al. 2020. "Impact of Viral Epidemic Outbreaks on Mental Health of Healthcare Workers: A Rapid Systematic Review." MedRxiv, https://doi.org/10.1101/2020.04.02.20048892.

Ridde, Valéry, Abena Asomaning Antwi, Bruno Boidin, Benjamin Chemouni, Fatoumata Hane, and Laurence Touré. 2018. "Time to Abandon Amateurism and Volunteerism: Addressing Tensions between the Alma-Ata Principle of Community Participation and the Effectiveness of Community-Based Health Insurance in Africa." *BMJ Global Health* 3, Supp. 3, https://doi.org/10.1136/bmjgh-2018-001056.

Roberts, A. H. 1979. "Life Expectancy and Causes of Death." In *Severe Accidental Head Injury*, 140–51, New York, NY: Macmillan, https://doi.org/10.1007/978-1-349-04787-1_12.

Robinson, James C. 2001. "Theory and Practice in the Design of Physician Payment Incentives." *Milbank Quarterly* 79 (2): 149–77, https://doi.org/10.1111/1468-0009.00202.

Rocha, Romero, and Rodrigo R. Soares. 2010. "Evaluating the Impact of Community-Based Health Interventions: Evidence from Brazil's Family Health Program." *Health Economics* 19 (S1): 126–158, https://doi.org/10.1002/hec.1607.

Rohde, Jon, et al. 2008. "30 Years after Alma-Ata: Has Primary Health Care Worked in Countries?" *The Lancet* 372 (9642): 950–61, https://doi.org/10.1016/S0140-6736(08)61405-1.

Romano, Max J., Jodi B. Segal, and Craig Evan Pollack. 2015. "The Association Between Continuity of Care and the Overuse of Medical Procedures," *JAMA Internal Medicine* 175 (7): 1148–54, https://doi.org/10.1001/jamainternmed.2015.1340.

Saberi, Parya, et al. 2012. "The Impact of HIV Clinical Pharmacists on HIV Treatment Outcomes: A Systematic Review." *Patient Preference and Adherence*, Dove Press, https://doi.org/10.2147/PPA.S30244.

Sakeah, Evelyn, et al. 2014. "Can Community Health Officer-Midwives Effectively Integrate Skilled Birth Attendance in the Community-Based Health Planning and Services Program in Rural Ghana?" *Reproductive Health* 11: 90, https://doi.org/10.1186/1742-4755-11-90.

Santarone, Kristen, Mark McKenney, and Adel Elkbuli. 2020. "Preserving Mental Health and Resilience in Frontline Healthcare Workers during COVID-19." *American Journal of Emergency Medicine* 38 (7): 1530–31, https://doi.org/10.1016/j.ajem.2020.04.030.

Schweich, Emily. 2020. "Cambridge Health Alliance Develops COVID-19 Community Management Model." America's Essential Hospitals, April 29, https://essentialhospitals.org/quality/cambridge-health-alliance-develops-covid-19-community-management-model/.

Scott, Richard, and Maurice Mars. 2015. "Telehealth in the Developing World: Current Status and Future Prospects." *Smart Homecare Technology and TeleHealth* 3: 25–37, https://doi.org/10.2147/shtt.s75184.

Sheikh, Kabir, Prasanna S. Saligram, and Krishna Hort. 2015. "What Explains Regulatory Failure? Analysing the Architecture of Health Care Regulation in Two Indian States." *Health Policy and Planning* 30 (1): 39–55, https://doi.org/10.1093/heapol/czt095.

Shridhar, Krithiga, et al. 2015. "Cancer Detection Rates in a Population-Based, Opportunistic Screening Model, New Delhi, India." *Asian Pacific Journal of Cancer Prevention* 16 (5): 1953–58, https://doi.org/10.7314/APJCP.2015.16.5.1953.

Sills, Billie W. 2015. "Meaningful Recognition: Recognizing the 'Soft Skills' of Nursing." *Tenn Nurse* 78 (2): 3.

Simoens, Stevens. 2004. "Experiences of Organization for Economic Cooperation and Development Countries with Recruiting and Retaining Physicians in Rural Areas." *Australian Journal of Rural Health* 12, 3:104–11, https://doi.org/10.1111/j.1440-1854.2004.00569.x.

Simonsen, Marianne, Lars Skipper, Niels Skipper, and Peter Rønø Thingholm. 2019. "Discontinuity in Care: Practice Closures among Primary Care Providers and Patient Health." *Economics Working Papers*, 2019-08, Department of Economics and Business Economics, Aarhus University.

Smith, Peter C., and Kalipso Chalkidou. 2017. "Should Countries Set an Explicit Health Benefits Package? The Case of the English National Health Service." *Value in Health* 20 (1): 60–66, https://doi.org/10.1016/j.jval.2016.01.004.

Smits, Helen, Anuwat Supachutikul, and Kedar S. Mate. 2014. "Hospital Accreditation : Lessons from Low- and Middle-Income Countries," *Globalisation and Health* 10, 65. 10.

Soler, Jean Karl, Hakan Yaman, Magdalena Esteva, Frank Dobbs, Radost Spiridonova Asenova, Milica Katic, Zlata Ozvacic, and others for the European General Practice Research Network Burnout Study Group. 2008. "Burnout in European Family Doctors: The EGPRN Study," *Family Practice* 25 (4): 245–65, https://doi.org/10.1093/fampra/cmn038.

Somanathan, Aparnaa, Elyssa Finkel, and Aneesa Arur. 2019. "Strengthening Integrated Care in Central and Eastern Europe." Health, Nutrition, and Population Discussion Paper, World Bank, Washington, DC.

Some, David, et al. 2016. "Task Shifting the Management of Non-Communicable Diseases to Nurses in Kibera, Kenya: Does It Work?," *PLoS ONE* 11 (1): 1–9, https://doi.org/10.1371/journal.pone.0145634.

Sparkes, Susan P., Antonio Durán, and Joseph Kutzin. 2017. "A System-Wide Approach to Analysing Efficiency across Health Programmes," Health Financing Diagnostics & Guidance No. 2, Geneva: World Health Organization.

Sparkes, Susan P., Joseph Kutzin, and Alexandra J. Earle. 2019. "Financing Common Goods for Health: A Country Agenda," *Health Systems and Reform* 5 (4): 322–33, https://doi.org/10.1080/23288604.2019.1659126.

Starfield, Barbara, Leiyu Shi, and James Macinko. 2005. "Contribution of Primary Care to Health Systems and Health," *Milbank Quarterly* 83 (3): 457–502, https://doi.org/10.1111/j.1468-0009.2005.00409.x.

Stenberg, Karin, Odd Hanssen, Melanie Bertram, Callum Brindlye, Andreia Meshreky, Shannon Barkley, and Tessa Tan-Torres Edejer. 2019. "Guide Posts for Investment in Primary Health Care and Projected Resource Needs in 67 Low-Income and Middle-Income Countries: A Modelling Study." *The Lancet Global Health* 7 (11): e1500–1510, https://doi.org/10.1016/S2214 -109X(19)30416-4.

Stone, Robyn, and Mary F. Harahan. 2010. "Improving the Long-Term Care Workforce Serving Older Adults." *Health Affairs* 29 (1): 109–15, https://doi.org/10.1377 /hlthaff.2009.0554.

Strasser, Roger. 2016a. "Delivering on Social Accountability: Canada's Northern Ontario School of Medicine." *The Asia Pacific Scholar* 1 (1): 3–8, https://doi .org/10.29060/taps.2016-1-1/oa1014.

Strasser, Roger. 2016b. "Students Learning Medicine in General Practice in Canada and Australia." *Australian Family Physician* 45 (1): 22–25.

Strasser, Roger, John C. Hogenbirk, Bruce Minore, David C. Marsh, Sue Berry, William G. McReady, and Lisa Graves. 2013. "Transforming Health Professional Education through Social Accountability: Canada's Northern Ontario School of Medicine." *Medical Teacher* 35 (6): 490–96, https://doi.org/10.3109/0142159X.2013.774334.

Strasser, Roger, Paul Worley, Fortunate Cristobal, David C. Marsh, Sue Berry, Sarah Strasser, and Rachel Ellaway. 2015. "Putting Communities in the Driver's Seat: The Realities of Community-Engaged Medical Education." *Academic Medicine* 90 (11) 1466–70, https://doi.org/10.1097/ACM.0000000000000765.

Strasser, Roger, John Hogenbirk, Kristen Jacklin, Marion Maar, Geoffrey Hudson, Wayne Warry, Hoi Cheu, Tim Dubé, and Dean Caron. 2018. "Community Engagement: A Central Feature of NOSM's Socially Accountable Distributed Medical Education." *Canadian Medical Education Journal* 9 (1): e33–e43.

Strasser, Roger, et al. 2018. "Challenges of Capacity and Development for Health System Sustainability." *Healthcare Papers* 17 (3): 18–27, https://doi.org/10.12927 /hcpap.2018.25505.

Stubbs, Brenda W., et al. 2014. "Evaluation of an Intervention Providing HPV Vaccine in Schools." *American Journal of Health Behavior* 38 (1): 92–102, https://doi .org/10.5993/AJHB.38.1.10.

Sukhanberdiyev, Kanat, and Larissa Tikhonova. 2017. "Kazakhstan." Kazakhstan Case Study: Fostering Cooperation between the Health and Social Sectors to Deliver Better Nurturing Care Services, https://nurturing-care.org/resources /nurturing-care-case-study-kazakhstan.pdf.

Sulat, Jaelan Sumo, et al. 2018. "The Impacts of Community-Based HIV Testing and Counselling on Testing Uptake: A Systematic Review." *Journal of Health Research* 32 (2): 152–63, https://doi.org/10.1108/JHR-01-2018-015.

Sumer, Safir, Joanne Shear, and Ahmet Levent Yener. 2019. "Building an Improved Primary Health Care System in Turkey through Care Integration." World Bank, Washington, DC, https://doi.org/10.1596/33098.

Suzuki, Teppei, et al. 2020. "Possibility of Introducing Telemedicine Services in Asian and African Countries." *Health Policy and Technology* 9 (1): 13–22, https://doi .org/10.1016/j.hlpt.2020.01.006.

Tandon, A., and Adrien Dozol. 2019. "Purchasing Integrated Care: Concepts, Trends and Policy Implications." World Bank, Washington, DC.

Tangcharoensathien, Viroj, et al. 2015. "Achieving Universal Health Coverage Goals in Thailand: The Vital Role of Strategic Purchasing." *Health Policy and Planning* 30 (9): 1152–61, https://doi.org/10.1093/heapol/czu120.

Tangcharoensathien, Viroj, et al. 2019. "The Political Economy of UHC Reform in Thailand: Lessons for Low- and Middle-Income Countries." *Health Systems and Reform* 5 (3): 195–208, https://doi.org/10.1080/23288604.2019.1630595.

Teerawattananon, Yot, and Nattha Tritasavit 2015. "A Learning Experience from Price Negotiations for Vaccines." *Vaccine* 33, Supp. 1: A11-A12, https://doi.org/10.1016/j.vaccine.2014.12.050.

Terwindt, Frank, Dheepa Rajan, and Agnes Soucat. 2016. "Priority-Setting for National Health Policies , Strategies and Plans." In *Strategizing National Health in the 21st Century: A Handbook*, edited by Gerard Schmets, Dheepa Rajan, and Sowmya Kadandale, 179–253, Geneva: World Health Organization.

Tesson, Geoffrey L., Geoffrey L. Hudson, Roger Strasser, and Dan Hunt, eds. 2009. "The Making of the Northern Ontario School of Medicine." *Canadian Family Physician* 56 (7): 685.

The Nation–Thailand. 2017. "400,000 Schoolgirls to Be Vaccinated against Human Papilloma Virus." *The Nation*, https://www.nationthailand.com/in-focus/30310318.

Thomas, Latoya, and Gary Capistrant. 2017. *State Telemedicine Gaps Analysis: Physician Practice Standards & Licensure*. Arlington, VA: American Telemedicine Association.

Tsolekile, Lungiswa Primrose, Shafika Abrahams-Gessel, and Thandi Puoane. 2015. "Healthcare Professional Shortage and Task-Shifting to Prevent Cardiovascular Disease: Implications for Low- and Middle-Income Countries." *Current Cardiology Reports* 17: 12, https://doi.org/10.1007/s11886-015-0672-y.

UN General Assembly, Resolution 74/2, Political Declaration of the High-Level Meeting on Universal Health Coverage: Moving Together to Build a Healthier World. 2019. A/RES/74/2 (Oct. 10), https://undocs.org/en/A/RES/74/2.

Vazirani, Anuraag A., et al. 2020. "Blockchain Vehicles for Efficient Medical Record Management." *Npj Digital Medicine* 3 (1), https://doi.org/10.1038/s41746-019-0211-0.

Vimalananda, Varsha G., et al. 2015. "Electronic Consultations (e-Consults) to Improve Access to Specialty Care: A Systematic Review and Narrative Synthesis." *Journal of Telemedicine and Telecare* 21 (6): 323–30.

Viswanathan, Vidya. 2014. "The Rise of the M.D./M.B.A. Degree." *The Atlantic*, September 29, https://www.theatlantic.com/education/archive/2014/09/the-rise-of-the-mdmba-degree/380683/.

Wang, Huihui, et al. 2016. *Ethiopia Health Extension Program*. Washington, DC: World Bank Group, http://Dx.Doi.Org/10.1596/978-1-4648-0815-9.

Wang, Lexin. 2002. "A Comparison of Metropolitan and Rural Medical Schools in China: Which Schools Provide Rural Physicians?" *Australian Journal of Rural Health* 10 (2): 94–98.

Wang, Xuan, et al. 2014 "Effect of Publicly Reporting Performance Data of Medicine Use on Injection Use: A Quasi-Experimental Study." *PLoS ONE* 9 (10): 1–7, https://doi.org/10.1371/journal.pone.0109594.

West, Michael, et al. 1999. "Developing Collective Leadership for Health Care." *Anaesthesist* 48 (9): 607–12.

White, Franklin. 2015. "Primary Health Care and Public Health: Foundations of Universal Health Systems." *Medical Principles and Practice* 24: 103-16, https://doi.org/10.1159/000370197.

WHO (World Health Organization). 2008. *Task Shifting. Global Recommendations and Guidelines*. Geneva, Switzerland: World Health Organization.

WHO (World Health Organization). 2010. *The World Health Report: Health Systems Financing: The Path to Universal Coverage."* World Health Organization, Geneva.

WHO (World Health Organization). 2013. "Transforming and Scaling up Health Professionals' Education and Training." Guidelines, World Health Organization, Geneva.

WHO (World Health Organization). 2016. "Framework on Integrated, People-Centred Health Services: Report by the Secretariat." World Health Organization, Geneva.

WHO (World Health Organization). 2018a. "Multisectoral and Intersectoral Action for Improved Health and Well-Being for All: Mapping of the WHO European Region Governance for a Sustainable Future: Improving Health and Well-Being for All." World Health Organization Regional Office for Europe, Copenhagen, Denmark.

WHO (World Health Organization). 2018b. "Building the Primary Health Care Workforce of the 21st Century." Technical Series on Primary Health Care, World Health Organization, Geneva, Switzerland.

WHO (World Health Organization). 2018c. "Health and Sustainable Development: Telehealth." WHO, http://www.who.int/sustainable-development/health-sector/strategies/telehealth/en/.

WHO (World Health Organization). 2018d. "Budget Matters for Universal Health Coverage: Key Formulation and Classification Issues." Health Financing Policy Brief 4, World Health Organization, Geneva, Switzerland.

WHO (World Health Organization). 2018e. "From Alma-Ata to Astana: Primary Health Care – Reflecting on the Past, Transforming for the Future." Interim Report from the WHO European Region to the Global Conference on Primary Health Care, World Health Organization, Geneva, Switzerland, https://www.who.int/docs/default-source/primary-health-care-conference/phc-regional-report-europe.pdf?sfvrsn=cf2badeb_2.

WHO (World Health Organization). 2019a. *World Health Statistics 2019: Monitoring Health for the SDGs: Sustainable Development Goals.* Geneva, Switzerland: World Health Organization. https://apps.who.int/iris/bitstream/handle/10665/324835/9789241565707-eng.pdf?sequence=9&isAllowed=y.

WHO (World Health Organization). 2019b. "Global Spending on Health: A World in Transition 2019." Global Report, World Health Organization, Geneva, Switzerland.

WHO (World Health Organization) and Asia Pacific Observatory on Health Systems and Policies. 2013. "Dual Practice by Health Workers in South and East Asia: Impact and Policy Options." Policy Brief, World Health Organization, Geneva.

WHO (World Health Organization) and UNICEF (United Nations Children's Fund). 2018. "A Vision for Primary Health Care in the 21st Century." World Health Organization, Geneva, Switzerland.

Williams, Gemma A., Claudia B. Maier, and Giada Scarpetti. 2020. "What Strategies Are Countries Using to Expand Health Workforce Surge Capacity to Treat COVID-19 Patients?" *COVID-19 Health System Response Monitor: Cross-Country Analysis*, https://analysis.covid19healthsystem.org/index.php/2020/04/23/what-strategies-are-countries-using-to-expand-health-workforce-surge-capacity-to-treat-covid-19-patients/.

Williams, Gemma A., Claudia B. Maier, Giada Scarpetti, Antonio Giulio de Belvis, Giovanni Fattore, et al. 2020. "What Strategies Are Countries Using to Expand Health Workforce Surge Capacity to Treat COVID-19 Patients?: Cross-Country Analysis." *COVID-19 Health System Response Monitor*, https://apps.who.int/iris/bitstream/handle/10665/336296/Eurohealth-26-2-51-57-eng.pdf.

Williams, Robert L. 2004. "Motherhood, Apple Pie, and COPC," *Annals of Family Medicine* 2 (2): 100–02, https://doi.org/10.1370/afm.70.

Wilson, David, and Daniel T. Halperin. 2008. "'Know Your Epidemic, Know Your Response': A Useful Approach, If We Get It Right." *The Lancet* 372 (9637): 423–26, https://doi.org/10.1016/S0140-6736(08)60883-1.

Wiwanitkit, Viroj. 2011. "Mandatory Rural Service for Health Care Workers in Thailand." *Rural Remote Health* 11, 1:1583, https://pubmed.ncbi.nlm.nih .gov/21348551/.

Wodchis, Walter P., Peter C. Austin, and David A. Henry. 2016. "A 3-Year Study of High-Cost Users of Health Care." *Canadian Medical Association Journal* 188 (3): 182–88, https://doi.org/10.1503/cmaj.150064.

World Bank. 2005. "Review of Experience of Family Medicine in Europe and Central Asia." Vol. I, World Bank, Washington, DC.

World Bank. 2016. "UHC in Africa: A Framework for Action." World Bank, Washington, DC. https://openknowledge.worldbank.org/handle/10986/26072. License: CC BY 3.0 IGO.

World Bank. 2017a. "Second Annual UHC Financing Forum: Greater Efficiency for Better Health and Financial Protection: Background Paper." World Bank, Washington, DC.

World Bank. 2017b. "Lao PDR: Health Governance and Nutrition Development Project— Additional Financing." World Bank, Washington, DC.

World Bank. 2017c. "Tobacco Tax Reform at the Crossroads of Health and Development: Technical Report of the World Bank Group Global Tobacco Control Program (Vol. 2): Main Report." World Bank, Washington, DC, https://documents.worldbank.org/en/publication/documents-reports /documentdetail/491661505803109617/main-report.

World Bank. 2018a. "Turkish Health Transformation Program and Beyond." World Bank, Washington, DC, https://www.worldbank.org/en/results/2018/04/02 /turkish-health-transformation-program-and-beyond.

World Bank. 2018b. *Rethinking Lagging Regions: Using Cohesion Policy to Deliver on the Potential of Europe's Regions*. Washington, DC: World Bank.

World Bank. 2018c. *Human Capital Project*. World Bank, Washington, DC, https://www.worldbank.org/en/publication/human-capital.

World Bank. 2019a. "High-Performance Health Financing for Universal Health Coverage (Vol. 2): Driving Sustainable, Inclusive Growth in the 21st Century." World Bank, Washington, DC. http://documents.worldbank.org/curated /en/641451561043585615/Driving-Sustainable-Inclusive-Growth-in-the-21st -Century.

World Bank. 2019b. *World Development Report 2019: The Changing Nature of Work*. Washington, DC: World Bank, https://www.worldbank.org/en/publication /wdr2019.

World Bank. 2020. "The Human Capital Index 2020 Update: Human Capital in the Time of COVID-19." World Bank, Washington, DC, https://doi.org /10.1596/34432.

World Bank and WHO (World Health Organization). 2019. *Healthy China: Deepening Health Reform in China: Building High-Quality and Value-Based Service Delivery*. Washington, DC: World Bank and WHO, https://doi.org/10.1596 /978-1-4648-1263-7.

Yang, Lianping, et al. 2014. "Public Reporting Improves Antibiotic Prescribing for Upper Respiratory Tract Infections in Primary Care: A Matched-Pair Cluster-Randomized Trial in China." *Health Research Policy and Systems* 12: 61, https://doi.org/10.1186/1478-4505-12-61.

Yazbeck, Abdo S., and Agnès Soucat. 2019. "When Both Markets and Governments Fail Health." *Health Systems and Reform* 5 (4): 268–79, https://doi.org/10.1080/23288604.2019.1660756.

Yazbeck, Abdo S., William D. Savedoff, William C. Hsiao, Joe Kutzin, Agnès Soucat, Ajay Tandon, and Adam Wagstaff. 2020. "The Case against Labor-Tax-Financed Social Health Insurance for Low-and Low-Middle-Income Countries." *Health Affairs* 39 (5), https://doi.org/10.1377/hlthaff.2019.00874.

Zhang, Yi, Martin Salm, and Arthur van Soest. 2018. "The Effect of Retirement on Healthcare Utilization: Evidence from China." *Journal of Health Economics* 62: 165–77, https://doi.org/10.1016/j.jhealeco.2018.09.009.

Zou, Huachun, Zunyou Wu, Jianping Yu, Min Li, Muhtar Ablimit, Fan Li, and Katharine Poundstone. 2013. "Internet-Facilitated, Voluntary Counseling and Testing (VCT) Clinic-Based HIV Testing among Men Who Have Sex with Men in China." *PLoS ONE* 8 (2); e51919, https://doi.org/10.1371/journal.pone.0051919.

Chapter 5

POLICY
RECOMMENDATIONS

Introduction

The preceding chapters were designed to (1) summarize evidence for primary health care (PHC) as the cornerstone of high-performing health systems, while showing why PHC needs to evolve; (2) identify structural shifts that most PHC models need to undertake to improve outcomes, contain costs, and support system-wide change; (3) propose proven reform steps and implementation strategies that countries can use to drive shifts in care organization, the health workforce, and health financing; and (4) show how countries can optimize domestic and external technical and financial resources to "walk the talk" on reimagined PHC.

Reconfiguring health systems around fit-for-purpose PHC poses major technical challenges, but it is above all a political problem. Solving that problem will depend on buy-in from influential stakeholders, perhaps especially those identified with the health system status quo. Achieving this buy-in, in turn, demands a policy adoption and implementation road map to engage payers, providers, and patients. The road map will vary across countries, reflecting national starting conditions, health and development priorities, political economy, and the path dependency of change processes within each health system. Systems centered around hospitals and specialists will pose particular difficulties for PHC-focused redesign. In all settings, PHC reform will be easier said than done.

As argued throughout this report, the COVID-19 (Coronavirus) tragedy may facilitate PHC-centered health system reform. Indeed, it has to do so, or the tragedy is destined to repeat itself. By exposing flaws in health systems worldwide, the pandemic has shown that these systems need to change—profoundly. To those who have traced the COVID-19 crisis to its roots, the importance of PHC for pending health system reform is clear. As countries complete the emergency phase of pandemic response, both future crisis preparedness and population health outside of crisis times depend on the ability of countries to "integrate core public health functions into a health system based on primary health care with universal health coverage" (WHO 2020, p. 33).

Prerequisites for action

There are three practical prerequisites for translating reimagined PHC into actionable policies and implementation in the wake of COVID-19:

+ **Whole-of-government commitment and leadership**. Building shared political commitment can begin with a data-driven review of the strengths and weaknesses of a country's existing PHC model (Borgès Da Silva et al. 2013). A policy paper or white paper can follow as a basis for consensus building among stakeholders. The dialogue should encompass actors within the health sector (for example, hospitals, medical associations, health insurance funds, and patients' organizations) and beyond it (for example, ministries of finance, agriculture, and the environment and local government authorities). Leaders need both tenacity and tact to maintain the momentum for reforms while incorporating diverse viewpoints. Diversity will ultimately enable broad ownership and successful implementation.

+ **Readiness to invest**. Implementing reimagined PHC will involve significant upfront investment and recurring costs. The COVID-19 crisis makes mobilizing these investments more challenging but also more important than ever. Resources will need to be secured through additional budgetary allocation, reallocations within the health sector, and/or donor financing. Chapter 4 emphasized that general government revenue is the appropriate primary source for PHC financing. In resource-constrained contexts where government funds were already overstretched before COVID-19, external financing from development partners may play a significant role, supporting countries to bridge the gap through interim financing. Long-term sustainability will ultimately require rebalancing resource allocation from hospitals to PHC.

+ **Accountability for outcomes**. Translating vision into action requires a formal accountability framework that sets out agreed roles and responsibilities for stakeholders. A strong framework incorporates tools to measure and evaluate implementation and outcomes, preferably through a set of customized PHC metrics.

With these prerequisites in place, countries can move confidently to design and roll out PHC reforms. What policy actions will governments need to prioritize, and how can development partners help? The remainder of this chapter offers recommendations.

The policy guidance formulated here aligns with the reimagined PHC reform matrix in table 5.1. In the following pages, a first set of recommendations addresses national policy makers. It outlines priority steps for national governments to implement PHC-centered reforms within their health systems. Apart from one consideration about managing the reform process itself, these recommendations are grouped under the three axes discussed in chapter 4: care organization and delivery, health workforce, and financing.

Table 5.1 Key recommendations for fit-for-purpose primary health care

	SERVICE DELIVERY	HEALTH WORKFORCE	FINANCING
For Countries	• Situation assessment (MoH) • Tailor team-based PHC service delivery model to country and local needs[a] (MoH) • Develop implementation plan for team-based service delivery model (with M&E) (MoH, MoF, local governments) • Use data and technology to drive adoption of team-based service delivery model[c] (MoH, MoF, insurance, MoT).	• HRH review[b] and gap analysis, aligned to team-based service model (MoH) • Refresh HRH strategy and policies (including M&E) (MoH, MoL, MoF) • Workforce changes for emergency preparedness and response (MoH, MoF, MoI) • Launch multidisciplinary medical education reforms (MoE, MoH) • Compensation models to promote generalist care and rural practice (MoH, MoF) • Tiered accreditation, tied to reimbursement (MoH, insurance authority, MoF, MoE) • Regulatory reform for telemedicine and labor mobility (MoH, MoL, MoT, insurance)	• Align HF strategy to team-based PHC service model. Prioritize financing from general government revenue. Eliminate user fees. Introduce or raise pro-health taxes (MoH, MoF, insurance authority). • Build emergency planning into HF strategy (MoH) • Adapt benefits package for equitable PHC coverage (MoH, MoF, insurance). • Implement resource mapping and costing for team-based care and PHC benefits package. Develop political strategy for PHC financing goals (MoH, MoF, insurance). • Implement payment reform to promote team-based care, coordination, and quality (MoH, MoF, insurance). • Integrate financing and service delivery data platforms for accountability (MoH, MoF, insurance, MoT).

(Continued)

Table 5.1 Key recommendations for fit-for-purpose primary
health care *(continued)*

	SERVICE DELIVERY	HEALTH WORKFORCE	FINANCING
For Global partnership through the SDG3 Global Action Plan PHC Accelerator	• Support documentation, measurement, evaluation, and learning on country experiences in team-based PHC service delivery, HRH, and financing • Support situation assessment and gap analysis in service delivery, HRH, and financing • Support countries' strategy refresh in HRH, health financing, service delivery, and governance • Provide advisory and technical assistance for country reforms. Support design and implementation of team-based service delivery and related HRH and financing solutions • Align external financing with country-led system-strengthening efforts, on budget to avoid fragmentation • Foster innovations, technology adoptions, and new initiatives through financial support and partnership • Support integrated data platforms to enable team-based service delivery and value-based payment, while building in-country analytical capacity		
World Bank	• Lending: easing access to finance for PHC • Learning: curating and mobilizing PHC knowledge and training • Leadership: crafting policy options through dialogue		

Note: (a) Key features of a team-based service delivery mode include the following: team composition, team-member roles, catchment area, empanelment, scope of services, management and reporting, referral mechanism, communication platforms, integration with the community, public health function/surveillance, and the role of the private sector, among others. (b) The HRH review would encompass existing staff numbers, availability, distribution, and competencies. (c) New technologies can facilitate interaction between patients and providers (for example, through e-consultation, patient portals, population health management tools), as well as interactions among providers (through e-referral, communication, and integration across providers).

HF = health financing; HRH = human resources for health; M&E = monitoring and evaluation; MoE = Ministry of Education; MoF = Ministry of Finance. MoH = Ministry of Health; MoI = Ministry of the Interior; MoL = Ministry of Labor; MoT = Ministry of Technology; PHC = primary health care; SDG3 = Sustainable Development Goal 3.

After formulating recommendations for governments, this chapter proposes action priorities for the international health community, in particular, the World Bank and its global health partners. These recommendations reflect the strategic directions adopted by the World Bank's Health, Nutrition and Population (HNP) Global Practice in its 2021 Strategy Refresh (World Bank 2007). At the end of the chapter, an integrated table summarizes the main steps for governments and partners to walk the talk for reimagined PHC.

Recommendations for countries

Management of the reform process

1. **Create an inclusive leadership group to drive PHC reforms**. This group will be responsible for delivering PHC reform on the path to UHC. It will work through dialogue and seek consensus, while recognizing the imperative for bold decisions and timely action. In most instances, the leadership group will include high-level representation from ministries of finance, health, and planning, among others; members of parliamentary health, finance, and budget committees; and representatives of professional associations, civil society organizations, and other stakeholder groups. Typically, the leadership group will be mandated to set up additional committees, commission reports, conduct public hearings, and initiate other activities to gather data and work toward consensus for decision-making.

Team-based care organization and delivery models

1. **Assess health workforce strengths and gaps, and plan the transition to team-based delivery**. Although all countries should aspire to build multidisciplinary care teams to deliver PHC, the specifics of team composition and empanelment strategies should be tailored to the local context. Contextual factors to consider include national and local epidemiologic profiles and socioeconomic determinants of health (Borgès Da Silva et al. 2013). To start, each country—supported by technical partners and donors, as appropriate—can undertake a situation assessment encompassing the following: (1) the current structure and composition of the health workforce; (2) how well the workforce matches health and health care needs; (3) people's care-seeking patterns across different provider types and levels of care; and (4) payment/financing mechanisms.

   Building on the situation assessment, countries can develop a transition plan to organize existing health worker cohorts into teams; establish managerial relationships and reporting chains; and empanel populations to care teams. Empanelment approaches should be responsive to local contexts and engage the private sector, depending upon the level of their engagement in PHC that is often socially stratified in low- and middle-income countries (LMICs). These countries often have private and deregulated low-technology clinics and pharmacies for the poor and the rural areas, as well as higher-cost and often insurance-driven private care facilities complementing and competing with the public health sector on quality, amenities, and more personalized care (Private Sector Health Alliance of Nigeria n.d.). Transition planning may consider short-, medium-, and long-term workforce and financing reforms to expand the comprehensiveness of care, extend the PHC teams' outreach into the community, and support integrated service delivery within care teams and across levels of care.

2. **Equip care teams to engage communities**. Reimagined PHC depends on care teams that are able to connect deeply with communities. Dedicated, skilled staff build community connections and trust through outreach and communication activities. These activities clarify local health needs and priorities; boost health literacy; and progressively empower local people to manage their own health. Such efforts may use surveys, community forums, and other tools to understand the socio-cultural and economic characteristics of the local population, as well as the health-related beliefs, attitudes, and behaviors. Teams will be able to use this knowledge to tailor messaging and action in public health, health promotion, and disease prevention.

3. **Strengthen and integrate information technology on the PHC front lines**. Reimagined PHC involves broadening access to digital platforms and leveraging data analysis capabilities to improve outcomes. Interoperable and integrated digital platforms are needed to create a culture of transparency and accountability in PHC. Doing this will empower patients and providers alike. The COVID-19 crisis has confirmed the importance of harnessing technology to monitor population health on the front lines, detect threats early, and facilitate knowledge sharing and care coordination. These needs are experienced within local care teams and across levels of care in both public and private sectors. As empowered co-producers of their own health, patients should ultimately be able to access, review, and export their personal health data on demand; in the long run, they should be able to generate and contribute their own health data, including through mobile applications and self-monitoring of health indicators.

Countries can score efficiency gains by upskilling data analysis capabilities within local care teams. Teams that collect more data and know how to use them can boost the quality of care for the populations they serve. Better data-analytic capabilities will allow technology-enabled care teams to track and understand population health in real time, including identification of potential outbreaks; undertake risk stratification to inform patient-specific outreach and care strategies; and more actively manage the empaneled patient list.

Multidisciplinary health workforce development

1. **Launch multidisciplinary medical education reforms**. Following a workforce needs assessment, countries can develop and implement a multipronged, multidisciplinary set of medical education reforms to plug gaps and optimize training for community-focused, team-based care. As described in detail in chapter 4, countries should address lopsided allocations of human resources for health through educational reforms

designed to attract workers to locations where they are needed most. These include strategies to build medical education campuses within rural or underserved areas; recruit local students from those same communities; prioritize and elevate the prestige of community care; and promote generalist practice. A reformed medical curriculum should be designed to prepare health workers for service in the team-based PHC environment by emphasizing collaborative practice. Training programs should also support development of new health workforce competencies, including data analysis and interpretation; disease surveillance; risk stratification; team management and coordination; and soft skills for effective patient engagement, outreach, and partnership. Depending on the local context and results of the health workforce assessment, countries may also need to invest in building new medical education programs to expand the health workforce and meet evolving workforce needs. Indeed, reforming the existing medical education platform for the full health workforce may be needed; a fit-for-purpose health workforce for reimagined PHC requires a core team that also includes community health workers (CHWs), registered nurses (RNs), and administrators. The expanded PHC team in more resource-rich settings would also involve the same core team—albeit with enhanced skills—but also pharmacists, dentists, psychologists and other mental health workers, lab technicians, and other health care providers whose services may be enhanced by the use of information and communications technology (ICT).

2. **Reform provider compensation models to promote rural practice and generalist care**. In addition to medical education reforms, countries can address compensation imbalances that exacerbate inequitable allocation of the health workforce, especially in those with a predominant private sector. Governments should ensure that the compensation for health workers (such as salaries or reimbursement rates) in rural or underserved areas is at least equivalent to the compensation in more saturated urban regions. Depending on the local context, leaders may also consider additional compensation or in-kind benefits to offset quality-of-life concerns. Reimbursement and salary reform is also needed to address the substantial differential between generalist and specialist physicians, thereby encouraging entry into generalist career paths and addressing the shortage of primary care physicians, as well as containing perverse and collusive dual practice in loose regulatory settings.

3. **Expand tiered accreditation systems tied to reimbursement policy**. In countries with mixed health systems, governments need to strategically engage with the private sector to leverage its workforce and infrastructure, while improving the quality of care and protecting citizens from out-of-pocket expenditures. Governments may leverage reimbursement

and strategic purchasing for universal health care (UHC) to incentivize private sector participation in a tiered accreditation system. A minimum accreditation tier would qualify private providers to receive reimbursement with public funds; achieving progressively higher accreditation tiers could be tied to higher reimbursement rates or reimbursement coverage for a broader range of services. Public providers should also be required to participate in the accreditation system and be subjected to the same standards.

4. **Reform regulations on telemedicine and labor mobility**. To best leverage their entire workforce and promote technology-enabled care, countries can review the regulatory landscape and identify the barriers to telemedicine expansion and labor mobility. Once the barriers are recognized, countries can critically assess which regulations are necessary and remove or reform those that are not. Countries that have already relaxed such regulations due to COVID-19 can review that experience with the goal of incorporating productive reforms into permanent policy.

5. **Support the frontline workforce**. The COVID-19 pandemic has placed extraordinary stress on frontline workers, but work-related stress and burnout are common issues across the health workforce, even outside of crises. Governments need to ensure that those in the PHC workforce receive financial, practical, and psychosocial support to manage the unique pressures of their jobs, during normal times and particularly during emergencies. Governments, care teams, and institutions engaged in medical education should have regular touchpoints to assess the physical and psychosocial welfare of the health workforce and troubleshoot challenges.

Financing and resource mobilization

1. **Develop a political strategy to deliver PHC financing goals**. Health officials tend to analyze financing options in technical terms, but financing and resource allocation are inherently political. Securing funds for reimagined PHC requires building commitment and buy-in across government. Achieving this will not happen without a deliberate political strategy. Leadership informed by such a strategy is key to translate countries' formal commitment to UHC under the Sustainable Development Goals (SDGs) into practical policies and resource allocation. The evidence is strong that public health-enabled PHC is the health care organization model most apt to improve the efficiency, resilience, and sustainability of public spending on health, thereby promoting equity and shared prosperity. Such evidence is vital but insufficient. A political plan is needed to ensure its uptake by those with the power to deliver change.

2. **Craft a tailored investment plan**. Fit-for-purpose financing for public health-enabled PHC must be rooted in a comprehensive package of services that meets the priority health needs of communities and is free at the point of service. The benefits package needs to be designed through a participatory and fair process. A gap analysis based on the assessment of existing service delivery capacity (access, quality, and cost) with respect to the defined service package is essential. Such analysis should lead to a country-driven investment plan for strengthening PHC platforms that includes infrastructure, human resources, routine operations, overhead, removal of user fees, and other features.

3. **Finance PHC without user fees through general government expenditure**. As discussed in chapter 4, the source of financing for PHC has important implications for equity, financial risk protection, and resilience to financial shocks. To ensure equitable and comprehensive coverage—given existing socioeconomic inequities and widespread labor informality—PHC should be financed through general government revenue. Government efforts to achieve UHC should consider how to transition away from suboptimal sources of PHC financing. These include social health insurance contributions, private insurance premiums, and out-of-pocket health care expenditures—the most inefficient and inequitable form of health financing. In most countries, funding from these suboptimal sources can be progressively replaced with routine allocations from the government budget. PHC services should be free at the first point of contact with health services.

4. **Implement pro-health taxes on tobacco, alcohol, and sugar**. Even as countries move to finance PHC from general government revenue, they can often boost tax revenue by implementing or increasing pro-health taxes on harmful products—especially tobacco, alcohol, and sugar. These taxes can create additional fiscal space, including to support PHC, while reducing the burden of common noncommunicable illnesses like hypertension, cancer, and diabetes, along with related health system costs.

5. **Ensure comprehensive and equitable coverage of PHC services through an affordable benefits package**. Countries' UHC benefits package needs to facilitate equitable provision of comprehensive PHC services. Countries need to reconcile the scope of the benefits package with the available resource pool, moving from implicit rationing to explicit and accountable priority setting for sustainability. A participatory benefits package design process offers a lever to rebalance overall health expenditure toward PHC in settings where PHC has been historically underprioritized.

6. **Leverage payment reform to promote team-based care, coordination, and quality**. Countries can expand the use of strategic/value-based

purchasing to facilitate team-based care models and incentivize care coordination and quality. (See chapter 4.)

7. **Create an accountability framework that links resources to results**. Resource mobilization (whether through additional allocations or reprioritization) tends to be more successful when accompanied by a strong accountability framework built on interoperable data platforms. Reliable and transparent measurement of PHC financing, which has been a weak link in many countries, will be critical to hold providers accountable to health system investors—including international and domestic funders and, most importantly, a country's citizens. Results need to be regularly monitored and the accountability framework itself adjusted to changing circumstances and priorities, including emergencies.

8. **Explore value-based purchasing**. Countries can leverage this approach to promote multidisciplinary teamwork, encourage collaboration across sectors, and incentivize better care quality and coverage. Patients' voices should be heard when provider payment mechanisms are being designed, thereby empowering health service users to participate in decision-making. Development partners may support countries to build measurement and monitoring capacity, enhance data platforms, and pilot and incubate innovations to improve accountability in PHC financing.

Recommendations for donors and the international health community

1. **Support documentation, evaluation, and learning on country experiences with multidisciplinary team-based care**. Despite a consensus favoring team-based care models for PHC, the literature still offers few practical examples and detailed evaluations to guide team design. Donors and the wider international community can enable countries' reform strategies by supporting systematic documentation, evaluation, and learning around different team-based care models, including transition processes. Donors could finance evaluations or reviews of specific country experiences; they could also support a community of practice for practitioners and policy makers at different stages in the reform process. In the long run, building on a growing donor-supported evidence base, international norm-setting bodies can establish standards and guidelines for PHC care teams—including the size, composition, and catchment population—that are tailored to local contexts and resource constraints.

2. **Support country-led digital integration**. In each country, donors can provide financial and technical support to integrate fragmented health data

platforms and/or ensure their interoperability. Any support donors provide to health management information systems (HMIS) should respect the long-term agenda for a single integrated or interoperable health information plat-form in each country. In the immediate term, donors should "walk the talk" by ensuring that any vertically organized data collection platforms are made interoperable with the national HMIS—such that national HMIS systems can access all donor-supported data (while respecting patient privacy).

3. **Align with a WHO-endorsed international standard for community-based medical education**. The international community should work collabo-ratively to raise international recognition of community-based medical education and qualifications. One practical step would be to align with a set of WHO-endorsed standards and guidelines for community-based medical education and certification. Like existing medical and nursing degrees, these qualifications would be broadly recognized across borders and hold equal prestige—ultimately including earning power—with tradi-tional medical education.

4. **Fund country-led multidisciplinary medical education reform**. Develop-ing new norms, content, and pedagogy for multidisciplinary medical edu-cation will require investment. Existing institutions will work together in new ways, while in some cases new institutions or facilities will be created. In addition to supporting the normative aspects of reforms, international partners may contribute financial resources to accelerate critical phases of the process. Capital investments in new medical education institutions may be a particularly good fit for multilateral development banks.

What will the World Bank do?

COVID-19 has opened a new era of global uncertainty and risk. Precisely for that reason, now is the time to advocate for, invest in, and work with countries to deliver reimagined PHC—the cornerstone of the health system transformations that the pandemic has shown are needed in countries at all income levels.

The World Bank is working with its partners to meet this challenge. Through its COVID-19 Multiphase Programmatic Approach (MPA) financing facilities, the World Bank has accelerated support to countries to tackle the pandemic while strengthening health systems fundamentals. Now, in a Strategy Refresh for the post-COVID world, the World Bank's Health, Nutrition and Population (HNP) Global Practice has prioritized ensuring universal and equitable access to affordable, people-centered, and integrated quality care with reimagined PHC. This agenda goes hand in hand with strengthening public health functions, including pandemic preparedness, and investing in health beyond health care under a whole-of-government approach (World Bank 2007).

In the years ahead, the World Bank will use three main mechanisms to help countries deliver the promise of reimagined PHC. These mechanisms match the World Bank's principal areas of added value in health, as identified in the 2021 Strategy Refresh: Lending, Learning, and Leadership. These priorities also underscore the World Bank's commitment to partnerships that have proven their value for countries, including the Global Action Plan PHC Accelerator, Primary Health Care Performance Initiative (PHCPI), Joint Learning Network (JLN), and others (WHO 2019).[1,2] As countries and partners continue to grapple with the health and economic "double shock" of COVID-19 (Tandon et al. 2020), the World Bank's approach is parsimonious. It does not aim to create new structures that might duplicate what already exists. Instead, it seeks to work within existing structures and alliances in more effective ways.

1. **Lending: ease access to funding for PHC reforms**. The World Bank will work with the Global Finance Facility (GFF) and other partners to make it easier for countries to quickly access the funds they need for PHC-oriented system reforms. Before COVID-19, investment in health system strengthening and public health-enabled PHC was constrained by the difficult transition to domestic health financing in some countries, together with the continued appeal of donor funding for disease-specific programs. COVID-19 has underscored the limits of such models and the need for new solutions. However, the crisis has also complicated resource mobilization for ambitious PHC-centered system reforms. The World Bank is well-positioned to help shift this dynamic, drawing lessons from financing and technical support innovations under the COVID-19 Multiphase Programmatic Approach (MPA) (World Bank 2020). As was the case of COVID-19, the World Bank can combine financial backing for PHC reforms with policy and technical advice that will inform leaders on emerging options and equip them to select, finance, and deliver the best approaches for country needs. The World Bank can move quickly to initiate conversations with its International Development Association (IDA) and International Bank for Reconstruction and Development (IBRD) clients and to raise the profile of PHC. Advancing PHC assertively in COVID-19 health system strengthening operations and GFF Essential Services Grants will be a "win-win" for countries and for the World Bank's programs, as both can achieve desired results more efficiently through PHC.

2. **Learning: mobilize practice-relevant PHC knowledge**. Together with analytic and financial partners, the World Bank will strengthen global knowledge hubs for PHC and ensure that they are equipped to deliver the actionable information that countries need in formats they can use.

Since PHCPI's creation in 2015, the initiative's databases and PHC improvement tools have advanced PHC learning and practice.[3] This and other PHC knowledge hubs, such as that maintained by JLN,[4] can achieve even more in the years ahead. More can be done to share PHC knowledge in user-friendly forms and to tailor information for policy makers and implementers facing specific challenges on the ground. Through collaboration in these efforts, the World Bank will capture and disseminate learning around PHC "hardware" (for example, digital technology, technology-equipped PHC workers) and "software" (for example, team-based organizational care models, risk pooling, value-based purchasing). It will help compile and assess country experiences and facilitate their dissemination through tailored global, regional, and country-specific training courses and other activities. World Bank technical assistance to countries will support the integration and operationalization of PHC knowledge in policies and programs. Recently, a new PHC performance framework from WHO and the United Nations Children's Fund (UNICEF) and the Organisation for Economic Co-operation and Development's (OECD) Patient-Reported Indicator Surveys (PaRIS) have advanced PHC performance measurement (OECD n.d.). The World Bank will work with these and other partners on a country-friendly measurement toolbox for PHC-related inputs, outputs, and outcomes. The World Bank will also expand the place of PHC in its learning platforms, such as flagship courses.

3. **Leadership: develop policy options in dialogue with ministers**. To support national leadership in PHC reform and facilitate a whole-of-government approach, the World Bank HNP Global Practice will establish a dedicated platform for policy dialogue, advice, and technical assistance to ministries of health and ministries of finance. The platform will include high-level policy seminars on country-selected topics, linked to the World Bank/International Monetary Fund Annual Meetings. Flagship courses will be tailored to senior decision-makers. The platform's initial agenda will focus on analyzing the political economy dynamics of PHC reform in the post-COVID-19 era, capturing the range of country experiences and emerging solutions. Platform dialogue will identify entry points and strengthen relationships for subsequent country-level technical collaboration and financial support. This initiative builds on and further leverages the GFF country leadership program that aims to bolster country leadership to drive transformational changes for health system reforms, as well as partner alignment with government priorities.

As the World Bank works with countries to build high-performing, equitable, and resilient PHC systems, it is not about creating new administrative structures, logos, and hashtags. Rather, it is about concretely "upping our game" with trusted partners and within structures that are largely in place, so that countries can get the support and the results they need, quickly, and at manageable cost. As with PHC itself, this is easy to say and harder to achieve. We set out together now, with hope and humility, to walk the talk.

Conclusion: Summary table of policy recommendations

Table 5.1 presents an integrated overview of the report's policy recommendations for countries and international partners. The proposed sequencing of the actions is reflected in the order of their presentation, that is, actions at the top of the table occur first.

Notes

1. See the PHCPI website at https://improvingphc.org.

2. See the Joint Learning Network website at https://www.jointlearningnetwork.org.

3. Primary Health Care Performance Initiative. n.d. "Improvement Strategies," n.d. at https://improvingphc.org/improvement-strategies.

4. Joint Learning Network. n.d. "Resources," n.d.

References

Borgès Da Silva, Roxane, Raynald Pineault, Marjolaine Hamel, Jean-Frédéric Levesque, Danièle Roberge, and Paul Lamarche. 2013. "Constructing Taxonomies to Identify Distinctive Forms of Primary Healthcare Organizations." International Scholarly Research Notices, https://doi.org/10.5402/2013/798347.

OECD (Organisation for Economic Co-operation and Development). n.d. "Patient-Reported Indicator Surveys (PaRIS): OECD," accessed May 29, 2021, https://www.oecd.org/health/paris/.

Tandon, Ajay, Tomas Roubal, Lachlan McDonald, Peter Cowley, Toomas Palu, Valeria de Oliveira Cruz, Patrick Eozenou, et al. 2020. "Economic Impact of COVID-19: Implications for Health Financing in Asia and Pacific." Discussion Paper, World Bank, Washington, DC.

WHO (World Health Organization). 2019. "The Global Action Plan for Healthy Lives and Well-Being for All." https://www.who.int/initiatives/sdg3-global-action-plan/about.

WHO (World Health Organization). 2020. "A World in Disorder: Global Preparedness Monitoring Board Annual Report 2020." World Health Organization, Geneva.

World Bank. 2007. *Healthy Development: The World Bank Strategy for Health, Nutrition, and Population Results*. Washington, DC: World Bank, https://openknowledge.worldbank.org/handle/10986/6843.

World Bank. 2020. "COVID-19 Strategic Preparedness and Response Program (SPRP) Using the Multiphase Programmatic Approach (MPA) Project: Additional Financing (English)." World Bank, Washington, DC.